PERVERSE SPECTATORS

JANET STAIGER

PERVERSE SPECTATORS

The Practices of Film Reception

New York University Press • *New York and London*

NEW YORK UNIVERSITY PRESS
New York and London

© 2000 by New York University

Library of Congress Cataloging-in-Publication Data
Staiger, Janet.
Perverse spectators : the practices of film reception / Janet Staiger.
p. cm.
Includes bibliographical references and index.
ISBN 0-8147-8138-1 (alk. paper) — ISBN 0-8147-8139-X (pbk. : alk. paper)
1. Motion picture audiences. 2. Film criticism. 3. Motion pictures—
Philosophy.   I. Title.
PN1995.9.A8 S69 2000
791.43'01'5—dc21   00-008433

New York University Press books are printed on acid-free paper,
and their binding materials are chosen for strength and durability.

Manufactured in the United States of America

10 9 8 7 6 5 4 3 2 1

Contents

IV   Interpretation and the Representation of the Real

Introduction

This is a collection of essays which, with one exception, have been written since I published *Interpreting Films: Studies in the Historical Reception of American Cinema* in 1992. As a group they constitute a continuation of the research agenda that I presented there—a historical materialist approach to audiences and media reception. I believe that contextual factors, more than textual ones,[1] account for the experiences that spectators have watching films and television and for the uses to which those experiences are put in navigating our everyday lives. These contextual factors are social formations and constructed identities of the self in relation to historical conditions. These contexts involve intertextual knowledges (including norms of how to interpret sense data from moving images and sounds), personal psychologies, and sociological dynamics. The job of a reception historian is to account for events of interpretation and affective experience.

What constitutes my advancement in this collection is an attempt at a more felicitous way of describing the specific acts of reception and making of personal meaning. This schema for considering reception events is developed in chapters 1, 2, and 3. It is an attempt at a synthesis of research done on reception but also recent work on fans, stars, and, in general, cultural studies. As far as I am aware, no one has tried to go beyond describing readers' responses in either a very general way (readers take up the position offered by the text, they resist it, or they negotiate it) or very specific ways (at best, lists of what readers do in creating alternative texts or in identifying with stars).

I am describing the rest of the essays as case studies, which does not mean that patterns are not presented. In every case, I link the specific traces of reception to broader historical circumstances. What is not possible to argue is a "master narrative": for example, that social class is the fundamental cause for all responses to films. That is because I believe that individuals have multiple (albeit socially constructed) identities. These identities, as well as specific historical situations, intersect to produce groups of responses that may be linked to broader dynamics of class, race and ethnicity, generation, gender, and sexuality identities (to name the most obvious).

I have titled this collection *Perverse Spectators*. Although I develop and clarify that concept in chapter 2, an introduction is a good place for an author to attempt to insist that the concept be interpreted as she imagines she intended. By *perverse* I wish to denote a turning away from dominant notions of "right" or "good." As I discuss in the first three chapters here and in *Interpreting Films*, speculation about real readers based on *academic* readings of texts does not take us very far before running up against rampant and remarkable deviations. In cultural studies, the triad of "preferred," "negotiated," and "opposi-tional" readings quickly became only a hypothetical when applied to various historical events. Almost every reading became "negotiated," thus losing much of the relational implications of that term. I might well have titled this book *Negotiating Spectators,* but the term suggests to me too much of an acceptance of, or knowledge of, textual "intent" by the spectator who must then find a special way through the expe-rience. In some ways *perverse* has the same implications, but I want to highlight the contradictory tension that term implies to me. Perver-sion can imply a willful turning away from the norm; it may also sug-gest an inability to do otherwise. Thus, the term distinguishes itself from the cultural studies triad—based as much cultural studies is on a rejection of psychoanalytical theories. In the reception studies I pur-sue here, I find several theoretical paradigms, including psychoanaly-sis, useful for explaining events of interpretation and experience. The term *perverse* also keeps me from necessarily assuming that deviance is politically progressive. Sometimes it is, sometimes it is not; each case must be described and evaluated with care and within the his-torical intersection in which it exists.

Indeed, this collection of essays will be theoretically mixed. I will use typical tools for textual analysis, describing written and aural ex-pressions around a specific event. These expressions will always be placed within wider historical debates and discursive flows and con-tradictions (a good example is chapter 6's discussion of shifting defini-tions of "obscenity"). However, I will often also turn to psychoanalyti-cal, cognitive psychology, and sociological theories to enrich my inter-pretation of what seems to be occurring. Sigmund Freud, Jerome Bruner, Mary Douglas, and Victor Turner may show up in the same essay. Frankly, my view is that several sorts of analysis contribute to understanding these events. Reception occurs to an individual as both a psychological and a sociological experience; only the arbitrary separation of concepts such as self and group inhibits a recognition that experiences cannot be isolated as either psychological or sociological.

Two organizational dynamics structure this collection. One is the dynamic apparent in the table of contents. A second dynamic exists in relation to fig. 2–1, "Viewers' Presumed Normative Reception Activities," presented in chapter 2. Fig. 2-1 is my attempt to characterize possible interpretative acts. It is deeply and gratefully indebted to the work of David Bordwell who, himself, has profited much from the research of many contemporary literary theorists. However, as I discuss in chapter 2, major problems exist in several assumptions underpinning the "normative reception" account of spectatorship. Among these questionable presumptions are that spectators are primarily interested in cognitive acts—especially the act of solving a problem—and that spectators are "knowledgeable and cooperative." I present in chapter 2 examples of perverse—at least in relation to the normative account—reactions to films. What constitutes, then, the pattern of the rest of my case studies are further examples of these perversions and their implications within a potential history of reception.

The normative account for the classical Hollywood film (and a TV program) would assert that the primary activity of a knowledgeable and cooperative spectator would be to try to solve the problems presented by the plot (in fig. 2-1, [1] Chronological or Narrative Chain). Other possible activities would receive secondary attention and would be understood by the spectator to contribute to the primary goal of understanding the story. These other activities revolve around the conceptual categories of (2) characters (or human agents for nonfictional films); (3) verisimilitude and "real world" expectations; (4) affective and emotional experiences; (5) aesthetic order and variation; (6) narrational source; and (7) discourse.

The case studies illustrate as a whole how much these other activities matter for spectators. Chapters 7, 8, and 9 introduce issues about spectators and characters. Chapter 7 analyzes Louis Althusser's theory of how Ideological State Apparatuses function to reproduce the relations of production. The chapter discusses interpellation for nondominant members of a social formation, specifically Jeanie Bueller and two parking lot attendants in *Ferris Bueller's Day Off*. Considering audience responses regarding identification, I ask with whom and for whom identification is occurring, and then I consider the implications that identification might have for the usefulness of Althusser's model.

Chapter 8 engages the historical function of underground cinema of the 1960s within the context of gay liberation politics and argues that this cinema provided a visible and increasingly approved community for gay identities that were considered less acceptable than ones promoted by liberals in the 1960s sexual liberation movement. "Flaming creatures" were elevated to the status of camp and pop culture, preparing the way for interpreting what was "radical" in the Stonewall revolt. Chapter 9 also focuses on relations between spectators and characters. Tracing the varied discussions of the gender and sexuality of Clarice Starling in *The Silence of the Lambs*, the chapter argues that variable readings of her character occurred. These variations helped overdetermine the response of concern by some gay men that people might interpret the film as, once again, stereotyping deviant sexual murderers as homosexuals.

Verisimilitude and "real world" expectations of spectators are examined in chapters 11 and 12. In chapter 11, I discuss the intertextual strategies by which readers tried to justify *The Return of Martin Guerre* as historically accurate. In nearly an opposite problem, in chapter 12, I review the controversy surrounding the docudrama *JFK*, directed by Oliver Stone. There some writers representing journalistic sources that accepted the official Warren Commission report seemed quite threatened by the unofficial popular sentiment, expressed through Jim Garrison's story in the film, that Lee Harvey Oswald was not the lone assassin of John F. Kennedy. Here these writers' problem was to deny the validity of a strong popular/social memory of a real event.

Affective and emotional experiences and pleasures probably underpin every act of reception, or maybe the better verb here is "drive." However, two chapters particularly bring to the forefront activities within this category. Chapter 6 discusses the exceptionally antagonistic responses to *A Clockwork Orange* because of the film's representations of sexual violence. However, since the film appeared to be part of an attemp at "liberation" from the censorship of sexual imagery and was the work of a major director, Stanley Kubrick, many people also desired an authorization to view such materials. The debates are typical of the strategies adopted in such a situation and are often repeated with other *auteur* films that breach taboos. This case study also considers why a camp cult appropriation of *A Clockwork Orange* might soon become possible for some viewers of the film.

Chapter 10 also considers aesthetic pleasures, in this case a particularly perverse reading of *The Texas Chain Saw Massacre* as a comedic adaptation of *Psycho*. Both this chapter and chapter 9 are good instances of how both psychoanalytical and sociological theory help explain the reception.

Part of the dynamics invoked in the case of *The Texas Chain Saw Massacre* is the powerful influence of intertextual projections by a reader. Referring to other texts, to notions of "authorship," and to genres and formula lies within the category of "aesthetic order and variation" activities. While nearly every chapter contributes examples of the importance of this to reception, chapter 4 is an excellent instance in which a spectator's ideas of similar texts to the one being watched influence the articulation of the spectator's reception, and may contribute to interpretations in which figuring out a plot and testing hypotheses matter much less than the pleasures of formula coherence (and deviation). Chapter 4 stresses as well that enjoying the mix of genres and formulas is not a recent innovation in spectatorship; rather, in the history of experiencing Hollywood movies, viewers have always found in a single film many similarities with movies they categorize as belonging to several genres or formulas.

Chapter 5 also discusses how important and useful aesthetic order and variation through intertextual comparisons may be in understanding the possible interpretations reasonably available to a spectator. Here the intertexts are not other movies but stories about the real lives of stars or novelizations of the movie plot. Chapter 5 is somewhat speculative, but it suggests that public knowledge about Marlene Dietrich around the time of the release of *Blonde Venus* might permit a reading of it as a comedy of desire rather than the more obvious melodrama evident through textual analysis without context. Moreover, if the spectator read the novelization of the film, the interpretation might even shift the generic assignment to that of a "romance" story, with a very different assessment of the plot of the movie. Hence, contextual knowledge might have an influence on what intertext is deemed relevant, and the impression of the plot of the story would significantly change.

Narrational source is another category of spectatorial activity. Indeed, contexts which suggest particular originations for a movie can determine interpretations. Two examples (also involving intertextuality since the "source" of the text is assumed to be the director) are the studies of *A Clockwork Orange* and *The Texas Chain Saw Massacre* (chapters 6 and 10). I suggest that various parts of the reception of these texts involve assuming the director to be responding to another text (in the case of *A Clockwork Orange,* the original novel by Anthony Burgess; for *The Texas Chain Saw Massacre, Psycho* directed by Alfred Hitchcock).

The last category of spectatorial activity in fig. 2–1 is "discourse." This category covers meaningful messages or personal significances[2] that an individual may derive for him or herself from a film or television program. The *A Clockwork Orange* case is probably the best example in this set of studies since as a part of a wave of early 1970s screen violence the film provoked excessive public concern about audience effects. As in our current discussions about the effects of media on youth, *A Clockwork Orange* precipitated public discussion of the relation of media violence and real-life behaviors. Would people imitate the antics of the characters? Could the aestheticization of violence desensitize viewers to the brutality of physical aggression? The defenses of film seem familiar: writers argued the film was merely duplicating the original novel that was its source; the violence was "realistic" or it was "mythically real"; and the film was art. Coming as the film did at the beginning of U.S. second-wave feminism, it also solicited early ideological readings that focused on its association of sexuality and violence. The potential significance of the film took up a major portion of the interpretative energy.

In summary, then, this collection of essays continues lines of research into the history of American film reception. Although I do no studies of television, on the whole I think much of what I present here is applicable to TV, with the addition of perhaps some consideration of the contextual and media-specificity problems of "flow," "least objectionable viewing," and technologies such as the VCR, cable, and remote control. Those are not minor issues, but my hypothesis is that TV-viewing options enhance spectatorial opportunities to be perverse spectators. If anything, TV viewing is even less reliant on the pleasures and values of sorting out stories and solving problems than is film.

A few words about the status of these essays. Chapters 1, 2, and 3 are revised versions of papers first published as conference proceedings. I consider this text to be the best source for the ideas expressed there. The individual case studies (chapters 4 through 12) are self-contained and have almost no overlap with each other. Moreover, since they were (with one exception) written since *Interpreting Films,* I found next to nothing in them that I thought I wanted to change. Correcting small grammatical errors and creating conformity in documentation are the primary changes from the original publication version. My hope is that by centralizing these studies from the rather wide-flung original publication sites and by pointing out their contribution to an overall view about writing the history of American film reception, their collectivity will make the whole now greater than the sum of the parts. Do not expect, however, any more profound master narrative than that real spectators are usually perverse spectators.

Numerous acknowledgments are due, and I once again thank everyone I mention in the notes both specifically for help on an individual essay and in general. I sincerely appreciate the faith in this and my other work shown by Eric Zinner of New York University Press. Both support and professionalism are hard to come by, and so I thank him for this rare combination. I appreciate as well the editorial assistance of Daisy Hernández, Cecilia Feilla, and Despina Papazoglou Gimbel throughout the process of moving this from some variant computer files to a final book.

NOTES

1. I have insisted that no immanent textual meaning exists. This has been read as suggesting that I do not believe a text exists. In fact, I believe that a physical object with sense data does exist. However, beyond that, language (if you use linguistic theories of the epistemology of film and television) or a schema (if you employ cognitive psychology approaches) intervenes. Moreover, prior expectations will "start" the interpretation before the film or TV show begins. At times, I will write as though a text exists (see my descriptions, for instance, of *The Return of Martin Guerre*). In those moments, I am assuming that readers all hold the same codes or schemata, thus permitting the *appearance* of a stable, "authentic" text. However, that *appearance* relies on a presumption of the homogeneity of the spectators, a presumption that I would finally refute. Thus, any description of a film or television program is merely a strategic maneuver in order to focus on something about the interpretations, but it is not a theoretical position or contradiction.

2. On the distinction between meaning and significance, see Janet Staiger, *Interpreting Films: Studies in the Historical Reception of American Cinema* (Princeton: Princeton University Press, 1992), 24.

PART I

HISTORICAL THEORY AND RECEPTION STUDIES

I

Modes of Reception

IN 1994 TWO films graphically representing violence and violent people were released. One was *Pulp Fiction,* directed by Quentin Tarantino; the other was *Natural Born Killers,* directed by Oliver Stone. Beyond the similarity of subject matter, affective resemblances exist: both films treat spectators to persistent sudden explosions of violence within the everyday.

Yet the two films are also quite different. *Pulp Fiction* is a convoluted story with long passages of dialogue between major characters and is shot in a classical Hollywood style. While also a narrative film, *Natural Born Killers* consistently uses transgressive cinematic strategies to call attention to the film as film. Although for various reasons *Pulp Fiction* was praised and prized over *Natural Born Killers,* commentators generally ignored the formal and stylistic differences between the films. Moreover, that both films might be said to exemplify quite deviant strands of narrative film practice and reception was taken for granted. Why should this be so?

The answer to this question might seem obvious, but I want to use these two films as contemporary markers to consider the problem of writing the history of film reception. Two major questions about the history and the future of cinema are, what are the experiences of cinema viewing for the audiences? And what are the meanings of those experiences? Although questions about the industrial and social institutions of cinema and about cinematic form and style retain their interest, scholars recognize that questions of reception are equally significant for sociological, cultural, and aesthetic theory. In the past twenty years, scholars have provided various speculations about going to the movies. These speculations have been provocative and useful in opening up research about the reception of movies, but it is now time to reconfigure the histories that are being written. It is time to move beyond some conceptual restrictions underpinning these speculations and to create more complex descriptions of film reception.

What I shall point to is that the binary oppositions structuring speculations by three major writers cannot be parsed out by historical period; the binary oppositions exist continually throughout the history of cinema. To have *Pulp Fiction* and *Natural Born Killers* exist at the same time is not controversial because such apparent opposites, and the experiences they might provoke, have existed throughout the past one hundred years, and likely will continue well into the next century. Moreover, these binary oppositions may now be limiting our descriptive possibilities.

THREE SPECULATIVE HISTORIES OF RECEPTION

For my purposes here, I want to look at three speculations that have been influential in film studies: those by Tom Gunning, Miriam Hansen, and Timothy Corrigan. All three writers have offered theories that purport to account for the entire history of U.S. cinema.[1]

Gunning sets up a distinction between a cinema of attractions and a narrative cinema (see fig. 1-1).[2] The cinema of attractions emphasizes presenting a series of disjointed and sometimes specular views, while the narrative cinema emphasizes storytelling. Based on earlier structuralist and semiotic distinctions between spectacle and narrative, Gunning's binary system adds a requirement of shock or astonishment to the spectacle side of the opposition. Thus, he can stress audience effect in his series of contrasts. Moreover, recently he has connected this cinema to the experience of modernity. The result for the cinema of attractions is a filmic experience in which confrontation with and critical involvement of the spectator occur, and this is opposed to the narrative cinema, in which the experience consists of an absorption into an illusion. Gunning further equates these two modes of reception with, respectively, the popular and the bourgeois.[3] The history Gunning writes has this popular, attraction-filled cinema dominant during the early years of the movies as modernity is arriving; submerged within classical Hollywood narrative film until the present; but reappearing sporadically in the cinemas of the avant-garde and modernism, some genres such as the musical, and recent action-adventure pictures.

FIG. 1-1. Tom Gunning's Speculations

CINEMA OF ATTRACTIONS	CINEMA OF NARRATIVE
Dates of Dominance	
pre-1906, continues in: avant-garde modernist practices some genres (e.g., musicals) recent spectacle cinema (e.g., Spielberg-Lucas-Coppola)	post-1906 dominant cinema
Spectator Address	
identification with camera but to display views arouse and satisfy visual curiosity direct address to spectator	identification with camera but to tell a story pose enigma that demands a resolution no acknowledgment of spectator
Psychoanalytical Address	
exhibitionist	voyeurist
Formal and Stylistic Features	
absence/presence of device to become framed	device is built into larger pattern
Mode of Reception/Effect on Audience	
confrontation astonishment spectator joins in, is critical	absorption into illusion follow drama "static," passive observer
Ideological Categorization	
popular	bourgeois

Hansen's speculation follows Gunning's in many respects, although Hansen slightly alters portions of the argument (fig. 1-2).[4] She indicates a bit more skepticism about the ideological empowerment of early modern cinema, which she calls "at once modernist bricolage and ideological mirage."[5] Hansen holds this view because she believes this cinema invites the formation of an "ideal public" through the wide intertextual horizon of the films themselves, but more important through the active engagement of its audience. The bustle that exists within the theater and the varied genres of movies and live events provide a variety of competing spectacles rather than the closed-down

FIG. 1-2. Miriam Hansen's Speculations

EARLY MODERN AND POSTMODERN CINEMA	CLASSICAL CINEMA
Dates of Existence	
through use of live sound postmodern cinema	1930s–1950s & to present
Spectator Address	
direct address as member of social, public audience	address as "invisible, private consumer"
diverse languages	universal language
appeal to "ideal public"	appeal to "isolated, alienated individuals"
identify with public event	identify with events on screen as unified spectator
Psychoanalytical Address	
exhibitionist	voyeurist
Formal and Stylistic Features	
presentational	representational
displays attractions	articulation of a story
short-term and incessant sensorial stimulation	lengthy observation of single event or object
many genres	genres are variants of a relatively homogeneous mode of representation
ruptures of self-enclosed world	keyhole, fetishistic distance
large intertextual horizon	narrative as self-contained
aestheticization of display of erotic persona of male stars	
Mode of Reception/Effect on Audience	
distraction, diversion instantiation of modernity transforms spatial perception mobilizes self	contemplation, concentration
Mode of Exhibition	
variety of competing spectacles	long, single feature
Ideological Categorization	
from vaudeville	from traditional arts
critique of bourgeois culture but connected to modernity ("at once a modernist bricolage and ideological mirage")	complicit with consumer society
potential female public sphere	patriarchal economy structurally masculinized

experience of the "voyeuristic" lengthy observation of a single, narratively self-contained feature film.[6] These positive attributes of early modern cinema are counterbalanced by the problem that this cinema also promotes commodified desire, in part through the aestheticization and erotic display of male stars for women spectators.

Although many similarities exist between Gunning's and Hansen's work, Hansen deviates from Gunning by arguing more fervently that the early modern cinema was a potential public sphere with more possibilities for women spectators, albeit one of these possibilities was to be socialized into a consumer culture. Hansen also treats the early modern cinema as a much longer phenomenon than Gunning does, suggesting that it exists until the era of synchronized sound when the commotion of the theater is regulated to the quiet, homogenous watching of classical films. Recently, Hansen has also referenced Corrigan's work as she has extended her argument to incorporate some recent cinema. Like Gunning and Corrigan, she thinks that the potential public sphere of the early modern cinema has reappeared in the experiences surrounding what is called postmodern cinema.

The third speculation is from Corrigan who sets up a tripartite division of U.S. film history (fig. 1-3).[7] Corrigan creates the categories of "pre-classical cinema" (1895 to circa 1917), "classical and modernist cinema" (1917 to the present and 1950 to the present, respectively), and "postmodern cinema" (1970s to the present). Like the other theorists, Corrigan creates his system focusing on the experience of the spectator. Emphasizing an opposition between the "glance" and the "gaze,"[8] he argues that preclassical and postmodern cinema encourages sporadic attention to the screen, while classical and modernist cinema is a gaze cinema. The gaze cinema creates a fixed subjectivity and unified identity through its narrative continuities, closures, central characters, and flexible realism. For the spectator, the gaze cinema is a cinema of interpretation and reading, while a glance cinema is one of performance.

Unlike Gunning but like Hansen, Corrigan seems to suggest that preclassical cinema "disappears" with the emergence of classical cinema, rather than viewing some practices as dominating others, as Gunning argues. Like Gunning, Corrigan argues that some recent films display a reemergence of audience effects similar to those of the preclassical era, a thesis Hansen has recently adopted.

How can we examine these speculations to understand which one(s) might be right or whether another speculation might provide a

FIG. 1-3. Timothy Corrigan's Speculations

PRE-CLASSICAL CINEMA	CLASSICAL CINEMA (CC) AND MODERNIST CINEMA (MC)	POSTMODERN CINEMA
	Dates of Existence	
1896–ca. 1917	CC—1917 to present MC—1950 to present	1970s to present
	Spectator Address	
dispersion of views fragmented identities	fixed subjectivity unified identity	dispersion fragmented
	Formal and Stylistic Features	
diverse spectacles	narrative continuity closure central characters flexible realism CC—invisible narration MC—visible narration	illegible dramatization of multiple identities
	Mode of Reception/Effect on Audience	
active, less coded relationship performance glance attention sporadic	interpretation, reading reading gaze attention sustained CC—stable viewer participating in CC MC—stable viewer opposing CC	performance glance attention sporadic "beyond engagement because they are nowhere and everywhere at once"
	Mode of Exhibition	
going more important than what is seen	social ritual	"outing"

better theory of the history of U.S. cinema? One place to start is to re-consider some empirical evidence in relation to the central propositions upon which these speculations hinge their arguments. None of the writers argues these claims based on the history of modes of production. Rather, they base their claims on changing modes of spectator address and changing conditions of exhibition. Thus, they claim that permutations in how the films address the audiences or how the audiences experience the films create different cinemas at sequential historical moments. Modes of address or modes of exhibition produce variant historical modes of reception. I would like to reexamine the two larger sets of data—modes of address and modes of exhibition—to determine the initial validity of these claims. Like my colleagues, I shall focus on U.S. cinema only. I will then question briefly whether the causal proposition (modes of address or exhibition cause modes of reception) is adequate to understand historical spectatorship.

MODES OF ADDRESS

This is where I return to *Pulp Fiction* and *Natural Born Killers*. I would argue that these two films are contemporary examples of the oppositions constructed by Gunning, Hansen, and Corrigan. *Pulp Fiction* is narrative/classical cinema par excellence. It requests of the viewer an identification with the camera to follow the convoluted enigma of what happens to Vincent and Jules. Voyeurism of *expected* violence absorbs us into the narrative's drama. We watch, à la Hansen, lengthy scenes of a single event or object. Despite instances of intertextual references to consumer products such as Big Macs and Sprite—the references are simply "l'effet du réel"—the film is basically a limited intertextual horizon, self-contained narrative; we need no extensive exterior allusions to create or debate a meaning for the movie. It is a film for reading, with a stable viewer participating in gazing in sustained attention to it.

Natural Born Killers, however, is the opposite. Although admittedly it has a narrative, it is predominantly a cinema of attractions and a postmodern cinema in which identification with the camera permits us to view a variety of popular visual materials quite diverse in their genre and style. News programs, popular music, television sitcoms, westerns, crime drama, and more intermingle simultaneously on the screen, in color and in black and white, on film and on television, and in canted angles that prevent any sense of an illusionist text. Director Oliver Stone not only frames these diverse texts within single shots but also uses intellectual montage to cut between 1990s killers Mickey and Mallory and 1950s TV viewers who, unlike the spectators in the movie houses, express great shock when witnessing these events. This is an exhibitionist text. This is a text that confronts and shocks the spectator, who must rely on his or her knowledge of popular culture and modern media to perform the text in its fragmentation and outward dispersion. One can only glance from here to there in several viewings to begin to see this text. It is a film in which the manipulation of space and time can surely be linked to modernity, while its popular cultural references run to one strand of middle-class intellectualism. It is "beyond engagement" because the spectator is "nowhere and everywhere at once."[9]

Whereas *Pulp Fiction* throws us into a narrative, circling us around its vortex, *Natural Born Killers* throws us out of the movie through intertexuality into a public world we must consider anew. *Pulp Fiction* plays with story and plot to intrigue the spectator, but never confronts a homogeneous, coherent narrative world. *Natural Born Killers'* limits are the virtual world of images where all popular culture is available for a multimedia collage.

Why both films now? Is this some kind of historical anomaly? Gunning, Hansen, and Corrigan all indicate formal and experiential affinities exist between the filmic address of an attractions/early modern/preclassical cinema and a postmodern cinema, and they also suggest that between the early years and these later years narrative/classical cinema sharply submerged or eliminated this address. Gunning tempers this by suggesting that some narrative genres such as the musical might display this address. Surely he would want to add some types of comedies, for instance, a film like the Marx Brothers' *Duck Soup* or even the dramatic collage text of *Intolerance*. I shall return to this issue below, but at least temporarily I want to posit that something seems not quite right with a theory that various historical periods produce different modes of filmic address, especially if an older one reemerges so forcefully some one hundred years later.[10]

MODES OF EXHIBITION

Let me turn to the other set of data: modes of exhibition. Hansen devotes great attention to the conditions of moviegoing as influencing the mode of reception and affect on the audience. In particular she suggests that the vaudeville format presenting a variety of competing materials was "at once modernist bricolage and ideological mirage." Moreover, the general liveness of the event, enhanced by real musicians until the coming of mechanically synchronized sound, sustained the sense of a public sphere even though the mode of address had already shifted into the classical narrative cinema.

Here, then, I want to consider the history of what it was like to go to the movies in the United States, starting with an account produced by Vachel Lindsay in his 1915 book *The Art of the Moving Picture*. Lindsay was a middle-class, populist, and progressive poet, who saw in movies the same great potential public sphere that Hansen also privileges. Lindsay argues for a "conversation theater" approach to film exhibition:

> I suggest suppressing the orchestra entirely and encouraging the audience to talk about the film. . . . With Christopher Morley . . . I was trying to prove out this [thesis]. As the orchestra stopped, while the show rolled on in glory, I talked about the main points in this book, illustrating it by the film before us. Almost everything that happened was a happy illustration of my ideas. But there were two shop girls in front of us awfully in love with a certain second-rate actor who insisted on kissing the heroine every so often, and with her apparent approval. Every time we talked about that those shop girls glared at us as though we were robbing them of their time and money. Finally one of them dragged the other out into the aisle, and dashed out of the house with her dear chum, saying, so all could hear, "Well, come on, Terasa, we might as well go if those two talking pests are going to keep this up behind us." The poor girl's voice trembled. She was in tears. She was gone before we could apologize or offer flowers.[11]

This story is of interest because the two groups are engaging in the wrong behaviors for their respective classes. The bourgeois middle-class male is supposed to be advocating a silent, attentive response to the movies, not talking through it; the working-class woman is not supposed to be the audience engaging in a quiet, gazing mode. If at least one early report of cinema viewing goes against the grain of the speculations, that does not invalidate the general principle.

However, at least for viewing in the United States, I would argue that the entire event of going to the movies does not change dramatically after the arrival of synchronized sound. More examples will be given in chapter 3, but here I want to survey just briefly some key points. Movie houses during the post-synchronized-sound era provided a variety of introductory materials before the feature (this exhibition format was standardized by the late teens and derived from vaudeville and other nineteenth-century amusements).[12] This variety format did not taper off until the 1950s, when television was able to provide shorts in greater numbers, and topical information could be distributed more quickly.

Moreover, during the 1930s and 1940s many live events still occurred in movie houses: at the start of the Depression, bingo and give-aways were part of the evening's events; into the war years, bond drives were routine. Since theaters were viewed as family entertainment, lots of children were present—certainly not contributing to an uninterrupted environment.[13]

Even if moviegoers were supposed to be trained to be quiet during the classical narrative cinema period, it is clear they were not always so obedient. According to studio records, at the initial preview of Orson Welles's *The Magnificent Ambersons* in Pomona, California, "the audience detested the picture, laughing in the wrong places, talking back to the screen and decrying its 'artiness' in their preview card comments."[14] In fact, it is also the case that exhibitors sometimes encouraged such interaction, at least in subsequent-run houses. Research into how exploitation movies of the 1920s through 1960s were exhibited indicates that a great amount of activity occurred in the halls, from lecturers interrupting the movies to explain events to nurses handing out educational pamphlets. I even have an example of a major Texas theater chain, the Interstate, suggesting to their exhibitors that they handle a particularly bad movie as "corny," as the worst film ever, with vocal audience participation encouraged.[15]

During the 1950s, as television provided a more relaxed social environment in opposition to the movie theater, drive-ins flourished as public sites and social environments for many people.[16] Although Linda Williams wishes to credit *Psycho* with allowing "audiences [to take] pleasure in losing the kind of control they had been trained to enjoy in classical narrative cinema," the *Psycho* experience was just part of a larger rowdiness permitted and encouraged by theater exhibitors competing with television.[17]

No, it is not at all clear to me that the conditions of exhibition for the classical narrative cinema uniformly promote a voyeuristic cinema, an absorption into an illusion, and a "static," passive spectator. Nor, of course, is all contemporary cinema a cinema of attractions or postmodern experiences. In fact, some of the so-called postmodern movies such as action-adventure pictures are shockingly constrained in the variety of their intertextual reception horizons (necessary for Hansen's public sphere cinema). So where do we go from here?

A NEW SPECULATION: MODES OF RECEPTION

The answer, I think, comes from André Bazin. In one of his most famous essays, "The Evolution of the Language of Cinema," he points out that it might be a mistake to divide the history of cinema by the coming of mechanically synchronized sound. Rather, he notes that a better way to conceive of cinematic history is to note the difference between those directors who have a faith in the image and those who have a faith in reality.[18] Bazin goes on to create a complicated, dialectical analysis of the relations between style and subject matter from the early years through the 1940s, but I think his basic point that the fault line of cinematic history is not technological change is well taken.

Let me make the proposition that every period of history (and likely every place) witnesses several modes of cinematic address, several modes of exhibition, and several modes of reception. Moreover, any individual viewer may engage *even within the same theatergoing experience* in these various modes of reception. In trying to clarify his position and avoid impossible claims, Corrigan writes, "[W]ithin the conditions of contemporary culture, there are many kinds of films that seem to have little to do with postmodernism." Corrigan also acknowledges that not all viewers are postmodern spectators.[19] I would add, nor is any viewer always one kind of spectator. What I am proposing is a renewed, complex history of moviegoing that avoids trying to demarcate these features by binary oppositions and rigid historical periods.

With this reconceptualization what happens, then, to some of the anomalies discussed above? How well would this approach handle the aberrant data? First of all, as to modes of address, it seems apparent to me as a spectator that I like all sorts of films. Although I do tend to prefer certain genres, my tastes are quite eclectic. Although I disapprove of *Pulp Fiction* for ideological reasons (its reliance on violence as a device to move the plot forward), I was a thoroughly engaged spectator at my first screening—in fact so much so that it was hard eventually for me to step back to criticize the film. *Natural Born Killers* is for me one of the great moments in moviegoing, for the sheer audacity that it displays. Never for a moment was I anything other than a distracted, critical viewer.

The history of movies is a history of diverse modes of address. Accepting for a moment the binaries constructed by the three theorists, I would even go so far as to say that some genres might be said to be more in the gaze/narrative mode; others in the glance/attractions mode. For example, "gaze" genres are the detective, romance, melodrama, thriller, and gangster movies. "Glance" genres are action-adventure films, many comedies, fantasies, specular science fiction, westerns. Horror films and musicals might exist in either group, depending on how they operate. In fact, comedies of remarriage might be gaze movies, while slapstick or gag comedies could be considered glance films. Since these genres have existed more or less from the start of cinema, they have all been available for all spectators to enjoy as they desire.

Connected to the modes of address that are said to influence reception are the modes of exhibition. Within a single evening at the theater in 1942, a filmgoer might move from a distracted, specular start while watching newsreels, shorts, and animated, highly intertextual cartoons, especially if they were from Warner Bros.—then settle back into an absorbed experience with a melodrama. It is not surprising to me that certain types of theatrical sites become associated with specific genres: if drive-ins are constructed as glance environments, their ultimate association with glance genres makes sense.

It is the case that certain variations of these cinematic modes of exhibition and reception become associated with notions of "high" and "low" taste, and this might be worth historical research. However, it is not yet clear to me that individuals in particular class, gender, sexual orientation, or ethnic/racial categories are socially constructed to adhere fully to the reception-mode categories to which some scholars have assigned them.

This binary opposition of "gaze" versus "glance" (or narrative versus attractions), however, really handicaps description of modes of reception. In a discussion of modernity at the turn of the century, Jonathan Crary argues that the increasing stimuli in the everyday world created a concern for attention. How might one discipline focus with so many competing sights? Modern capitalism had to contend with "pushing attention and distraction to new limits and thresholds . . . and then responding with new methods of managing and regulating perception."[20] Randolph Starn argues for a tripartite categorization of "modes of visual attention."[21] These are (1) "the glance," which is initiated by an image's "appeal to a visual exchange where considerations of seeing and knowing are practically inseparable" (p. 210), but which is a brief exchange; (2) "the measured view," which "imposes a strict visual discipline in return for the image of a finite world mastered by the beholder and proportioned to the beholder's eye" (p. 220); and (3) "the scan," which is a "sweeping way of seeing that picks up a pattern, distinguishes, and then pieces together the shape of a design" (p. 222). Starn's schema may have problems, but it does suggest that if modes of address are related to issues of spectators' attention and focus, a richer description of this part of reception might be developed than has operated in the binaries emphasized to date.[22]

Yet the issues of attention produced by modes of address and modes of exhibition are only one small part of what might count as influences on modes of reception. Reception also includes emotional and cognitive behaviors and activities, not clearly derived from physiological, psychological, or social facts of attention. Hansen has recently argued that examining the horizons of reception within a public sphere theory can be a useful theoretical tool for examining modes of reception.[23] Hansen's use of that theory, however, tends to the binaries described above, which are based on external stimuli (the conditions of viewing, the intertextual horizons presented by the film).

In *Interpreting Films*, I have argued for a historical materialist approach to modes of reception.[24] Such an approach considers cognitive and affective activities of spectators in relation to the event of interpretation. A historical materialist approach acknowledges modes of address and exhibition, but it also establishes the identities and interpretative strategies and tactics *brought by spectators to the cinema*. These strategies and tactics are historically constructed by particular historical circumstances. The historical circumstances sometimes create "interpretative communities" or cultural groups such as fans who produce their own conventionalized modes of reception.

A historical materialist approach goes beyond the tripartite division of "preferred," "negotiated," and "oppositional" reading strategies commonly used in some cultural studies scholarship. Instead it describes the processes and phenomena in more specific details. It might, for instance, consider whether the spectator is reading for a plot or watching favorite stars; whether verisimilitude matters or what counts as verisimilitude; whether costume and visual display provide clues to a lesbian or gay subtext; how ethnicity and race might produce "oppositional" gazes or "call-and-response" behavior in a theater.

The more I study spectators, the more perverse I find them to operate, relative to what academics claim are the real or appropriate moviegoing behaviors. For instance, historians of theatrical entertainment now recognize the variety of modes of reception all classes have participated in and the impossibility of disassociating popular culture from elite culture[25]—a binary thesis film studies once tried to establish. This is not to suggest that certain modes of reception do not have different ideological implications, only that I do not think we have sorted this problem out yet.

What I am proposing then is that we use the initial speculations of Gunning, Hansen, Corrigan, and others but that we reconfigure the history of U.S. cinema as a diverse set of modes of address, modes of exhibition, and modes of reception that have always been concurrent even if certain parts of these modes are in dominance in particular situations (the addresses of a film, the conditions of exhibition, the parts of the program being watched, the personal interpretative behaviors of the spectator). Because I believe these modes of address, exhibition, and reception precede cinema by at least one hundred or more years, I would also venture to argue that the future of cinema and the new media of computers and the Internet will be a continuation of this variety of stimuli and activities.

What I think we need is a historical affective and cognitive epistemology and aesthetics of cinema rather than a reductive and ultimately unsatisfying binary opposition that tries to push the diversity of filmgoing experiences into either/or, reductive categories. This shift in speculations about the experiences of moviegoing may provide a better possibility for eventually coming to terms with sociological, aesthetic, historical, and political meanings of those experiences.

NOTES

I wish to acknowledge with thanks my fall 1995 graduate class in American Film History, the audience at the Association Québécoise des Études Cinématographiques 1995 colloquium "Le Cinéma cent ans après," and Walter Metz.

1. The writers focus on U.S. cinema. All of them would likely (and rightly) hesitate to generalize their views beyond the United States. Other theorists exist but make claims only for portions of the history of U.S. cinema. See particularly arguments of the 1970s around Brechtian cinema, for example.

2. Tom Gunning, "The Cinema of Attraction: Early Film, Its Spectator and the Avant-Garde," *Wide Angle* 8, nos. 3/4 (1986): 63–70; Tom Gunning, "'Primitive' Cinema—A Frame-Up? or the Trick's on Us," *Cinema Journal* 28, no. 2 (Winter 1989): 3–12; Tom Gunning, "'Now You See It, Now You Don't': The Temporality of the Cinema of Attractions," *The Velvet Light Trap* no. 32 (1993): 3–10; Tom Gunning, "Tracing the Individual Body: Photography, Detectives, and Early Cinema," in *Cinema and the Invention of Modern Life*, ed. Leo Charney and Vanessa R. Schwartz (Berkeley: University of California Press, 1995), 15–45. Also see Tom Gunning, "The World as Object-Lesson: Cinema Audiences, Visual Culture and the St. Louis World's Fair, 1904," *Film History* 6, no. 4 (Winter 1994): 422–44.

3. Other film scholars who have recently been constructing modernity as partially an onslaught of sensory inputs include Mary Ann Doane, "Technology's Body: Cinematic Vision in Modernity," *Differences* 5, no. 2 (1993): 1–23; Ben Singer, "Modernity, Hyperstimulus, and the Rise of Popular Sensationalism," in *Cinema and the Invention of Modern Life*, ed. Charney and Schwartz, 72–99. On the issue of the effect of this on spectator attention, see below.

4. Miriam Hansen, *Babel and Babylon: Spectatorship in American Silent Film* (Cambridge: Harvard University Press, 1991); Miriam Hansen, "Early Cinema, Late Cinema: Permutations of the Public Sphere," *Screen* 34, no. 1 (Spring 1993): 197–210. Also see Miriam Bratu Hansen, "America, Paris, the Alps: Kracauer (and Benjamin) on Cinema and Modernity," in *Cinema and the Invention of Modern Life*, ed. Charney and Schwartz, 362–402.

5. Hansen, *Babel and Babylon,* 30.

6. This thesis of the nickelodeon as a potentially positive experience for women was originally advanced by Judith Mayne, "Immigrants and Spectators," *Wide Angle* 5, no. 2 (1982): 32–41.

7. Timothy Corrigan, *A Cinema without Walls: Movies and Culture after Vietnam* (New Brunswick, NJ: Rutgers University Press, 1991).

8. Corrigan attributes the gaze/glance distinction to John Ellis, *Visible Fictions: Cinema, Television, Video* (London: Routledge, 1982), who uses it to distinguish between watching film (gazing) and watching television (glancing). Also see the synopsis in Sandy Flitterman-Lewis, "Psychoanalysis, Film, and Television," in *Channels of Discourse, Reassembled*, 2d ed., ed. Robert C. Allen (Chapel Hill: University of North Carolina Press, 1992), 16–25. This distinction has older roots. Randolph Starn, "Seeing Culture in a Room for a Renaissance Prince," in *The New Cultural History*, ed. Lynn Hunt (Berkeley: University of California Press, 1989), 217, indicates his tripartite system of

attention (see below) is influenced by Norman Bryson, "The Gaze and the Glance," in Bryson's *Vision and Painting: The Logic of the Gaze* (New Haven: Yale University Press, 1983).

9. Corrigan, *A Cinema without Walls*, 19. Compare this with Gunning's definition of modernity in his "Tracing the Individual Body," 16.

10. Essentially this is the problem Hansen struggles with in her "Early Cinema, Late Cinema" essay. Her explanation is that this openness exists during periods of transformation in capitalism and cultural formations.

11. Vachel Lindsay, *The Art of the Moving Picture*, rev. ed. (1922; rpt. New York: Liveright, 1970), 15–16.

12. On the heterogenericity of nineteenth-century amusements, see Margaret Cohen, "Panoramic Literature and the Invention of Everyday Genres," in *Cinema and the Invention of Modern Life,* ed. Charney and Schwartz, 227–52.

13. See chapter 3 for details.

14. Richard B. Jewell, "Orson Welles, George Schaefer, and *It's All True*; A 'Cursed' Production," *Film History* 2, no. 4 (November/December 1988): 330.

15. Eric Paul Schaefer, *"Bold! Daring! Shocking! True!: A History of Exploitation Films, 1919–59* (Durham, NC: Duke University Press, 1999).

16. See Mary Morley Cohen, "Forgotten Audiences in the Passion Pits: Drive-in Theatres and Changing Spectator Practices in Post-War America," *Film History* 6, no. 4 (Winter 1994): 470–86.

17. Linda Williams, "Learning to Scream," *Sight and Sound* [new], 4, no. 8 (December 1994): 15. Hitchcock was also not the source of "transform[ing] the previously causal act of going to the movies into a much more disciplined activity of arriving on time and waiting in an orderly line" (p. 15). That honor certainly goes to the Cinerama screenings and the spectacle biblical epics of the 1950s, where reserved seating as well as a fixed starting time replicated theatrical experiences—again, in competition with television.

Hansen assumes that theaters were quiet in the classical era and accepts the clichéd wisdom that talk in movie houses nowadays is due to the habit of watching television at home, in "institutionally less regulated viewing situations" ("Early Cinema," 198). This does not correspond to the evidence, nor does it lead to the most elegant explanation of the history of U.S. cinema.

18. André Bazin, *What is Cinema?* vol. 1, trans. Hugh Gray (Berkeley: University of California Press, 1967), 23–40.

19. Corrigan, *Cinema without Walls*, 3.

20. Jonathan Crary, "Unbinding Vision: Manet and the Attentive Observer in the Late Nineteenth Century," in *Cinema and the Invention of Modern Life*, ed. Charney and Schwartz, 47.

21. Starn, "Seeing Culture in a Room for a Renaissance Prince," 210.

22. Here psychobiological or cognitive theories might be useful.

23. Hansen, "Early Cinema."

24. Janet Staiger, *Interpreting Films: Studies in the Historical Reception of American Cinema* (Princeton: Princeton University Press, 1992).

25. See Leo Lowenthal and Marjorie Fiske, "The Debate over Art and Popular Culture: English Eighteenth Century as a Case Study," in *Literature, Popular Culture, and Society*, by Leo Lowenthal (Englewood Cliffs, NJ: Prentice-Hall, 1960), 54; James B. Twichell summarizing Lawrence Levine's *Highbrow/Lowbrow: The Emergence of Cultural Hierarchy* in *America in Carnival Culture: The Trashing of Taste* (New York: Columbia University Press, 1992), 28–36; Peter Jelavich, "Popular Dimensions of Modernist Elite Culture: The Case of Theater in Fin-de-Siècle Munich," in *Modern Intellectual History: Reappraisals and New Perspectives,* ed. Dominick LaCapra and Steven L. Kaplan (Ithaca, NY: Cornell University Press, 1982), 220–50.

2

The Perversity of Spectators

Expanding the History of the Classical Hollywood Cinema

IN THE EARLY 1980s while David Bordwell, Kristin Thompson, and I were writing *The Classical Hollywood Cinema: Film Style and Mode of Production to 1960*, we were concerned to make an intervention into lines of argumentation posed in what we now rather broadly call "Screen theory." Our initial idea articulated over dinner in 1978 was to write a hundred-page monograph that would create what we thought would be a much more nuanced historical argument about why the overall output of Hollywood was so consistently similar. Using materialist theory about the production of art, we hoped to write a critical sociology of the mode of production that would explain the film form and style prevalent throughout a set of films.

At the time, we were explicitly countering claims about this set of films uniformly positioning the audience spectator into a complicit passivity with a text's discourse. The representational form and style labeled "classical bourgeois realism" was said to create a spectator that was removed from the "realm of contradiction."[1] Moreover, that position assumed that the text caused the effect. As Colin MacCabe writes with pride about his analysis, "the text has no such separate existence [from the spectator]. If we dissolve the reader into the text in the system of identification which I have outlined in this article, it is impossible to hold text and reader . . . separate."[2]

Bordwell and Thompson rejected these correlations based, as they were, so heavily on claims about visual design and a particular theory of the subject. Image choice, narrational voice, identification, and audience subjectivity fell into a domino theory of causal reasoning. Two historically based reasons for questioning this logic existed. For one thing, Bordwell and Thompson rejected depictions of those films by that position as inadequate to describing the design of the formal and stylistic norms of classical Hollywood cinema. For another, they believed that audiences were much more historical (that is, influenced by their time in history) and interactive with the text than Screen theory suggested. They had another idea about what happened between the movie and the audience members.

At that time, it seemed important to criticize the descriptions of Hollywood cinema and to offer an alternative view of the text-effect. I shall return to the Bordwell-Thompson position in a moment. However, I want first to stress that much like Screen theory, we tended to assume that *textuality* determined what people did. Given historical circumstances and a "knowledgeable and cooperative spectator," people would spontaneously interact in particular ways with a given text. Still, we acknowledged that our focus in *The Classical Hollywood Cinema* might be inadequate to describing what audiences really did. We wrote:

> If we have taken the realms of style and production as primary, it is not because we consider the concrete conditions of reception unimportant. Certainly conditions of consumption form a part of any mode of film practice. An adequate history of the reception of the classical Hollywood film would have to examine the changing theater situation, the history of publicity, and the role of social class, aesthetic tradition, and ideology in constituting the audience. This history, as yet unwritten, would require another book, probably as long as this. While we have not treated reception fully, the present book does introduce certain issues—e.g., the activities which the Hollywood film solicits from the spectator, or the importance of early advertising in establishing classical canons—which we believe to be necessary to any future study of how the classical film has been consumed under specific circumstances.[3]

To what degree *The Classical Hollywood Cinema* disrupted the equations of Hollywood equals classical bourgeois realist cinema equals positioned spectator depends on how one charts current arguments about early, classical, and postclassical Hollywood. In many ways, the Screen position continues apace. Arguments that attempt to revise the earlier position often suggest that the variety of types of films produced by Hollywood during the past one hundred years is more complex, but that at a certain point classical bourgeois realist cinema takes over (or dissipates). Additionally, newer theories of identification, desire, and fantasy have complicated some early presumptions. Nuances come as well from observations that some aspects of the sites of exhibition can interrupt the subject effect. Or scholars can claim that this scenario works only for Anglo heterosexual males, but that women, people of color, or gays and lesbians can resist this textual colonization.

Bordwell has continued his refutation of the Screen position in subsequent books and essays. A good place to see this is in his *Narration in the Fiction Film*, where he asserts more explicitly that film form and style will "solicit" knowledgeable and cooperative spectators to process the information cognitively in routine manners.[4] There he broadens his argument by looking at other modes than the classical Hollywood mode of narrating fictional films.

In some ways, I find the original Bordwell, Staiger, and Thompson account of the classical Hollywood cinema still completely persuasive—for what it wants to describe. Recall that our original goal was to describe a sociology of production: what the filmmakers wanted to achieve. Our study of the discourse of the industry went after what the workers thought would create a product that would be acceptable, entertaining, and compelling to as many people as possible. The filmmakers articulated a set of rules to achieve a standardized product for a mass audience.

Where perhaps our account falls short is that we failed to stress how frustrated these workers were when all their carefully laid plans failed. Or when what they often thought of as the mystery of the process produced a success they had scarcely anticipated. As Bordwell and Thompson put it, the filmmakers through the films solicited a response, that response being customer satisfaction. What we did not understand in the early 1980s was how perverse a spectator might be, because we, like people in the Screen theory paradigm, placed too much emphasis on texts creating effects.

Ultimately, I have gone another way. In *Interpreting Films* I disagree with the Screen and Bordwell positions, and argue that context is more significant than textual features in explaining interpretative events.[5] This context most certainly includes the sense data of the film, but it also includes the interpretative strategies used by a spectator. These strategies are influenced by, among other things, aesthetic preferences and practices, knowledges and expectations prior to attending to the moving images, and experiences in the exhibition situation. The context also includes the "historically constructed 'imaginary selves,' the subject positions taken up by individual readers and spectators" (p. 81). Whether I am thinking of myself as a professor or a woman or a neo-Marxist or an American influences what happens while I watch a movie.

The study of the use function of films has prompted new attention to the variety of engagements spectators make with visual media. Although the producers of some dramatic classical Hollywood cinema sought to achieve certain cognitive and emotional experiences for their audiences, clearly the actual circumstances of exhibition, the variety of modes of address, and the pleasures sought by people in their attendance at the movies are much more perverse than our standard text-focused and institutional-based histories have been able to acknowledge. This is no error, for the process of writing histories is one of transitions and, to some degree, building on previous work. Now that the normative expectations are fairly well described, scholarly research needs to expand that history to describe and account for the exceptional number of variations—so exceptional as perhaps even to be the norm.

To go further here, I have already criticized the strategy of describing readings as preferred, negotiated, or resistant.[6] While useful at the start of cultural studies, this triad has numerous problems. For the sake of brevity, I will simply state here the most pertinent to this situation— the triad isn't very descriptive. To rectify this deficiency and to increase further our knowledge of spectators and audiences, I want first of all to lay out a chart that describes what have been assumed as the normative acts of a knowledgeable and cooperative spectator. This chart has the advantage of having much more descriptive power for viewer activities than other systems. The chart is based on the work of the Russian Formalists, Meir Sternberg, Bordwell, and Thompson. However, I take full responsibility for its current organization and its potential problems. After describing this chart, I will provide examples of apparent spectatorial perversity. My purpose will be to indicate how this chart helps us consider the ideology imbedded in the "normative" presumptions.

I need to say a word here about my use of the term "perversity." Perversity has connotations of turning away from what is right or good, i.e., perverted. The term also is suggestive of obstinately persisting in an error or fault, being wrongly self-willed or stubborn. One dictionary even includes characterizations of perverse individuals as having a disposition marked by opposition and contradiction, of being "cranky" and "peevish."

I reject these connotations, based as they are on ideologies of a natural morality, an it-goes-without-saying correctness, and proper subordination. By choosing the term "perversity," I wish to highlight the willfulness of the spectator while also avoiding the implicit, but false, conjunction that doing something different is necessarily politically progressive. Such a conjunction often comes with the terms "resistant" or "insubordinate."[7] That assumption of political progressiveness seldom comes with the notion of "perversion." Rather, I believe that each act of deviant (*and normative*) viewing requires historical and political analysis to locate its effects and "judge" its politics.

I shall not try to explain the causes of these instances of deviance here. However, if I were to make such an attempt, I would turn to ideological and discursive presuppositions by those creating the supposed norms. I do not think that these instances of deviance consist of anything more than spectators' finding their own pleasures, which might be explained by theories used by scholars of the Screen tradition or might find explanations in cognitive, social, or other sciences. Peoples' acts of apparent rebellion are not conscious or obstinate in the face of figures of authority, since the rules laid out as "normative" aren't those of many people. The rules of normative behavior come mostly from just the scholars of textual poetics. Even the members of the classical Hollywood mode of production were perverse in their creation of the movies, often deviating from the rules because they found pleasure and entertainment in what they had produced.

VIEWERS' PRESUMED NORMATIVE
RECEPTION ACTIVITIES

Bordwell and Thompson posit that five general types of textual organization exist: chronological/narrative, the categorical, rhetorical, abstract, and associational. The focus here is on the chronological/narrative text. This focus on organizational form has no bearing on the issue of whether the text is fictional; I subsume that problem under one of the subordinate categories of reading (verisimilitude). In Bordwell's, Thompson's, and others' work, the presumption is that knowledgeable and cooperative readers and viewers of texts normally do certain things with the sense data of a film, depending on the type of sense data they receive.

I shall discuss the chart in fig. 2-1, "Viewers' Presumed Normative Reception Activities for a Chronological/Narrative Film," first in terms of the classical Hollywood film. However, I will also describe briefly what Bordwell posits for readers when they confront art cinema, historical materialist cinema, or parametric cinema.

The proposition for a chronological/narrative film in the classical Hollywood mode is that viewers will participate by predominantly considering compositional features (specifically the chronological or narrative chain of events and the characters). Secondarily and relatedly, they will make choices and hypotheses about verisimilitude, aesthetics, narration, and discourse. The chart lists more specific viewing acts, which often develop in the order that I have listed here, but need not occur necessarily in order to achieve the final dominant goal—to guess what happened and what will happen in the story.

For a classical Hollywood film, Bordwell argues that the primary goal of the knowledgeable and cooperative spectator is to resolve the plot's hermeneutics. Who did what to whom, and why? The activities listed beneath the first category, "Chronological or Narrative Chain," are the most obvious acts required to achieve the outcome of figuring out the story. Connected to constructing the chain of events is the viewer's engagement with the characters (or human agents, if this is a nonfiction story). For Bordwell, figuring out who the protagonist is and what he/she knows is most significant for creating schemata about why the character acts as he/she does. Bordwell might recognize that some viewers are interested in other relationships with characters/human agents (such as empathizing, identifying, desiring, or disidentifying); however, since those are affective activities, Bordwell would subsume those activities as less pertinent to the goals of the classical Hollywood film and to his knowledgeable and cooperative spectator and would likely also relegate them to the affective realm, which he excludes from theoretical consideration.

As Bordwell and Thompson argue, the classical Hollywood cinema is at its best when the other aspects of the viewing experience can be supportive of the compositional goals of the text. In the weighting of choices, classical Hollywood filmmakers will alter reality, downplay

FIG. 2-1. Viewers' Presumed Normative Reception Activities
for a Chronological/Narrative Film
(for fiction and nonfiction normative acts, not necessarily in the
following order; order depends on type of text—CHC,
art cinema, parametric, and so forth)

Compositional

1. Chronological or Narrative Chain
narrative has causality among events as well as temporal sequence
   - determine place (space)
   - find order to events (place into a chronology)
   - determine causality
   - seek relations between plot and subplot(s)
     - e.g., causal; thematic
   - predict events
   - seek closure

2. Characters/Human Agents
   - determine "focalization"—whose story is this?
   - seek causes/motivations for behavior
   - seek relations with characters/human agents
     - empathy (feel for)
     - identification (feel "like")
     - object-choice interest ("desire")
     - disidentify with villains
   - consider character transformations

Verisimilitude

3. Real World Expectations
   - determine relation between text and real world
     - if text is believed to making claims about real world,
       - then categorize as nonfiction
       - proceed relative to personal narrative about real world
       - expand or revise own knowledge or disagree with information
     - if text is believed to make partial claims about real world,
       - then categorize as docudrama
       - proceed relative to personal narrative about real world, but less critical of knowledge-claims of text
     - if text is believed to make no claims about real world,
       - then categorize as fiction
       - proceed with no expectations of match to real world
       Instead:
       - determine expectations about textual genre and its conventions
       - consider breaks from objective realism as possible subjective realism
       - compare acting to
         - real life
         - conventional acting
   - examine mise-en-scène for information about physical environments
     - learn historical information
     - "window shop"

Aesthetics

4. Affective and Emotional Experiences
desire, surprise, sadness, repulsion, joy, etc.

5. Order and Variation
   - look for patterns, repetition and variation, parallels within the text (i.e., "style")
   - look for intertextuality ("genre" used to predict)
     - look for adherence or difference
   - look for allegory, symbolism, symptomatic interpretation

---

Narration

6. Source
   - determine supposed source of narration
     - "internal" source of the text
     - "external" source of the text: hypothesized "authorship"
   - judge internal source's tone
     - self-conscious . . . unself-conscious narration
   - judge internal source's intentions
     - omniscient . . . restrictive
     - omnicommunicative . . . suppressive
     - reliable . . . unreliable

Discourse

7. Messages/Ideology
   - determine textual meanings (meaning)
     - referential, explicit, implicit, symptomatic [Bordwell's system]
   - determine personal significance (significance)

---

aesthetics (such as symbolism), subdue narrational voice, and avoid "sending a telegram" (in the parlance of Samuel Goldwyn). Determining verisimilitude, aesthetics, narration source, and meanings (and significance) is part of the viewer's activities but less significant overall when a viewer is experiencing the classical Hollywood mode of cinema.

Bordwell argues that other cinemas engage viewers in different ways,[8] and this chart in fig. 2-1 can also be used to report for those encounters. Art cinema—which has a loosened causal chain, no deadlines, weak or low closure, and inconsistent character behavior—creates a verisimilitude of either excessive realism or subjective realism. Additionally, narrational sources from a hypothesized author are much more pertinent to viewing. Thus, the knowledgeable and cooperative art cinema spectator will reduce his or her concerns about figuring out a story and will focus on viewing activities related to connecting the story to a "real world" and to a narrational message. Historical materialist knowledgeable and cooperative viewers will subordinate the composition and verisimilar aspects of the text to reading for textual meanings. Parametric knowledgeable and cooperative viewers will focus on order and variation within aesthetic exchanges.

EXAMPLES OF "PERVERSION"

Recent research on the activities of viewers or groups of viewers calls into question many of the descriptions of the viewing process that this chart delineates. While most people likely do view films with some of these behaviors intact, a good amount of evidence questions how truly representative a normative reading of this chart is for the typical viewer. A brief survey of just a bit of the literature on actual reception behaviors is suggestive.

One of the most typical and often cited examples of the classical Hollywood cinema is *The Big Sleep* (1946). The film's notoriety, however, stems from the supposed lack of clarity of its causal chain. Who killed whom is hard to decipher. In fact, one of the great anecdotes of film history is that the director stopped filming in order to contact the original story's author to ask what happened. Even the author wasn't very sure. Literature about the film has emphasized this opaqueness and anecdote as evidence of the Hollywood drive toward causal reasoning. But, if causal clarity were really the expectation of watching *The Big Sleep*, we would expect the reviewers of the period to reject the film outright for its failure. However, only the *New York Times* concentrated on the confusing plot. The other reviewers of the film noticed the problem, but then focused on other features of the text which the writers deemed much more than adequate compensations. For example, *Variety* noted, "There are six deaths to please whodunit fans, plenty of lusty action, both romantic and physical, as Bogart matches wits with dealers in sex literature, blackmail, gambling and murder." *Time* wrote, "Actually, the plot's crazily mystifying, nightmare blur is an asset, and only one of many. By far the strongest is Bogart." And *The New Republic* claimed, "It all has the feeling of an opium smoker's fantasy." No, plot is not important provided the film compensates with spectacles of violence or sex, or the acting of a male lead.

It is my opinion that most viewers of the classical Hollywood film, any classical Hollywood film, would agree: a satisfying affective realm may dominate any pleasures from mastering a complicated story line. My view is further substantiated by the research on viewers of soap operas and romances.[9] The purported classical Hollywood viewer should expect that characters will remain consistent throughout the story, or that if they change, the change will be motivated by their realizing another way to deal with the obstacles confronting them. Soap opera and romance readers do not seem to require that kind of consistency of character. What matters is either fitting the actions into a fantasy of a happy ending or, in the case of an ongoing television program, adjusting to external production needs (such as the replacement of an actor playing a character so he or she can do a movie). Television viewers seem quite savvy that these are constructed fictions, and verisimilitude is hardly a high priority.

Indeed, knowing that fictional narratives are produced permits many viewers to concentrate on narrational issues related to the production of the text. A study of some 1950s gay male viewers of *A Star Is Born* (1954) revealed that they were much more interested in constructing the story of the *production* of the film (when did Judy Garland shoot which scene) than in the film's plot—which at any rate was already "known."[10]

Viewers also project their personal, sometimes marginalized, identities into the sense data. Elizabeth Ellsworth reports that radical feminist viewers of *Personal Best* (1982) created a new conclusion to the film that had the alienated women lovers back together. The viewers also reprioritized the "normative" hierarchy of characters, placing the lesbian in the role of protagonist, against the grain of the more obvious reading.[11] A final example is the camp readings that so many skillful viewers perform on texts.[12] A talented camp reading of a classical Hollywood film would ignore causality but read for spectacle. The villain(ess) would be constructed into the hero(ine) role. The less verisimilitude the better.

In general, then, a couple of rules regarding the classical Hollywood cinema and perverse spectators do exist. These are:

1. Perverse spectators don't do what is expected.
2. Perverse spectators rehierarchize from expectations.

Some of the rehierarchizing has to do with genre preferences. This is, I believe, because critical systems of taste hierarchies prefer some types of films to others, and the normative system was built on those tastes. For example, taste cultures privilege drama over melodrama, sophisticated comedy over slapstick, eroticism over pornography. But not all viewers have the same taste preferences.

WHY THE NORMATIVE DESCRIPTION FALLS SHORT

Once I start looking for nonanticipated behavior, it is everywhere. Why, then, does the normative description fall so short? Among the reasons are the following:

1. *The normative description has been created by a specific group of people:* academic scholars, often with an Arnoldian sense of the purpose of experiencing literature.

2. *The normative description is built on a small set of types of narrative making.* The normative system privileges genres with high cognitive and low excessive-affective demands, which mirrors the interests of the Russian Formalists, whose aesthetic preferences were also for game playing and norms and deviance. But these preferences do not represent the tastes of large numbers of people.

3. *The normative description is specific to the period of its development.* Its appearance in the last half of the 1800s and the early part of the 1900s results in its focus on a particular type of storytelling while paying less heed to earlier and later forms of narration. Thompson is quite explicit about this when she describes how the classical Hollywood cinema came about as a consequence of "a major shift in assumptions about the relation of spectator to film."[13] These assumptions involved (1) moving the spectator from outside the mise-en-scène of a theatrical audience to "within or on the edge of the narrative space," and (2) using 1880s and 1890s models of short-story and well-made-play writing to form the narrative and narration.

Meanwhile, however, spectators continue to use all sorts of strategies of engagement with texts. Bordwell's work on alternative modes of narration helps somewhat to avoid Bordwell, Staiger, and Thompson's original focus on just the mode of interacting with the classical Hollywood cinema, but historical work shows that spectators do not follow the procedures he describes for those modes either.

Jonathan Culler discusses this issue of historical contingency in a good case study of the critical reception of the novel *Tom Jones*.[14] The earliest interpreters of the novel emphasized plot, with characters considered constituents of the plot. Later, a critical inversion occurred, with incident interpreted as revelation of character. In the twentieth century, when seeking a unifying vision of the world is a hallmark of great literature, scholarly interpretations focused on thematic codes as the integrative function. Finally, the impact of modernism produced readings that foregrounded narrational voices of irony and self-referentiality to integrate the devices. In fig. 2-1, this is a shift in emphasis from narrative chain to characters to discourse and, finally, to narration.

4. *The normative description does not take into account a variety of viewers.* Several ways to approach this point exist, but as an example let me point out that textual characters have multiple attributes: age, race/ethnicity, biological sex, gender, sexual preference, occupation, national identity. A character might do certain acts, but a viewer may associate those acts with any one of the attributes of the character's identity. For instance, a cop in command may turn dirty work over to subordinates who are Chicanos. The Anglo, working-class reader may understand this as the "top" man's avoidance of dirty work rather than as an act implicated in a racial discourse.

Readers have different strategies in reading. George Dillon suggests three types. The "Character-Action-Moral" reader does not care much about meaning and significance but sees the event chain linked to the "main character's traits, motives, thoughts, responses, and choices." The "Digger-for-Secrets" reader assumes the narrator has hidden secrets and derives a subtextual meaning from the textual events. The "Anthropologist" reader has the least interest in the events. Instead, this reader focuses on translating the characters' actions and statements into expressions of implicit cultural norms and values.[15]

While I would back away from such generalized theories as Dillon presents, I would underline that the normative description assumes a very limited range of interests for readers and indulges in the construction of an "ideal spectator," a notion well criticized.[16]

5. *The normative description does not take into account the alibi.* Films are often supposedly about one thing when in fact they are easily read as another. Take, for instance, the classical exploitation films of the 1930s and 1940s. Purportedly presented to educate the viewer, these films were there for spectacles of the taboo, forbidden, and gross. This is where polysemy is to the benefit of both the producers and the viewers.

6. *The normative description functions from a very limited set of reasons why spectators might watch a film.* The normative accounts of all four types of cinema—classical, art, historical materialist, and parametric—all dwell on pleasures derived from cognitive mastery or education. Lots of people do not care about that pleasure but enjoy other emotions.

7. *The normative description assumes that spectators are knowledgeable and cooperative.* It assumes as well that spectators are interested in being

logical, thoughtful, coherence seeking, interested in a narrative climax rather than in multiple moments of excess, and so forth. This strikes me as perhaps one of the most salient causes for the failure of the normative description. In an excellent theoretical book, Ellen Schauber and Ellen Spolsky lay out a sequence of activities to describe how readers sort texts into genres. For instance, for a text to be assigned to a functional genre such as "romance," it will need to meet the requirements of being "well formed" relative to the generic prototype and of having a sufficient number of gradient necessary and gradient typicality conditions.[17] This process allows for the most coherent interpretation to emerge.[18] While spectators might go to a film because they think it will be a romance, it is not likely that their interaction with the text will concentrate on that, nor will failure of the film to cohere to their expectations necessarily be troublesome or even noteworthy, provided other parts of the experience compensate. As Manfred Naumann suggests,

> [A work of art] becomes for [the reader] a means of knowledge, of extending his [sic] acquaintance and information; a means of assistance in life, of finding his identity, of realizing and confirming himself; a means of amusement, diversion, and play, of edification and consolation; a means of getting to know an author better, of enlarging his aesthetic and historical knowledge of literature, of penetrating into the beauties of poetic language, or into literary laws and technique.[19]

CONCLUSION

I pointed out at the start of this chapter that the logic Bordwell, Thompson, and I wished to understand when we wrote *The Classical Hollywood Cinema* was the logic of the mode of production. We focused on the practices filmmakers employed in their attempts to produce a type of film that would provide a spectator with an enjoyable experience, and part of those practices involved constructing a particular type of narration. As in Screen theory, however, when we moved to arguments about the textual effects for the spectator, we made unjustified assumptions, easily summarized in the phrase "knowledgeable and cooperative spectator." We did not account for the perverse spectator.

To write the history of the classical Hollywood cinema from the perspective of its reception is not to overthrow those original findings.

Rather it is to recognize how far the filmmakers were from understanding—at least in terms of their discourses, but perhaps not in terms of some of their practices—what their audiences might enjoy. To write the history of the reception of the classical Hollywood cinema is to examine the interplay between the produced films and their consuming publics.

NOTES

I wish to thank particularly my graduate students in "American Media Reception" (1997) for helping me work through material used in this essay. Also, I appreciate the suggestions and reactions to earlier versions of this chart by audiences at the University of Copenhagen (1997), the University College London (1998), the University of East Anglia (1998), the Watershed Media Centre at Bristol, particularly Martin Barker (1998), and the Kansas University–University of Missouri at Kansas City Conference (1998).

1. Colin MacCabe, "Theory and Film: Principles of Realism and Pleasure," *Screen* 17, no. 3 (Autumn 1976): 7–27; Peter Wollen, "Godard and Counter-cinema: *Vent d'Est*," *Afterimage* 4 (Autumn 1972), rpt. in *Readings and Writings* (London: Verso, 1982), 79–91.

2. MacCabe, "Theory and Film," 25.

3. David Bordwell, Janet Staiger, and Kristin Thompson, *The Classical Hollywood Cinema: Film Style and Mode of Production to 1960* (London: Routledge & Kegan Paul, 1985), xiv.

4. David Bordwell, *Narration in the Fiction Film* (Madison: University of Wisconsin Press, 1985).

5. Janet Staiger, *Interpreting Films: Studies in the Historical Reception of American Cinema* (Princeton: Princeton University Press, 1992).

6. Staiger, *Interpreting Films*, 72–76.

7. Robert C. Allen suggests a different triad in his *Horrible Prettiness: Burlesque and American Culture* (Chapel Hill: University of North Carolina Press, 1991), 36. He posits an ordination/subordination/insubordination trilogy to describe production acts. While this has some value in more aptly describing the real political effect of certain behaviors, the Allen triad still falls short in descriptive felicity.

8. Bordwell, *Narration in the Fiction Film*.

9. Mary Ellen Brown, "Knowledge and Power: An Ethnography of Soap-Opera Viewers," in *Television Criticism: Approaches and Applications*, ed. Leah R. Vandeberg and Lawrence A. Wenner (New York: Longman, 1991); Janice Radway, *Reading the Romance: Women, Patriarchy and Popular Culture* (Chapel Hill: University of North Carolina Press, 1984).

10. Staiger, *Interpreting Films.*

11. Elizabeth Ellsworth, "Illicit Pleasures: Feminist Spectators and *Personal Best,*" *Wide Angle* 8, no. 2 (1986): 45–56.

12. Jane Feuer, "Reading *Dynasty*: Television and Reception Studies," *South Atlantic Quarterly* 88, no. 2 (Spring 1989): 443–60; Pamela Robertson, *Guilty Pleasures: Feminist Camp from Mae West to Madonna* (Durham, NC: Duke University Press, 1996).

13. Bordwell et al., *Classical Hollywood Cinema*, 158–67.

14. Jonathan Culler, *The Pursuit of Signs: Semiotics, Literature, Deconstruction* (Ithaca, NY: Cornell University Press, 1981), 63.

15. George L. Dillon, "Styles of Reading," *Poetics Today* 3, no. 2 (Spring 1982): 77–88.

16. Staiger, *Interpreting Films,* 24–27.

17. Ellen Schauber and Ellen Spolsky, *The Bounds of Interpretation: Linguistic Theory and Literary Text* (Stanford: Stanford University Press, 1986), 59.

18. Meir Sternberg, *Expositional Modes and Temporal Ordering in Fiction* (Baltimore: Johns Hopkins University Press, 1978), 253–45; Steven Mailloux, "Reader-Response Criticism?" *Genre* 10 (Fall 1977): 424–25.

19. Manfred Naumann, "Literary Production and Reception" [1973], trans. Peter Heath, *New Literary History* 8 (Autumn 1976): 117.

3

Writing the History of American Film Reception

IN CHAPTER 1, "Modes of Reception," I argued against a tendency in film studies to create two large categories of texts or exhibition situations, to pit those against each other, and then to make vast claims about spectator effect from that binary opposition.[1] Although that broad generalization might have been somewhat effective initially in studying American film, it does not hold up historically. Instead, the entire history of cinema in every period (and likely every place) witnesses several modes of cinematic address, several modes of exhibition, and several modes of reception. Moreover, any individual viewer may engage *even within the same theatergoing experience* in these various modes of reception.

In chapter 2, "The Perversity of Spectators," I provided an alternative system for examining the modes of reception.[2] My outline, based on the work of Russian Formalists, Meir Sternberg, David Bordwell, and Kristin Thompson, expanded upon what these scholars have claimed to be the reception activities for a narrative film of the "classical" type. However, research on actual viewers of classical films suggests an extensive variety of activities not conforming to these predictions. This system, then, is useful for noting types of strategies in richer detail than the triad of preferred, negotiated, and resistant readings. Additionally, one could also track the receptions of a film across a period of time.[3]

Another potential use of this system is in studying discourses around a culture event in which a film might participate. In "Taboos and Totems" (chapter 9), instead of studying a full set of discourses around the film *The Silence of the Lambs*, I discuss how a segment of readers—some gay men—used the film to try to "out" its star, Jodie Foster, as a lesbian.[4] My interest here is not in surveying all the receptions of the film but in exploring how the film could be appropriated by a specific group for a political act of resistance against what they perceived was the possibility of reading the serial killer as a homosexual.[5]

In this chapter, I want to take up the issue of "talk" and media reception in order to supply an extension of the system proposed in chapter 2. One of the major characteristics of the causal arguments of some scholars of reception is to create boundaries around the reception experience. That is, in discussing reception they consider only part of the process. One of the boundaries commonly created is the text as an artifact. What the text does to the audience is what is determinant. If the film is a classical Hollywood narrative, then the viewer takes up a voyeuristic reception mode, becoming absorbed in the plot and identifying with the characters. If the film is a text of spectacle and visual or aural stimulation, the viewer is positioned into an exhibitionist mode of reception and responds critically or with distraction.[6] Some scholars go on to argue that the latter type of film is popular (of the people) or modern or postmodern, with the classical film usually labeled bourgeois or premodern. The boundary constraining the audience in this theoretical framework is the stylistic practices of the text. However, if in fact the text were determinant, all of the perversions, changes, and appropriations that reception scholars have described would be impossible.

Even those scholars who argue that the viewing context can improve the possibility of a wider range of readings or audience experiences construct new boundaries. The two boundaries of contextual theorists that I will focus on are historical time periods (presound, sound/classical, postclassical) and audience identities (class, race, ethnicity, age, sexual orientation, gender). In the concluding part of the essay, I will consider a third boundary imbedded in many contextual studies.

TALKING IN THE THEATER

In an important and underrecognized essay published in 1982, Judith Mayne argued that the immigrant experience in the nickelodeon may be more complex than scholars had previously understood. She posited that while the immigrant was being familiarized with American culture and consumerism through the "shopping window" of the screen, the collectivity of the experience within the theater should also be considered as a potential force for promoting resistance to industrialization and, for women, to the patriarchal home.[7] The nickelodeons bestowed on immigrants an unprecedented status as worthy consumer. Moreover, the exhibition site functioned as a mediation between public and private spheres. Descriptions by contemporary writers such as Mary Heaton Vorse in 1911 indicate a lively exchange of commentary and debates within audiences at the exhibition scene, and it is just such an exhibition context that Mayne considers as lending more complexity to the reception of the movies being shown on the screens.[8]

Miriam Hansen has developed Mayne's original idea by drawing on German theories of the public sphere. She then combines Mayne's observations about the nickelodeon scene with the binary text-determinant reception theories.[9] What comes out of this is a bifurcated history in which exhibition situations that permit a "public sphere" dialogue among the participants have some potential for contemplative, distractive viewing, while exhibition situations that close down this dialogue reduce spectators to an absorbed, identifying viewing position. Hansen places great weight on the effect of the arrival of mechanically synchronized sound, which permitted on-screen diegetic dialogue. The screen's commanding talk shuts down the audience's chat. In her discussion of recent viewing situations, Hansen further states that watching films in homes in "institutionally less regulated viewing situations" has had some effect on increasing talk in four-wall theaters.[10]

The question I want to ask is, is the ability to talk during a movie an appropriate dividing line in the theorization of audiences and media reception? What do we know about talking in the American film theater? Did the arrival of sound cut off talk? Were some audience groups who would have liked to continue to chat constrained by other audience members who prohibited community dialogue? Were the contemplative, distractive opportunities shut down to an absorbed, identifying experience?

We do know that talk by minority groups has been occurring recently during some types of screenings. One of the most famous examples of this is the phenomenon around *The Rocky Horror Picture Show,* which started during the transitional postclassical time described by Hansen as renewing opportunities for this public-sphere experience. *The Rocky Horror Picture Show* opened in New York City in 1975; by 1976, "counterpoint dialogue" had started. Still going strong today, *The Rocky Horror Picture Show* scene has shifted in the minorities it serves. Once a haven for urban gay men, the current audience is predominantly young adolescents, and dialogue lines once extolling sexual freedom and gender bending are less common, while homophobic and misogynist remarks are common.[11]

The Rocky Horror Picture Show, however, came out of not a TV audience but a wider party scene in the New York underground cinema movement of the 1960s. From the early 1960s through the Warhol media events at the Dom in St. Mark's Place in 1966 and beyond, the late-night taboo-breaking exhibition situation was an environment appealing to nonconformist but often white, and usually male, hipsters and sexually liberated people. Often with a liberal to leftist agenda, but not necessarily nonsexist, films such as *Flaming Creatures* (1963), *The Chelsea Girls* (1966–67), and *Cocks and Cunts* (1963–66) challenged not only heterosexual, monogamous mores but very often taboos against interracial sexuality. Accounts of these screenings describe them as quite rowdy, with people vocally expressing their judgments of the films. Smoking and ingesting illicit drugs helped contribute to a casual viewing context.[12]

This underground scene was not the scene of the classical film, so it does not serve as an example of talk during the watching of classical films. The New York hip scene did, however, have its precedents in situations in which classical Hollywood films were screened. This context was the teenage filmgoing parties of the 1950s, where attendance at drive-ins or even in four-wall theaters at which showmanship gimmicks promoting grade-B horror and thriller films scarcely encouraged an absorbed, identifying spectator.[13] Accounts of the audiences encountering the surprise of buzzers under their chairs suddenly going off during *The Tingler* (1959) or a skeleton flying across the auditorium at the climax of *House on Haunted Hill* (1958) suggest some exhibitors of Hollywood movies were interested in a much more lively experience than the quiet expected at other 1950s screenings.[14] This history also reminds us that the dialogue activity for *Scream* (1996) is nothing new.

In fact, such teen screening (and screaming) parties even predate the 1950s. In studying the exhibition scene in the 1940s during World War II, I discovered that a major problem for theaters was the adolescent and preadolescent audiences. With a scarcity of day-care centers and more funds available to youth as a consequence of the war economy, kids attended the theater more often, stayed later—even to midnight on weeknights—and had no parental supervision. "Juvenile delinquency" became a common reported complaint. In Indianapolis, juveniles were "slashing seats, breaking light globes and committing other acts of vandalism." Chicago exhibitors reported smoking damage, screens "riddled with pins till they look like waffles," and kids dropping things from the balcony. Moreover, "sex crimes have been committed in dark houses with insufficient help to patrol them properly." Managers witnessed mothers dropping off children under the age of six and then heading off to shop.[15] Our image of 1940s audiences as quietly engrossed in the most recent Hollywood film needs to be revised.

So here are some examples of minorities which in certain circumstances use the exhibition site as a public space not only to talk to one another (an important aspect of community and the public sphere) but even to talk back to the screen. Minorities served by this community space include gays and straights, sexual and political liberals and conservatives, and teenagers. Most of the members of these example groups are marginalized by age, although studies also suggest that they are typically white and often middle-class.[16]

Talk at theaters isn't confined, though, to the white and middle- or working-class adolescent or young urban male. A less studied but important example is the "call-and-response" talk common among African American audiences. In a description of two recent screenings of *Independence Day* (1996), starring Will Smith, Kevin L. Carter writes:

> On screen, as a huge alien spacecraft hovers threateningly over downtown Los Angeles, weirdos and trendies party on the roof of an LA skyscraper and excitedly await the aliens' arrival. MAN and WOMAN in audience respond to the images on screen.
>
> MAN: Look at that. Do you notice one thing? There aren't any black people up there! We aren't stupid enough to stay around waiting for no aliens.
>
> WOMAN: They'd be on the way out of there.
>
> MAN: I know I'd be out of Dodge.[17]

The astute reference to the western genre by this male audience member suggests how savvy audiences are about what they are seeing.

Yet this is just resistant commentary among two audience members. Here's an example of "call-and-response" from a viewer who is surely neither contemplative, distracted, nor "oppositional":

Scene 2: Interior, local movie theater, weeknight showing of "Eraser."
VANESSA WILLIAMS has just made a harrowing escape from some BAD
GUYS and is panicked. The FEDS assure her that, even though she's risk-
ing her life to put the BAD GUYS in jail, she'll be protected.
> FED: Don't worry, you'll be fine.
> WILLIAMS: No, I'm not going to be fine.
> MAN IN AUDIENCE: Vanessa, you'll always be fine! (P. E6)

Carter continues in his discussion to suggest that not all African
Americans appreciate call-and-response; one fifteen-year-old woman
told him, "I think it's one of the rudest things someone can do. . . . It
makes it very hard for a listener to hear what's going on in a movie"
(p. E6). This reaction, as well as other studies of African American audiences, indicates that blacks are not homogenous. Often class identity or gender identity produces divisions within the racial/ethnic
identity.[18]

The examples of talk described so far might be characterized as belonging to members of minority groups, albeit of different identities. Is
it the case that the most obvious nonminority group—white, heterosexual, adult, middle-class males—are the listeners who act appropriately
at the movies? Once over the troublesome teen years, do they become
responsible bourgeois viewers? The answer is, not in all cases. In some
particular circumstances this audience will talk at the movies.

One circumstance is the all-male stag party or exploitation movie.
Now I have been to only one stag movie party where the audience was
mostly men, but silence was the last thing any of them wanted. Teasing,
joking, and general verbal showing off were the prevalent behaviors,
because if quiet resulted, the sexual tension and potential homoerotic
possibilities became too apparent. Other people's accounts of these
events reinforce the view that my experience was typical.

Another occasion when this category of people has been known to
talk during movies is while watching Hollywood movies at the front
during World War II. Research by Bill Fagelson indicates that soldiers
indulged in the same kind of cynical "call-and-response" back talk to
Hollywood movies that I have described for some African Americans.[19]
Moreover, the content of the back talk can be linked to the soldiers'
broader context. Often they criticized what they considered were the
unrealistic movie representations of the war conditions; they also re-
sented male stars who escaped induction into the service.

Both of these examples of talk by the most "dominant" audience group might be explained by their exhibition situations—illicit stag movie parties or ragtag, ad hoc screenings at the front. And one of these sets of movies certainly does not suggest any kind of "classical" text.

Evidence does exist, though, that talk by this dominant group occasionally occurred in exhibition situations in which appropriate behavior was expected, during the classical-sound era of Hollywood, and for classical films. One such occasion was discussed in chapter 1, the preview screening of *The Magnificent Ambersons* (1942) in Pomona, California. According to Richard Jewell's research, "The audience detested the picture, laughing in the wrong places, talking back to the screen and decrying its 'artiness' in their preview card comments."[20] A second example is during the early years of the art cinema movement in the United States. The *New York Times* reported in 1965 that at revivals of Humphrey Bogart films the audience "shouts the dialogue." The audience members were described by the reporter as "collegiate and postcollegiate—welter of dungarees, war-surplus coats and tweed jackets with a scattering of beards, mustaches and students in motorcycle boots."[21]

The hypothesis that classical Hollywood exhibitors took the exhibition scene totally seriously is also questionable. During the supposed heyday of the classical film—the 1930s and 1940s—auditoriums were used as community halls in which exhibitors promoted moviegoing by giving prizes for games, and they displayed their civic responsibility by soliciting for bond drives. Although the audience might settle down for the main feature, a public-sphere environment was not excluded but actually encouraged. Moreover, even the main feature during the high-classical era was susceptible to violation if audience needs demanded it. Arthur Frank Wertheim writes that the radio comedy *Amos 'n' Andy* was so popular in the early 1930s that "motion picture theaters installed loudspeakers in lobbies and stopped whatever film was being shown so that fans could hear the program over a radio placed on the stage."[22]

While many writers during all of these years complained about interference from people's talk, not all white, middle-class, bourgeois men supported the quiet-during-the-movie mode of spectatorship. As noted in chapter 1, the progressive poet and democrat Vachel Lindsay argued in the late teens for a "conversation theater." Lindsay went on to suggest that if readers planned to follow up on his suggestion of quietly chatting during a movie, perhaps they should sit toward the front of the auditorium so that only the conversants and "Little Mary" Pickford would hear what they had to say.[23]

Now this example is quite suggestive in upsetting the stereotypical view of American film reception. A middle-class, white man is urging talking during the film—albeit quietly and so as not to bother other people. In his account of one attempt at this conversation theater, working-class women are the ones attempting to constrain Lindsay and his friend's behavior with the classic tactic of the scathing gaze. They did in 1918 what we do in 1998. It is the case, I will grant, that the reason the women request that the men stop talking is that they cannot become absorbed in the romance unfolding before them. And I will grant as well that talk disrupts the illusionistic experience. But these sets of etiquette at the movies seem unconvincingly aligned with audience identities or with historical time periods. I have provided examples of all audience identities talking through all historical periods of the classical Hollywood film at many types of films—the horror, the thriller, the war movie, the male melodrama, and the romance. The boundaries of audience identity or historical time period are inadequate as dividing lines unilaterally to carve up film history and create a general theory of audience reception.

Interestingly, a recent study of the movement toward a quiet, attentive audience mode implies that while listening intently may be a bourgeois protocol, the configuration of relations may be different from what has been posited in film studies. James H. Johnson in *Listening in Paris* asks, why did the Parisian audiences become silent at musical events? During the era of Louis XV (the mid-1700s), the expected behavior of the aristocracy was to circulate throughout the theater, converse with friends, and occasionally enjoy the spectacle of the machinery, dancing, and *"filles d'opéra"* (the women dancers). Johnson writes that one "young nobleman explained to his guest that listening to the music with focused attention was 'bourgeois.' 'There is nothing so damnable,' he went on, 'as listening to a work like a street merchant or some provincial just off the boat.'" Johnson notes, "For these spectators, attentiveness was a social *faux pas*."[24]

Johnson ultimately concludes that while listening attentively became the dominant convention (as the bourgeoisie replaced the aristocracy at the theater), also important in the move to silence during the show were changes in the physical features of the hall (related to the politics of the French Revolution), the musical and theatrical qualities of the works, and altered desires and expectations about aesthetics. In the mid-1700s, music was supposed to be obvious, so that listening was not required; by the late 1700s, aesthetics and musical trends moved toward emphasizing emotionalism and personalized connections to the specta-cle. Expectations and appropriate behavior might include crying dur-ing an opera. By the 1800s, "Grand Opera was spectacle, an updated mix of revolutionary-era scenes of masses crowding the stage and Napoleonic glitter" (p. 250). The props and costumes were more realis-tic but also varied and plentiful; "hair-raising denouements" were praised; and the music was powerful and percussive. So much was going on that the new audience of the bourgeoisie needed to pay atten-tion. While Johnson connects silence in the auditoriums with the bour-geoisie, in his study spectacle, stimulation, and melodrama drive that choice. It is a choice away from talk, but it was the aristocracy and not the proletariat who had been the talkers—vainly showing off and gos-siping among their peers.[25]

This reminds us that talk-as-talk is not necessarily talk of the sort implied by the phrase "the public sphere." What determines talk in the theater? Certainly the context, and not the text. Who is watching, what the occasion is, and whether the situation is serious or play—all of these seem pertinent. But audience identity or exhibition situation (such as mechanically synchronized sound) will not always match up with a lis-tening or a talking audience. More important, though, if the question is really about the potential for progressive or conservative audience ef-fects, what is being said matters too. A lot of talk is not talk that pro-motes any democracy, intelligent dialogue, or progressive critique of the movie's plot. The boundaries of audience identity and historical time period do not help to write the history of American film reception nor does the existence or nonexistence of talk in the auditorium.

BEYOND TALKING IN THE THEATER

I suggested a third boundary may also be limiting the writing of film reception history. That third boundary is assuming the time spent watching the film is the context of the event. Some scholars of recep-tion write as though "experiencing" the text stops at the end of the show. Even if the audience has been perfectly bourgeois and quiet during the movie, talk happens afterward—and a great deal of it. To analyze the ideological, cultural, and personal effects of film viewing, we must also consider postmovie talk by spectators. Here the work of cultural studies and analysis of fans contribute to writing the history of American film reception.

Fig. 3-1, "*Beyond* Presumed Normative Reception Activities," supplements fig. 2-1. The first half of the chart, "Physical and Expressive Activities during the Event," lists possible external features of the spectator's activities during the movie. The second half of the chart, "Reception Activities after the Event," goes forward to break the boundary of the film-viewing event as the end of the reception process.[26]

I would like to compare fig. 2-1 and fig. 3-1 briefly before moving to consider the second half of fig. 3-1. Fig. 2-1 summarizes what might be said to be some of the activities going on *inside* the spectator during the movie—activities that are cognitive, affective, and emotional. Fig. 2-1 considers the spectators' production of meanings of the text. Fig. 3-1 synopsizes external activities that are not traditionally thought of as making meanings but which obviously feed into the consequences of fig. 2-1 or externalize the internal thoughts and feelings being developed within the spectator. Thus, on one side, an activity during the film of "metatalking"—discussing with a co-spectator what is occurring—would have consequences on an interpretation. Any of us can recall doing that—even though we are supposed to be nice, bourgeois audience members. On the other side, expressing sudden terror or laughing out loud indicates an affective and emotional state being experienced.

This chart does not attempt to explain why these activities occur. I believe that different activities have different explanations. Affective and emotional expressions may be better explained by psychological theories; sociological theories are more suited for accounting for

FIG. 3-1. *Beyond* Presumed Normative Reception Activities
(terminology based on film and television viewing,
but applicable to other types of texts)

Physical and Expressive Activities during the Event

Extent of this will depend on contextual factors such as
- Site of event: four-wall theater, exploitation house, drive-in, party, bar viewing night, home
- Genre of the text
- Social mix/dynamics: all-male stag party; adolescent males in a group with women; broadly viewed social ritual (such as televised wedding or funeral); date

Activities
- Metatalking—discussion of the narration and text-as-text
- Talking to characters
- Talking to "author"
- Talking with companions, such as
  - bringing them up to date on the events
  - explaining character motives
  - translating cultural ambiguities
- Repeating memorized lines of dialogue from film (repeat viewers)
- Expressing affective and emotional states—laughing, crying, screaming, becoming aroused
- Performing social roles—expressing terror or fortitude in face of horror
- Walking out temporarily or permanently

Reception Activities after the Event
- Viewers and Other Viewers—Discussion of the text with others
  - social interaction, bonding
  - "cultural forum"—discussion, debate
  - fan or "cult" involvement—more systematic or intensive exchange about the text
    - commentary—opinions of pleasure, displeasure; "dishing"
    - speculation—gossip and predictions, possibly using extra-textual information
    - request for and diffusion of information
- Viewers and Characters and/or Stars
  - Extracinematic practices include
    - attempting to resemble the physical features of the character and/or star
    - imitating the character's and/or star's actions
    - copying the star so as to become the star
  - write letters to character and/or star
  - attempt to get physically close to star
  - fantasize—from repetitive daydreams to accounts of paranormal encounters
- Viewers and the Production of New Materials
  - Narratives
    - recontextualize the story
    - expand the series timeline
    - refocalize the characters
    - realign the moral world
    - shift the genre
    - combine diegetic worlds
    - dislocate characters into new worlds
    - insert oneself into the story
    - build on an emotional crisis in the original narrative
    - create sexual stories between characters
  - Creation of songs, videos, academic articles, etc.
- Viewers, the Textual World, and the Real World
  - name children, pets, etc. after aspects of the textual world
  - take trips to places used in textual world
  - collect materials related to the text and its makers
- Viewers and Personal Significance
  - use information in film to guide behavior in everyday life
  - use film in personal memory as signpost to life's experiences
  - organize collected or created materials to stimulate memories of text, star, meanings in scrapbooks, fan newsletters, 'zines, web pages
- Go to the film again, perhaps bringing others to "initiate" them

much of the talk and some of the physical behavior. Yet both types of theories probably should be marshaled to explain any specific case being studied.

The second half of fig. 3-1 is a start toward outlining postmovie meaning making. I am not able here to discuss whether or not meanings made "after" the movie are more or less accurate than those made during the event. I assume anyone working in reception studies has already forsaken the belief in some immanent meaning to the text. What matters in either case (interpretations existing during or after the film) are the uses that the meanings have for people.

What the second half of fig. 3-1 supplies are some ideas about the possibilities of dialogue and connection among spectators after the movie, by which "talk" continues to process the text, reworking it for the use of the spectator. Part of that spectatorial use seems clearly to be personal, but other use values are social—the creation of communities of people who use the text as the object through which to construct networks of attachment, discovery, and, sometimes, authority and power.

While most studies of fans emphasize the positive features of exchange and empowerment deriving from interests in often marginal objects of pleasure, I would point out that scholars may need to shift their presumptions even here—although not back to the days when fans were considered pathological spectators. Without going that far, I would argue that some fans and fan communities might benefit from more critical social theory. The fan's attention to capturing the physical garments of a star or creating a web site with the most hits also bespeak desires for power and control. Fandom, like movies and like exhibition-site behavior, cannot be easily bifurcated into good and bad; the historian's responsibility is adequate description and thoughtful evaluation.

To write the history of American film reception, thus, requires avoiding unnecessary and unproductive boundaries that prevent scholars from considering a wide variety of factors that might explain what the relations are between spectators and films. The boundaries of the text as stimulus need to be removed. The boundaries of audience identity and historical time period also have to be questioned as scholars seek evidence of a variety of exhibition experiences during times presumed to "contain" spectators from being intelligent and thoughtful— or silly—viewers of the films. Scholarship also needs to avoid the boundary of the event of moviegoing itself. Working and reworking a text continue far beyond the walls of a theater.

I suggest then that (1) reception scholarship move away from a decade/period model of film exhibition to a set of practices that cross the years of filmgoing. Scholarship should note class practices, perhaps related to presumptions of taste such as "high" and "low." These class practices, however, need to be checked against the meanings being made. Ethnic and gender practices should also be tracked for patterns but not unreasonably homogenized. (2) Scholarship should investigate not just the event of filmgoing but the continual making and remaking of interpretations and emotional significances through the lives of individuals. Here work on popular and cultural memory is relevant. The use of a film such as *Gone with the Wind* to pin down the "meaning" of someone's life at a particular moment in her existence—just like the Kennedy assassination—will be part of the history of American film reception. (3) Scholarship must avoid correlating political effectivity with specific behaviors. The event as a whole—within its historical context and its historical consequences—must be considered before we make any kind of evaluative claims about whether the meanings are progressive or conservative. And for whom. Ideological evaluations should also avoid universalizations. Talk is not always progressive even in the public sphere. Talk can be quite incendiary. It can, however, also be binding and supportive. Writing the history of American film reception is only one of the kinds of writing about American film possible; for me, it is one of the most intriguing and complicated.

NOTES

1. Janet Staiger, "Modes of Reception," "Le cinéma cent ans après" colloquium, Montreal, Quebec, 15–19 November 1995 (forthcoming in conference proceedings). [Chapter 1 here.] The trends are observed in the work of Tom Gunning, Miriam Hansen, Timothy Corrigan, and others following in their footsteps.

2. Janet Staiger, "The Perversity of Spectators: Expanding the History of the Classical Hollywood Cinema," Visual Media: History, Aesthetics and Reception conference, Copenhagen, Denmark, 1–4 December 1997 (forthcoming in conference proceedings). [Chapter 2 here.]

3. Janet Staiger, *Interpreting Films: Studies in the Historical Reception of American Cinema* (Princeton: University of Princeton Press, 1992).

4. Janet Staiger, "Taboos and Totems: Cultural Meanings of *The Silence of the Lambs,* in *Film Theory Goes to the Movies,* ed. Jim Collins, Hilary Radner, and Ava Collins (New York: Routledge, 1993), 142–54. [Chapter 9 here.]

5. Janet Staiger, "An Archive of Emotions," Society for Cinema Studies Conference, San Diego, California, 4–7 April 1998.

6. Tom Gunning tends to use more formalist, "defamiliarization" language; Miriam Hansen draws on Brechtian language.

7. Judith Mayne, "Immigrants and Spectators," *Wide Angle* 5, no. 2 (1982): 32–41.

8. Mary Heaton Vorse, "Some Picture Show Audiences," *Colliers*, 24 June 1911, 441–47.

9. Miriam Hansen, *Babel and Babylon: Spectatorship in American Silent Film* (Cambridge: Harvard University Press, 1991); Miriam Hansen, "Early Cinema, Late Cinema: Permutations of the Public Sphere," *Screen* 34, no. 1 (Spring 1993): 197–210. Hansen is careful to suggest that the public sphere of the nickelodeons is not a perfect one; rather it is ambiguous with both progressive and conservative features.

10. Hansen, "Early Cinema," 198.

11. Based on my own observations in 1979 versus today.

12. See chapter 8.

13. On the midnight movie and *Rocky Horror* audiences, see J. Hoberman and Jonathan Rosenbaum, *Midnight Movies* (New York: Harper & Row, 1983), 1–76, 174–213; Bruce A. Austin, "Portrait of a Cult Film Audience: The Rocky Horror Picture Show," *Journal of Communications* 31 (1981): 43–54.

14. Mary Morley Cohen, "Forgotten Audiences in the Passion Pits: Drive-in Theatres and Changing Spectator Practices in Post-war America," *Film History* 6, no. 4 (Winter 1994): 470–86.

15. William Castle, *Step Right Up! . . . I'm Gonna Scare the Pants Off America* (New York: G. P. Putnam's Sons, 1976), 136–59. I thank Alison Macor for her research which introduced me to Castle's antics.

16. "Late Pix Menace to Kids?" *Variety*, 14 October 1942, 7; "Curfew Spreads," *Motion Picture Herald*, 5 December 1942, 9; "Curfew Cutting Grosses but Towns Want Strict Juve Delinquency Curb," *Variety*, 25 August 1943, 7; "Zoot-Suited Juveniles Run Amok in Detroit Theatres and Niteries," *Variety*, 23 November 1943, 7; "Parents' Responsibility," *Variety*, 14 November 1945, 9; "Chi Theatre Vandalism Up," *Variety*, 21 November 1945, 7.

17. Kevin L. Carter, "Black Audiences Don't Watch, They Talk to Movies," *Austin American-Statesman*, 26 July 1996, E6.

18. Thomas Cripps, "*Amos 'n' Andy* and the Debate over American Racial Integration," in *American History/American Television: Interpreting the Video Past*, ed. John E. O'Connor (New York: Ungar, 1983), 33–54; Norman F. Friedman, "Responses of Blacks and Other Minorities to Television Shows of the 1970s about Their Groups," *Journal of Popular Film and Television* 7, no. 1 (1978): 85–102; Jacqueline Bobo, "*The Color Purple*: Black Women as Cultural Readers," in *Female Spectators: Looking at Film and Television*, ed. E. Deidre Pribram (London:

Verso, 1988), 90–109; Cheryl B. Butler, "*The Color Purple* Controversy: Black Woman Spectatorship," *Wide Angle* 13, nos. 3/4 (1991): 62–69.

19. Bill Fagelson, unpublished seminar paper, University of Texas at Austin, Fall 1997.

20. Richard B. Jewell, "Orson Wells, George Schaefer, and *It's All True*: A 'Cursed' Production," *Film History* 2, no. 4 (November/December 1988): 330.

21. "Old Bogart Films Packing Them In," *New York Times*, 28 January 1965, n.p.

22. Arthur Frank Wertheim, *Radio Comedy* (New York: Oxford University Press, 1979), 48.

23. Vachel Lindsay, *The Art of the Moving Picture*, rev. ed. (1922; New York: Liveright, 1970), 15–16.

24. James H. Johnson, *Listening in Paris: A Cultural History* (Berkeley: University of California Press, 1995), 31.

25. Also see John F. Kasson, *Rudeness and Civility: Manners in Nineteenth-Century Urban America* (New York: Hill and Wang, 1990). Kasson suggests refinement of manners implied physical control of emotions; yet restraint of expression does not conflict with pleasure in having those feelings.

26. The chart in fig. 3-1 is indebted to a massive amount of research by many fine scholars. I apologize to those I fail to recognize in the following list: Denise Bielby and C. Lee Harrington, "Reach Out and Touch Someone: Viewers, Agency, and Audiences in the Televisual Experience," in *Viewing, Reception, Listening: Audiences and Cultural Reception*, ed. Jon Cruz and Justin Lewis (Boulder, CO: Westview Press, 1993), 81–100; John Champagne, "'Stop Reading Films!': Film Studies, Close Analysis, and Gay Pornography," *Cinema Journal* 36, no. 4 (Summer 1997): 76–97; John Fiske, *Television Culture* (London: Methuen, 1987); Stephen Hinerman, "'I'll Be Here with You': Fans, Fantasy and the Figure of Elvis," in *The Adoring Audience: Fan Culture and Popular Media*, ed. Lisa A. Lewis (New York: Routledge, 1992), 107–34; Henry Jenkins, *Textual Poachers: Television Fans and Participatory Culture* (New York: Routledge, 1992); Jackie Stacey, *Star Gazing: Hollywood Cinema and Female Spectatorship* (London: Routledge, 1994); Helen Taylor, *Scarlett's Women: Gone with the Wind and Its Female Fans* (New Brunswick: Rutgers University Press, 1989); Jennifer C. Waits, "United We Dish: The Construction of Reality in the Melrose Update Community," Popular Culture Association Conference, San Antonio, TX, March 1997; and the numerous papers from undergraduate and graduate students in the Department of Radio-Television-Film at the University of Texas at Austin.

PART II

INTERPRETATION AND HOLLYWOOD FILM HISTORY

4

Hybrid or Inbred

The Purity Hypothesis and Hollywood Genre History

TWO THESES IN recent film scholarship seem closely linked. One thesis is that films produced in Hollywood in the past forty years or so are persistently instances of genre mixing. For example, in discussing two films, *Back to the Future III* and *Dances with Wolves* (both 1990), Jim Collins writes,

> they represent two divergent types of genre film that co-exist in current popular culture. One is founded on dissonance, on eclectic juxtapositions of elements that very obviously don't belong together, while the other is obsessed with recovering some sort of missing harmony, where everything works in unison. Where the former involves an ironic hybridization of pure classical genres . . . , the latter epitomizes a "new sincerity" that rejects any form of irony in its sanctimonious pursuit of lost purity.[1]

Collins notes that John Cawelti noticed this generic transformation as long ago as the early 1970s. What Collins hopes to contribute is a description of the 1990s films as "ironic hybridization" and "new sincerity" as well as an explanation for the trend.

The second thesis in recent scholarship is that genre studies has been handicapped by its failure to sort out just exactly what critics are doing when they think about "genre." Examples of this thesis are excellent essays by Rick Altman, Tom Gunning, and Adam Knee in a 1995 issue of *Iris*. Interestingly, it was also in the early 1970s that Andrew Tutor provided a detailed discussion of the problems of doing genre studies, just when Cawelti noticed a rash of genre transformations occurring.[2]

This conjunction of theses about genre films and how to do genre studies in the 1970s and again in the 1990s might be explained in two different ways. One is that something different in Hollywood movies of the 1970s and 1990s provoked critical attention to how we categorize and define groups of films. Another—and the one I want to argue for—is that Hollywood films have never been "pure," that is, easily arranged into categories. All that has been pure has been sincere attempts to find order among variety.

Good reasons exist to find such order. For one thing, patterns of plot structure and conventions of representation do persist through-out decades (and some plot structures and conventions predate the emergence of cinema). To suggest, as I shall, that Hollywood films have never been pure instances of genres is not to say that Hollywood films do not evince patterns. Patterns do exist. Moreover, patterns are valuable material for deviation, dialogue, and critique. Variations from patterns may occur in order to make a text fresh or to comment on the issues raised within the standard pattern, and both aesthetic and ideological functions of variations make no sense without a no-tion of some pattern or order. Hence, although the tactics of grouping films by genre have been eclectic, grouping films can still be an im-portant scholarly act because it may elucidate what producers and consumers of films do. That is, they see films against a hypothesized pattern based on viewing other films. The process of comparison—which requires pattern—is crucial to communication and may con-tribute to enjoyment of a text.[3]

Finding order goes awry, however, when a subjective order visible in the present is mapped onto the past and then assumed to be the order visible in the past. This historicist fallacy is then compounded if the past pattern is assumed to be pure against a visible present that is not, and the visible present is assumed to be some transformation, deterioration, or hybridization of a pure essence and origin.

To claim that films produced in "New Hollywood" (hereafter "Post-Fordian Hollywood") are typified by a recombinant force is to misunderstand seriously "Old Hollywood" (hereafter "Fordian Holly-wood").[4] And the cause of the historical error is our own critical appa-ratus that has led us to believe erroneously that Hollywood films and genres were once pure. To make this argument more than an assertion, I want in this essay to review why the "genre" purity thesis is fallacious both theoretically and historically, and why the "hybrid" claim for Post-Fordian Hollywood is a particularly pernicious characterization.

A THEORETICAL JUSTIFICATION FOR THE
REJECTION OF THE PURITY THESIS FOR
FORDIAN HOLLYWOOD

Two ways exist to argue theoretically against a purity thesis for films created during the Fordian era of Hollywood. One argument is to note that the eclectic practices and failures of prior critics of genre suggest that any attempt to find a suitable method for describing genres is doomed: if critics could have done it, they would have already. The other theoretical argument is to take a poststructuralist position that any observed pattern will invariably criticize itself. Both arguments have recently been used to discuss the activity of genre study.

The eclectic-practices-and-failures argument is preferred by film scholars when tackling the difficulties of hypothesizing patterns across films. Indeed, this is the strategy employed by Tutor in his 1973 analysis of the pitfalls of doing genre work. Tutor notes four methods by which critics might try to group films, and he underlines the problems for each one. These methods, and my labels for them, are as follows: (1) find a film and judge other films against the pattern and conventions in that film (the *idealist* method); (2) determine from empirical observation the necessary and sufficient characteristics to include a film in the category (the *empiricist* method); 3) make an a priori declaration of the characteristics of the group (the *a priori* method); and (4) use cultural expectations to categorize the text (the *social convention* method).

Problems with the idealist method include finding ways to judge among various declarations of which film is the ideal from which the pattern should be derived. For the empiricist method, a circularity exists: The critic has already predetermined which films to include in the group in order to find the necessary and sufficient characteristics. The a priori method operates in a predetermined fashion as well as, like the idealist method, presents problems of settling debates among critics. Finally, the social convention method raises questions about how the critic finds evidence of expectations and determines cultural consensus. Moreover, for all four methods, characteristics can shift from grouping to grouping. Tutor notes that while the western is defined by "certain themes, certain typical actions, certain characteristic mannerisms," the horror film is defined by the above and the "*intention* to horrify."[5]

Tutor's reaction is to take the practical approach I have mentioned already: simply to live with the inconsistencies in method and "deficiencies" in the objects of analysis for the sake of what might be learned from textual comparison. Indeed, most film scholars know these theoretical shortcomings of genre study, and then just forge ahead anyway.

The inability of previous scholarship to find an appropriate method of genre categorizing has also been the focus of the recent essays by Gunning, Knee and Altman. They, too, note the eclectic practices and failures associated with genre criticism. Gunning particularly stresses that the groupings created by critics assume some kind of "preexistant phenomena" that critics "articulate."[6] These phenomena may be quite at odds with the use of genre terms by individuals charged with distributing and exhibiting films, who may have much to gain by expanding the categories into which a film might fit and thus widening the appeals to various audiences. Thus, he urges that scholars distinguish carefully between academic and industrial acts of genre classification.

In reviewing the sources of science fiction films of the 1950s, Knee details a variety of categories of films from which these movies drew their features. Among them are the war film of the 1940s and the postwar documentary. In fact, Knee eventually concludes that 1950s "science fiction in a sense functions both as a genre and as a mode of generic discourse, a rendering fantastic of other generic forms."[7] Such a view of the "adjectival" possibilities of genre categories has existed for some time among scholars of melodrama, who argue that melodrama is less a narrative formula and more a mode of vision, inflected upon many different narrative patterns.

Altman, too, outlines contradictions in categorizing films by genre. Expanding somewhat on Gunning's list, he details four different approaches to "genres": (1) a *model,* which becomes a formula of production; (2) a *structure,* which exists as a textual system in a film; (3) an *etiquette,* which is the category used by distributors and exhibitors; and (4) a *contract,* which is an agreement with spectators on how to read a film.[8] These four approaches then produce five disparities in the critical application of genres to individual texts or groups of texts: (1) words used for genres are sometimes nouns and sometimes adjectives; (2) producers try to reproduce the norm but also deviate from it; (3) genres defined by critics are different from genres perceived by audiences; (4) genre categories are sometimes historical and sometimes transhistorical; and

(5) genres defined by producers are different from genres analyzed by critics.

In all of these cases of attention to the eclectic practices and failures of critics to delineate clear, coherent, and consistent categories for films, the underlying premise is not that this cannot be done. Rather it is that until critics sort this out and everyone—from the authors to the distributors and exhibitors to the audiences and the critics—agrees on how to categorize films, no hope exists for genre study to function so that critics may find exemplars of the formulas, patterns, and conventions. Thus, this theoretical argument against a "purity" thesis operates from an assumption that human behavior and labeling can never be controlled so that critics would know a "pure" genre or genre film.

This practical approach to arguing against critical knowledge of "pure" genre films is quite different from a poststructuralist thesis. A poststructuralist thesis would argue that every text inherently displays what it is not. A good example of the application of this thesis to literary texts is Thomas O. Beebee's *Ideology of Genre,* and this method could fruitfully be applied to film studies as well. Like Tutor and Altman, Beebee finds four different approaches to genre: (1) as *rules,* which display the "authorial intention" in production of the text (adherence to or deviation from the conventions and patterns might occur); (2) as *species,* which is the historical and cultural lineage of a genre text; (3) as *patterns of textual features,* which exist "in the text itself"; and 4) as *reader conventions,* which exist "in the reader" (p. 3). Appealing to poststructuralism, Beebee suggests that every act of labeling is "always already unstable" (p. 27): "I argue that, since a 'single' genre is only recognizable as difference, as a foregrounding against the background of its neighboring genres, every work involves more than one genre, even if only implicitly" (p. 28). Thus, genre labeling by any of the above four approaches is "inescapable" (individuals cannot understand a text except in context with surrounding texts). Moreover, the text is inevitably impure because it cannot but be known by the context in which it exists. Beebee goes on to argue that genre texts often are in dialogue with their own definition by (fallacious) exclusion, creating moments of metatextuality and places for assessing ideological struggle (pp. 12–19).

Beebee's approach to the problems of genre and notions of the "purity" of a text is familiar from poststructuralist criticism that elucidates structuring absences ("what a text can not say but says in spite of itself"), evidences of overdetermination, and intertextual dialogues.

Since poststructuralism hypothesizes this breaching of boundaries and impurity to be features of every text, then any text located as an instance of genre would also, ipso facto, breach generic boundaries and display its excluded otherness. In other words, no genre film is pure.

Both the practical argument about eclectic practices and failures and the poststructuralist argument provide theoretical reasons why critics should reject the notion that Fordian Hollywood ever produced pure examples of genre films. Why is it, then, that the sense of a "transformation" in genres or an "ironic hybridization" and a "new sincerity" exists strongly enough in the era of Post-Fordian Hollywood to encourage special attention to generic instability as some new feature of the Post-Fordian era?[9] Cawelti believes the trend is due to an exhaustion and inability of the underlying myths of popular genres to deal with the post–Vietnam War era. Collins explains "ironic hybridization" and "new sincerity" as attempts to master "the media-saturated landscape of contemporary culture."[10] In cases of "ironic hybridization," the films explore the plurality of genre experiences through referential dialogues with their sources. In cases of "new sincerity," the films revert nostalgically to seek a lost "authenticity" (p. 257). Both textual strategies are methods to control a sensory experience of the "hyperconscious" (p. 248).

Another explanation exists as to why Cawelti and Collins find generic transformations and hybridizations in Post-Fordian Hollywood, and that is that they never interrogate the generic descriptions of Fordian Hollywood. As Gunning notes, genre classification by film critics began in the 1940s, particularly in the writings of Robert Warshaw and James Agee. Film genre study accelerated with the arrival in the universities of academic film studies and the critical methods of New Criticism, structuralism, and semiotics. The descriptions of Fordian Hollywood genres upon which Cawelti and Collins rely are ones constituted by film critics observing a limited set of films produced mostly between 1930 and 1960.[11] Additionally, those founding generic descriptions display the definitional fallacies described above.

Even more significantly, the generic descriptions are produced by critical methods that *by their very methodology* offer one genre category by which to label and analyze the text. New Criticism analyzes how great works overcome apparent contradictions to create a master coherence: All the parts are made to fit together by the critic, or the text is demeaned as a lesser artistic work. Structuralism finds one underlying binary opposition influencing the surface. Semiotics looks for narrative patterns and transformations that also reveal primary, if perhaps contradictory, structuring paradigms.

What Cawelti and Collins do not tackle is how arbitrary and inadequate those original generic descriptions are to the original texts. Fordian Hollywood genre texts appear to be suddenly transforming in the 1970s or hybridizing in the 1990s because the generic definitions were "fixed" by critics in the 1960s using critical methods that sought coherence and purity. This "fixing" of genre definition (and of text to genre category) ignored (or sought to overcome through critical argumentation of coherence) the industrial practice by Fordian Hollywood of providing at least two plots for every movie. And it is here that I turn to historical reasons to reject the purity thesis of Fordian Hollywood genres.

A HISTORICAL JUSTIFICATION FOR THE
REJECTION OF THE PURITY THESIS
FOR FORDIAN HOLLYWOOD

Several fundamental economic and ideological forces influenced the normative construction of the conventions of the classical film produced by Fordian Hollywood. Among these were the needs to (1) both standardize and differentiate products, and (2) market movies to many individuals. From the 1910s, Hollywood business people assumed several types of audiences: adult and child, male and female, urban and rural. They further assumed that certain genres had greater appeals to the various subgroups. Throughout the history of Fordian Hollywood, discourse is plentiful about the varying tastes. Moreover, a movie appealing to a variety of audiences was praised as having good potential box office. Reviewers often tried to describe what the various audiences would or would not find in a film.

The Fordian Hollywood film usually has two plots, one often being a heterosexual romance. What makes this dual plot "classical" is that the two plotlines hinge on and affect each other. The advantage of the dual plotline, I would argue, is that such a narrative structure permits appeals to multiple subgroups of taste. Moreover, the advantage of a heterosexual romance as one plotline is the presumptive appeal to women consumers (who the industry also assumed from the 1910s were major decision makers in family entertainment choices). Finally, add to this the need to differentiate product. Combinations and re-arrangements of formulas are quite simple if two conventional plotlines from different genres are merged together.

To test the thesis that Fordian Hollywood films are a mixture of multiple genres and not pure examples, I need to analyze them. However, since the theorists of genre point out how many different ways genres may be defined, I want briefly to show that no matter how I create the criteria by which genres are constructed, Fordian Hollywood movies will not stand up to the purity hypothesis. For the most part, I will make only gestures toward this proof, but I hope the evidence and argumentation will seem to have sufficient validity that common sense will take my argumentation to its conclusion.

For my purposes here, I will use Altman's set of four methods for defining genres that I described previously: a *model*, a *structure*, an *etiquette*, and a *contract*. To determine etiquette and contract, I will use film reviews as a sort of explicit statement of mediation among the distributors, exhibitors, and spectators. My presumption is that film reviewers are functioning as surrogate consumers, following up on the promotion and publicity generated by the studios and affirming or denying the proposed reading strategies to counsel viewers about what they will see. Thus, the reviews are one among several sites of evidence for both etiquette and contract.

How did Fordian Hollywood construct genres as models of production? It certainly did not construct them rigorously or neatly. One way to determine how studios perceived formulas would be to examine the work areas of associate producers for studios. In 1932, Irving Thalberg's associate producers were organized as follows: Al Lewin was in charge of sophisticated stories; Bernie Hyman, animal stories; Bernie Fineman, genre pixs and curios; Eddie Mannix, action films; Larry Weingarten, Marie Dressler films; Paul Bern, sex fables; and Harry Rapf, sad stories.[12]

Beyond the use of dualplot structures and the incoherency evident in MGM's allocation of work assignments (which is typical of all the studios) is the production source of stories. Since Fordian Hollywood found purchasing novels, plays, and magazine stories economical (the story came ready-made and possibly with some indication of consumer satisfaction and advance publicity), Fordian Hollywood dealt a good deal of the time with premade stories that might not fit any studio-produced formula.[13] The premade stories were usually reconfigured to adhere to Fordian Hollywood norms of storytelling, but their original sources outside the studio system contaminated them. Moreover, the value placed on innovation produced work in cycles, widely acknowledged by commentators on the Fordian Hollywood system.[14] No, the purity hypothesis most certainly would not hold up if I were to use the model method of defining Fordian Hollywood genres.

What about the *structure* method? Here is the method most likely to result in satisfactory findings, since the point of the structure method is to uncover underlying, nonconscious patterns that only the sensitive critic can reveal. Is Fordian Hollywood replete with examples of films that display pure genres with no interference by other patterns or formulas, no hybridizing? Here are how three critics deal with apparently prototypical genres or examples of genre films:

*Paul Kerr, in discussing film noir, writes: "Furthermore, the "'hybrid' quality of the film noir was perhaps, at least in part, attributable to increasing studio insecurities about marketing their B product (covering all their generic options, as it were, in each and every film)."[15]

*Dana Polan, discussing *In a Lonely Place* (1950, directed by Nicholas Ray), allocates the film to film noir, screwball comedy, and gothic romance categories.[16]

*Peter Wollen, discussing *Psycho* (1960, directed by Alfred Hitchcock) and *Marnie* (1960, Hitchcock), declares: "[the films are] hybrids of the fairy tale with a detective story."[17]

I do not mean to suggest that no critic could ever fail to find examples of "pure" structures of a genre. However, I would also argue that if another critic came along, that second, argumentative critic could likely make a case for contamination, influence, or degradation of the pure-case example. How to do this is neatly argued by David Bordwell in his *Making Meaning*.[18] Recalcitrant data exist in all Fordian Hollywood films to permit critical debate and perception of other patterns and formulas: see the second plotline just to begin. Moreover, the argumentative critic could easily dispute the pure-example critic's original definition of the pattern and conventions of the genre category as shown by the theoretical work of Altman, Gunning, and Beebee.

How easy this argumentation would be to do is evident when I turn to the etiquette and contract methods of genre definition. The routine effect of combination within Fordian Hollywood is obvious not only for apparent cases such as *Abbott and Costello Meet Frankenstein* but even for films that critics have labeled to be classics in a particular genre. Take, for instance, the classic "screwball comedy" *It Happened One Night* (1934). Contemporaneous reviewers described the movie as "a smooth blending of the various ingredients" with "a deadly enough familiarity all through"; using intertextual observations, they called the film "another long distance bus story" and a "Molière comedy," while the male protagonist was "one of those crack newspaper men frequently discovered in Hollywood's spacious studios."[19] Those remarks notwithstanding, the reviewers thought the film charming but not the start of a new movie pattern.

Little Caesar (1931) was a crime movie but the "modern criminal . . . thirsts primarily for power." Thus, it was also a "Greek epic tragedy," a gangster film, and a detective movie. *The Public Enemy* (1931) was a gang film, documentary drama, and comedy, but "in detail *The Public Enemy* is nothing like that most successful of gangster films [*Little Caesar*]."

Stagecoach (1939) was resolutely described in *Variety* not as a western (this would have been a derogatory term in 1939),[20] but instead as a "'Grand Hotel' on wheels," an "absorbing drama without the general theatrics usual to picturizations of the early west." Likewise, the *New York Times* labeled it a "frontier melodrama" and concluded with a pun on the film director's name: "They've all done nobly by a noble horse opera, but none so nobly as its director. This is one stagecoach that's powered by a Ford."

Casablanca (1942) would succeed because of the "variety of moods, action, suspense, comedy and drama." While it "goes heavy on the love theme," *Casablanca* also had "adventure" and "anti-Axis propaganda." "[Warner Bros.] is telling it in the high tradition of their hard-boiled romantic-adventure style" with "a top-notch thriller cast," and "they have so combined sentiment, humor and pathos with taut melodrama and bristling intrigue that the result is a highly entertaining and even inspiring film." It was another "*Grand Hotel* picture, a human crossroads." *Mildred Pierce* (1945) was a "drama," "melodrama," "frank sex play," "mother-love" story, and, of course, a "murder-mystery."

As several of the theoreticians of Hollywood suggest, the ways to create genre categories are multiple. By all of them, except the critical method by which a scholar can find a pattern within the text, I have argued that, historically, no justification exists to assume producers, distributors, exhibitors, or audiences saw films as being "purely" one type of film. In the case of the structural method, both the problems with traditional critical methods of genre study and evidence that critics have argued that genres are mixed in Fordian Hollywood cinema suggest that it too fails to locate "pure" examples of genres within Fordian Hollywood cinema. This is to suggest not that the pattern or genre is not "pure" but that Fordian Hollywood films do not provide clean examples of the critically defined genre.

THE PERNICIOUS HYBRID THESIS OF
POST-FORDIAN HOLLYWOOD

In the preceding two sections, I have argued that representing Fordian Hollywood films as fitting into neat, coherent genre categories is an inadequate thesis both theoretically and historically. Rather, films produced during that period were perceived by producers and audiences to belong potentially to several categories. No one worried about this. Instead, the lack of purity broadened the film's appeal in terms of both the likely audiences who might enjoy the movie and the film's originality.

The reason, however, to expend this much effort on the problem of the purity thesis for Fordian Hollywood cinema is that the purity hypothesis is then used to prove that a critical difference exists between Fordian and Post-Fordian Hollywood cinema. It is one thing to claim, as Cawelti does, that genres are transforming in the early 1970s. It is another to propose that Post-Fordian cinema is typified by its hybridity.

The reasons for my complaint are twofold. One is that this proposed difference just does not exist.[21] The second reason is that the use of the term "hybrid" for Post-Fordian cinema distorts and reduces the potential value that the theory of hybridity has for cultural scholars.

The notion of "hybridity" comes from botany and zoology and describes the crossbreeding of separate species.[22] An influential application of this organic concept to literature comes from Mikhail Bakhtin, who stresses the meeting of two different "styles" or "languages" derived from different cultures. He summarizes: "the novelistic hybrid is *an artistically organized system for bringing different languages in contact with one another*, a system having as its goal the illumination of one language by means of another, the carving out of a living image of another language."[23] Bakhtin particularly emphasizes that the event of hybridization permits *dialogue* between the two languages. In botany and zoology, the function of hybridization is to produce invigorated offspring by the crossbreeding, but the offspring may be sterile. So, too, the hybridized literary text (often a parody) may create a strong effect, but the hybrid itself does not generate a new family.

In accord with Bakhtin's original proposition, the recognition of textual hybridity has been fruitfully appropriated by postcolonial scholars to describe the outcome of cross-cultural encounters. Editors of *The Post-Colonial Studies Reader* write that an event of textual hybridity does not deny "the traditions from which [a hybrid text] springs," nor does a hybrid event signal the disappearance of the culture from which the hybrid derives.[24]

More significantly, however, a textual hybrid has effects on colonizers. Homi K. Bhabha points out that the colonizers' recognition of hybridity produced by the colonized must call into question the transparency of colonizing authority. In "Signs Taken for Wonders," Bhabha cautions,

> The discriminatory effects of the discourse of cultural colonialism, for instance, do not simply or singly refer to a "person," or to a dialectical power struggle between self and Other, or to a discrimination between mother culture and alien cultures. Produced through the strategy of disavowal, the *reference* of discrimination is always to the process of splitting as the condition of subjection: a discrimination between the mother culture and its bastards, the self and its doubles, where the trace of what is disavowed is not repressed but repeated as something *different*—a mutation, a hybrid. . . .
>
> . . . Hybridity is the sign of the productivity of colonial power, its shifting forces and fixities; it is the name for the strategic reversal of the process of domination through disavowal (that is, the production of discriminatory identities that secure the "pure" and original identity of authority).[25]

Bhabha's point here is clear: to recognize a hybrid forces the dominant culture to look back at itself and see its presumption of universality. Hybridity always opens up the discriminatory presumptions of purity, authenticity, and originality from which this textual hybrid is declared to be a deviation, a bastard, a corruption. Bhabha goes on to explain that "the hybrid object . . . revalues its presence by resiting it as the signifier of *Entstellung*—after the intervention of difference. It is the power of this strange metonymy of presence to so disturb the systematic (and systemic) construction of discriminatory knowledges that the cultural, once recognized as the medium of authority, becomes virtually unrecognizable" (p. 157).

To use the notion of hybridity for the mixing of genres in Post-Fordian Hollywood cinema is, thus, to pervert doubly its potential value for cultural studies. In the social and communicative sense that Bakhtin uses the term hybridity, the notion ought to be reserved for truly cross-cultural encounters. I have to ask, are the breedings of genres in Fordian and Post-Fordian Hollywood truly cross-cultural? Truly one language speaking to another? I seriously doubt that the strands of patterns that intermix in Hollywood filmmaking are from different species. Rather, they are in the same language family of Western culture. The breeding that occurs is not cross-cultural, but perhaps, and with a full sense of the derogatory implications involved, even a case of *inbreeding*.

Moreover, Bhabha's very particular political sense of hybridity suggests that when critics encounter a cross-cultural hybrid, the questions of power, of presumptive authority, purity, and origination of the dominant genre ought to be the focus of the analysis. Unlike Bakhtin, Bhabha stresses the historical fact of an inequality of cross-cultural contacts and communications.

I cannot, of course, do more than request that critics respect the possibility that narrowing the application of theories such as textual hybridity to a specific situation has value—both descriptive and explanatory—to scholars. However, I do make the plea. Despite all the theoretical and historical problems associated with categorizing films, perhaps the most valuable critical contribution that can be made is to analyze the social, cultural, and political implications of pattern mixing. In the above theoretical discussion, none of the writers ultimately declared the project of genre criticism impossible or unworthy—only fraught with scholarly difficulties. My rejection of the hybridity thesis for Post-Fordian Hollywood cinema is not a rejection of (1) the view that pattern mixing is occurring; or (2) the fact that Post-Fordian Hollywood cinema is producing hybrids both internally within the United States and externally throughout the world economy of signs. Internal hybrids[26] would be films created by minority or subordinated groups that use genre mixing or genre parody to dialogue with or criticize the dominant. Films by U.S. feminists,

African Americans, Hispanics, independents, the avant-garde, and so forth might be good cases of internal hybrids.

Both inbreeding and hybridizing need to be studied, and genre criticism has a contribution to make toward that work. Considering the implications of how critics apply theories can help in that cultural and critical work, but distinguishing between inbreeding and hybridity throughout the history of Hollywood has scholarly potential.

NOTES

1. Jim Collins, "Genericity in the Nineties: Eclectic Irony and the New Sincerity," in *Film Theory Goes to the Movies*, ed. Jim Collins, Hilary Radner, and Ava Preacher Collins (New York: Routledge, 1993), 242–43.

2. Rick Altman, "Emballage réutilisable: Les produits génériques et le processus de recyclage," *Iris* 20 (Fall 1995): 13–30; Tom Gunning, "'Those Drawn with a Very Fine Camel's Hair Brush': The Origins of Film Genres," *Iris* 20 (Fall 1995): 49–61; Adam Knee, "Generic Change in the Cinema," *Iris* 20 (Fall 1995): 31–39; Andrew Tutor, *Theories of Film* (London: Martin Secker and Warburg, 1973), rpt. as "Genre and Critical Methodology," in *Movies and Methods*, ed. Bill Nichols (Berkeley: University of California Press, 1976), 118–26; John G. Cawelti, "*Chinatown* and Generic Transformation in Recent American Films," in *Film Theory and Criticism*, 2d ed., ed. Gerald Mast and Marshall Cohen (New York: Oxford University Press, 1979), 559–79.

3. Tutor, "Genre and Critical Methodology," 119–21.

4. I reject the representation of Hollywood as "new" after World War II; rather I see Hollywood's industrial structure, modes of production, signifying practices, and modes of reception as an intensification of monopoly capitalism. Following contemporary theorists of global capitalism (e.g., Robins, Appadurai, Sreberny-Mohammadi), I am relabeling the period of Hollywood of 1917 to around 1960 as "Fordian Hollywood"; the Hollywood of post-1960 or so I will call "Post-Fordian Hollywood" to emphasize the strong linkages to the past as well as the industry's accommodations to late monopoly capitalism. Moreover, this labeling permits the possibility of a new descriptive term for Hollywood if it moves beyond "Post-Fordian" practices—which is less the case for a label such as "New." Kevin Robins, "Reimagined Communities? European Image Spaces, Beyond Fordism," *Cultural Studies* 3, no. 2 (1989): 145–65; Arjun Appadurai, "Disjuncture and Difference in the Global Cultural Economy," *Public Culture* 2, no. 2 (Spring 1990): 1–24; Annabelle Sreberny-Mohammadi, "The Global and the Local in International Communications," *Mass Media and Society*, ed. James Curran and Michael Gurevitch (London: Edward Arnold, 1991), 118–38.

5. Tutor, "Genre and Critical Methodology," 120.

6. Gunning, "'Those Drawn with a Very Fine Camel's Hair Brush,'" 50.

7. Knee, "Generic Change in the Cinema," 36.

8. Altman, "Emballage réutilisable," 14. This list is quite similar to Thomas O. Beebee's list summarized below; *The Ideology of Genre: A Comparative Study of Generic Instability* (University Park: Pennsylvania State University Press, 1994). Altman does not refer to Beebee, and I have no reason to assume influence: just the happy coincidence of intelligences.

9. Cawelti, "*Chinatown* and Generic Transformation"; James Monaco, *American Film Now: The People, the Power, the Money, the Movies* (New York: New American Library, 1979); Robin Wood, "Smart-ass and Cutie-pie: Notes Towards an Evaluation of Altman," *Movie* 21 (Autumn 1975): 1–17. Monaco writes that "*Easy Rider,* by all accounts one of the most significant movies of the decade, was a Chase-Caper-Road-Youth-Drug-Buddy film" (56) and that in the 1970s, "the lines of definition that separate one genre from another have continued to disintegrate" (56). Wood even uses the "hybrid" term: "[Robert Altman's] best films are hybrids, products of a fusion of 'European' aspirations with American genres" (7). As I shall discuss below in the third section, at least Wood's use of the term "hybrid" may have justification since he suggests an encounter between two "languages" (although whether European cinema is another language from Hollywood could be debated).

10. Collins, "Genericity in the Nineties," 243.

11. The lack of access to films prior to 1930 is an important cause for the limitations in these critics' descriptions of Hollywood genres.

12. "Metro-Goldwyn-Mayer," *Fortune,* 6 December 1932, rpt. in *The American Film Industry,* ed. Tino Balio (Madison: University of Wisconsin Press, 1976), 260.

13. Motion Picture Producers and Distributors of America, *Film Facts 1942: 20 Years of Self Government, 1922–1942* (New York: Motion Picture Producers and Distributors of America, n.d.), 52.

14. William J. Fadiman, "Books into Movies," *Publishers' Weekly,* 8 September 1934, 753–55.

15. Paul Kerr, "My Name Is Joseph H [*sic*] Lewis," *Screen* 24, nos. 4–5 (July–October 1983): 52.

16. Dana Polan, *In a Lonely Place* (London: British Film Institute, 1993).

17. Peter Wollen, "Hybrid Plots in *Psycho,*" *Framework* 13 (1980), rpt. in *Readings and Writings: Semiotic Counter-Strategies* (London: Verso, 1982), 37.

18. David Bordwell, *Making Meaning: Inference and Rhetoric in the Interpretation of Cinema* (Cambridge: Harvard University Press, 1989).

19. These quotations come from contemporary reviews in *Hollywood Reporter, Motion Picture Herald, New Republic,* the *New York Times, New Yorker, Saturday Review, Time,* and *Variety.*

20. *Variety* and *Motion Picture Herald* would not use "western" because of that genre's association with a rural taste, but the *New Yorker* does not hesitate.

21. Or both Fordian and Post-Fordian cinemas are hybridity cinemas, which is not the way I want to go. See below.

22. It can also apply to genera and family, so technically the term could be used for what we are discussing. However, see my remarks below.

23. M. M. Bakhtin, *The Dialogic Imagination: Four Essays* [1934–35, 1940, 1941], trans. Caryl Emerson and Michael Holquist (Austin: University of Texas Press, 1981), 361.

24. Bill Ashcroft, Gareth Griffiths, and Helen Tiffin, eds., *The Post-Colonial Studies Reader* (London: Routledge, 1995), 184.

25. Homi K. Bhabha, "Signs Taken for Wonders: Questions of Ambivalence and Authority under a Tree outside Delhi, May 1817," *Critical Inquiry* 12, no. 1 (Autumn 1985): 153–54.

26. The term "internal" implies accepting the notion of a "nation," which is a problem for theories of post-Fordian capitalism. This is an issue impossible to take to its appropriate conclusions here.

5

The Romances of the Blonde Venus

Movie Censors versus Movie Fans

THE TRADITIONAL VIEW of censorship has presented the regulation of content as a repression of forbidden knowledges. Censorship is regarded as inflicting the moral or epistemological view of one group on another, and the outcome of censored representations is the containment of possibilities for some members of the social whole.

Recently, these views of censorship have been reconsidered. Michel Foucault has refuted the repressive hypothesis by arguing that censorship proliferates talk about, and possibilities for, eroticism. Censorship opens up, rather than closes down, confessions, talk, absolution, and resistive transgressions. Additionally, critical-theory and cultural-studies scholarship theorizes that multiple voices exist within a text and multiple discourses pervade society. Thus, in terms of the availability of representations, many exist, some are ambiguous, and some are contradictory within themselves and with other representations. It is hardly surprising, then, that this revisionist scholarship may also argue that within a society multiple interpretations of a text are possible. These interpretations depend in part upon the subjectivity of the various readers, but also significantly upon the context of the experience of encountering the text.

The history of the research on regulation in moving images has reproduced this broader transformation. The traditional approach to film censorship examines what happens in the production of a script and its filming to create a moral discourse.[1] This emphasis on the events during production implies a mode of reception. Moral discourse "positioned" the spectator; thus, moral discourse "contained" possibilities of alternative representations (and behavior as a consequence of those representations). Concern was especially for women, but also men, gays and lesbians, and people of repressed races, ethnicities, classes, and beliefs.

The revisionist approach to film censorship has employed three arguments. The first is the poststructuralist argument, showing how texts are invariably filled with gaps or contradictions which permit readers to have more play with the meanings than is preferred by those attempting to regulate the text. The second argument is to situate the film within its surrounding historical discourses, and to realize that movies do not exist in isolation from other knowledges. Films are only one public discourse. Audiences were fully aware that movies produced by the major studios in the United States during the classical era were supposed to conform to a set of moral conventions. Around the publicity for Hollywood films were lots of other stories in newspapers and magazines and on radio describing the acts of regulation by official censors, the Hollywood studio bosses, or regulatory institutions such as the Motion Picture Producers and Distributors Association (MPPDA). These regulatory acts, of course, permitted scandals to proliferate. What the film once was prior to its regulation would be a pleasurable knowledge, in terms of knowing both what the scene or acts were that were changed or excised and that one knew what was being forbidden. Thus, regulation and censorship encourage "transgressive"[2] imaginations rather than blocking them.[3]

If these two arguments help our understanding of this social dynamic, revisionist film scholarship has also adopted a third argument: an observation that creates more complexity to the social formation. Although it may be the case that Hollywood films generally represent the views of the middle class in the United States, the entire complex of Hollywood film is heterogeneous in its class and ideological alliances. The product of Hollywood contains films ranging from conservative to liberal in their points of view. In a culture of consumption, it is handy for monopoly capitalism to expand economies of pleasure and to secure profit by proliferating objects of desire for multiple constituencies.[4]

To illustrate these revisionist strategies of studying film regulation, I wish to revisit an instance of this dynamic which has received wide attention: the film *Blonde Venus*, directed by Josef von Sternberg and released by Paramount in September 1932. The plot of the released film is simple. Helen Faraday (played by Marlene Dietrich) decides to go back into show business when her husband Ned (Herbert Marshall) needs money for a rare medical cure to save his life. Helen's return to her singing career enables Ned to travel to Europe for the cure. Yet money for this trip comes not only from work but apparently from Nick Townsend (Cary Grant), a man-about-town. Helen and Nick have an affair. When Ned discovers this upon his return, he demands custody of their son, but Helen flees with the boy, at times apparently resorting to prostitution to make their way. A detective eventually tracks her down, and she gives up the child to Ned. Helen becomes a big success, and in Paris Nick runs into her again. He takes her back to the United States where, while visiting her son, she and Ned are reconciled.

The released movie, however, is not what was originally presented for filming, and was rewritten to comply with demands from the film industry regulators. Yet other sectors of the film industry were *simultaneously* producing stories that they claimed to be the "truth" of the tale of the blonde Venus against the "falseness" of the film version. Thus, at the same time that the *Blonde Venus* movie was being presented as a *prescriptive moral story in fiction, a counterdescriptive amoral story of fact* was circulating. The true story might be told with an address of pseudomorality—"Isn't this awful?!" "Aren't you shocked?!"—but it was not forced into an ending with compensating moral values. Hence, the amoral story operated with much more suspense than the fictional one. Was there or was there not to be retribution for sexual/moral/normative deviance? Was there a God in heaven who would punish the wicked? Moreover, the case of *Blonde Venus* is particularly snazzy because a third story also was being disseminated. It was a *fictional story, but a "true" romance* which was also at odds with the regulatory film version.

Thus, while a publicly moral discourse is available, two publically subversive ones are also accessible. For the purposes of this essay, I shall label these three stories the melodrama of desire (the story of the regulators), the comedy of desire (a story of the movie fans), and the romance of desire (another story of the movie fans).

THE MELODRAMA OF DESIRE—*BLONDE VENUS* AND ITS REGULATION

This story is a story of seduction, fall, and redemption. It requires contextualization within contemporary production activities in terms of formula filmmaking and product differentiation, and it was the story found officially on the screens across the United States.

Amanda Anderson argues that in U.S. culture of the nineteenth century, bad women were women who lose control.[5] While this is amply demonstrated by Anderson, I believe that it is also the case that bad women were likewise those who have excessive control, who are not victims but victimizers. These bad women are the belles dames, vampires, and femmes fatales of the Victorian imagination. During the nineteenth century, explanations for these women were couched in religious or occult belief systems. However, in the twentieth century, as secular humanism and social science gained ascendancy, secular explanations for behavior became common. People had agency within their circumstances, and morality became something not predestined or inscrutable but a consequence of personal judgment and will. For the progressivist ideology,[6] people are evaluated on the basis of their actions once they know the difference between right and wrong within the social system. God has nothing to do with it. A third possibility, however, exists. That is a cynical realism, in which such moral discourse is irrelevant.

By the 1920s, secularism was evident in many Hollywood films, but the older ideologies of religion and occultism existed as well. Films where these ideologies commonly occur are within the formulas around the fallen woman. Fig. 5-1 schematizes a number of these possibilities. For example, the explanation for a woman's fall may be her victimization (she has too little control over her situation). In the twentieth century, this plot motivation produced stories of the working-class prostitute and the sacrificing mother. However, the explanation for her fall may be her behavior as a victimizer. While nineteenth-century representations tended to theorize the femme fatale as evil, twentieth-century stories provided more mundane explanations. A woman may desire money, social mobility, or revenge. By the 1920s, a woman may also be a desiring subject; she may have sexual relations with men to whom she is not married because she loves or lusts.[7]

By the late 1920s, a series of such narratives had appeared from the major studios and were labeled "sex stories." MGM distributed *Flesh and the Devil* in 1927. In this film, Felicitas (Greta Garbo) seduces her husband's best friend (John Gilbert) while her husband is gone, and then cannot restrain her desire when her husband returns. Felicitas eventually repents her behavior, but as she runs across a frozen lake to prevent a duel between the two men, the ice breaks and she drowns. Providence provides the moral justice required to end the story properly. *Possessed* (MGM, 1931) tells the story of the ambitious woman Mar-

FIG. 5-1. Fallen Women

WOMEN AS VICTIMS	WOMEN AS VICTIMIZERS (FEMMES FATALES)
1800s—Religious or Occult Explanations: Sin in a Moral Universe	
e.g., seduced and abandoned, the working-class prostitute, the white slave	e.g., la belle dame sans merci, the vampire
1900s—Secular Explanations: Behavior in a Nonmoral Universe ("humanization")	
Plots for Working-Class Women	
working-class prostitute	woman as desiring money or social mobility, e.g., vamp, golddigger, kept woman
Plots for Working-Class or Middle-Class Women	
sacrificing mother maternal melodrama maternal woman's film	woman as desiring subject married or non-married

ion (Joan Crawford), who determines to make her fortune in the big city. She meets rich man Mark Whitney (Clark Gable) and becomes his kept woman. When his bid for a political seat is threatened by their affair, Mark offers to marry her and let the voters decide. Marion is not punished because at one point she offers to give Mark up, thus redeeming herself.

However, by the early 1930s, several films dispensed with older religious, occult, and progressivist resolutions. *Red Headed Woman* (MGM, 1932) is perhaps one of the most notorious of these films. The secretary Lily (Jean Harlow) works her way up the status ladder through a series of bosses, and in the process destroys at least one marriage. Lily eventually heads off to Paris with a new rich boyfriend. The couple divorced as a consequence of Lily's intervention is reunited since the husband has learned his lesson, but Lily goes unpunished and seems only to profit from her behavior.

Blonde Venus was obviously to be in the general grouping of fallen women stories. As a Paramount poster advertised the film, "From the lips of one MAN to the arms of another!"[8] The question for director von Sternberg, star Dietrich, the studio, and the regulators was where in these categories would the blonde Venus fit and what ideology would prevail—religious/occult providence, progressivist redemption, or cynical realism. The first script was written by either von Sternberg or Dietrich.[9] It provided an explicit treatment of infidelity and prostitution. Studio executives were obviously worried by the screenplay, and conflict with von Sternberg developed. Those previewing the screenplay for the MPPDA thought the plot was unacceptable for the screen.[10]

The studio commissioned a second script. In it, Helen is in love with both her husband and Nick. The ending would reveal that her husband had had an affair as well, justifying a happy ending with Helen and Nick together. The industry regulators were unhappy with the latter part in particular and also with lyrics for proposed songs, "I'm Getting What I Want" and "I Couldn't Be Annoyed."[11]

A third script was tried: a studio revision in negotiation with the regulators. Dropped was the character motivation that Helen loved both men and that Ned had had an affair. The regulators approved the third version because Helen's affairs and prostitution were motivated as sacrifices for the husband and child, Helen was never happy in her life of luxury, and she was willing to drop her singing career when the possibility of returning home was available.[12] Thus, the third script creates a maternal melodrama with progressivist ideology. Although some revisions occurred between the third script and the final edited film, these main plot points were retained.

If this were the end of the story, it would be possible to argue from the traditional censorship approach that the narrative "contains" the possibilities for Helen by forcing her back into monogamy and the nuclear family through the film's fairy-tale ending, and, consequently, regulating women viewers as well into a conservative ideology. Indeed, the reviews of the film all said the plot was a "mother-love" story.[13] They assumed Helen was a kept woman and a prostitute, and that *Blonde Venus* was a maternal melodrama and working-girl story (woman as victim). Thus, if only reviews of the film are examined for the reception of this film, we would have to conclude that the regulation worked.[14]

However, in her study of *Blonde Venus*, Lea Jacobs argues, as a poststructuralist revisionist, that because of ambiguity and ellipses negotiated between the studios and regulators to avoid what the regulators saw as problems of representation, Helen's motivations for her behavior are never clear.[15] No visual representation of funds exchanged between Helen and Nick occurs. No dialogue explains why Helen takes a two-week trip with Nick before the return of Ned. Additionally, one particularly strong representation may invoke a counterimage of Helen. The "Hot Voodoo" number Helen sings could imply motives for her behavior beyond those of "wifely sacrifice and devotion." Finally, Jacobs argues, the fairy-tale ending would be read ironically by the audience.

Indeed, Jacobs' appeal to textual analysis is a strong argument for suggesting that audiences might read *Blonde Venus* not as a maternal melodrama, but as a melodrama of woman-as-desiring-subject. This would shift the film from one category of fallen woman to another, and, according to the regulatory conventions, upset the requirements of compensating moral values when Helen returns to her husband and child. This is so because Helen, woman-as-desiring-subject, never repents her illicit desire; rather, mother love simply triumphs.

While it is possible to employ the revisionist argument of textual polysemy in the case of *Blonde Venus*,[16] it is also possible to use the second and third revisionist arguments of placing the film in its historical discourses and recognizing the heterogeneity of the social formation. It is through these two arguments that the textual-analysis argument is confirmed, and the melodrama of desire becomes an obvious reading choice for many viewers.

THE COMEDY OF DESIRE—THE BLONDE VENUS AND HER FANS

If the film *Blonde Venus* vacillates about whether Helen loves Ned but also Nick, so does the public discourse around Helen's interpreter, Marlene Dietrich. Such auxiliary talk could feed into and support—at least in comparison with the preferences of the regulators—readings subversive of a mother-love interpretation of Helen's motives. A semi-autobiographical parallel between the film and Dietrich's life would be obvious to any devoted fan of the movies, of which there were hundreds of thousands in 1932.[17] The comedy of this story of desire requires examining the public discourse about Dietrich just prior to the release of *Blonde Venus*.[18]

The German Husband

At the time of Dietrich's move from Germany to the United States, she was married to Rudolf Sieber and had a daughter, Maria.[19]

Although she was a successful stage and film actress there and in the United States, initial star publicity stressed Dietrich's maternal nature and downplayed her status as a career woman who had left her husband in Germany to pursue her work. Describing Dietrich's life in Hollywood, an article in *Pictorial Review* in 1931 reported that she did not go to parties but stayed home reading the books her husband sent her and that she loved to cook.

> It develops, in fact, that Miss Dietrich's life . . . is focused as much upon her domestic duties as is that of any of her sisters undistracted by a career. Here she arises early—usually at eight or before—and oversees her maids. Sometime during the morning she takes her little girl out to the park, and when they return she is likely to prepare lunch with her own hands.[20]

The American Director

Dietrich came to the United States with director von Sternberg after the success of *The Blue Angel*. In the public discourse, von Sternberg is represented as her Svengali. *Photoplay* wrote in 1931, "Plucking her from a German musical comedy in Berlin for the leading feminine role opposite Emil Jannings in 'The Blue Angel,' Von Sternberg has guided her movie career from that moment with an unswerving devotion and intense zeal."[21] Indeed, von Sternberg's devotion to Dietrich is part of the myth of Hollywood. Dietrich's remarks are always ones of submission and appreciation for von Sternberg's mentoring.

Public discourse rapidly reported rumors that she and von Sternberg were having an affair. Von Sternberg's wife, Mrs. Riza-Royce, sued for alienation of her husband's affections. She lost, but the case was widely reported in the papers. Jokes appeared around the mythical star image of Dietrich as a devoted mother. Leonard (Old Snoop) Hall in November 1931 wrote a satire for *Photoplay* about one day in the life of Dietrich.

> 10 A.M.—Radio speech over a network of 150 stations, from the studio. "I luff my husband and my leedle girl. . . . *Herr* Von Sternberg— *ach*, he is a genius! Such a great director. I luff my husband and am happiest among my *schnitzel*. I want to make great pictures for the

American people. I luff the American people, and my husband and my leedle girl!" . . .

[At a photo opportunity] Other poses: Director Von Sternberg holding Marlene with one hand and her husband with the other, . . . while the little girl waves the German and American flags. . . . All four singing "Down by the Old Mill Stream."[22]

The French Star

If von Sternberg's wife's affections were being alienated, so possibly were his. By January 1932, new innuendoes appeared in fan magazines. Underneath a photo of Dietrich on a movie set with Maurice Chevalier leaning over her was the caption: "'How's the baby?' asks the lad from gay Paree. And dynamite Dietrich replies, 'Ach! Svell! You and your missus come for dinner and I bake somet'ing nice, yah?' And that's what Marlene and Maurice Chevalier talk about when they visit each other's sets. Or maybe they're just kidding us."[23] In February 1932, *Photoplay* reported that Dietrich might be trying to break away from the Trilby spell of von Sternberg. Moreover, "There was a young German actor who comforted Marlene during this time. There was also Maurice Chevalier, whose constant society Marlene sought. They lunched together and they danced together at the Ambassador Cocoanut Grove. What is more, they laughed together—a thing she never did with Von Sternberg. At first, it seemed a friendship merely."[24]

By August 1932, *Photoplay* chuckled, "Oh to be a grain of sand, when the glamorous Dietrich and the gay Chevalier, both visiting at a friend's house along the beach, fell into a friendly wrestling match! And wrestled and wrestled. So she wanted to wrestle, and all the time we wondered—. And friends claim Marlene won by an accent!"[25] And in September, the same month *Blonde Venus* was released, *Photoplay* reported that von Sternberg "is putting on a better act than ever these days," while "'We are divorcing to keep our friendship,' was the word from Yvonne Vallee, Maurice's charming little French spouse to whom he has been wed since 1927. 'Incompatibility' was the reason both agreed on."[26]

Thus, fans of movie magazines could read an autobiography into *Blonde Venus* if they wished. This story would be of a woman desiring a lover and participating in an affair, not out of duty to her husband and child but in spite of it. Although fans would know that the censors would contain the movie version with a moral ending, they may also have appreciated that ending as a public joke: that the melodrama of maternal love was a fictional construct, and the joke was on the censors for thinking they were being successful in promoting it. Instead, the story of the blonde Venus was a comedy of desire. This reading of desire was certainly abetted by studio publicity. An advertisement for *Blonde Venus* showed Helen as mom in the center of the image, and to the side her in the "Hot Voodoo" costume. The cut line was "Glorious Dietrich as a Flaming Woman Who Longed for the Love that Tortured Her!"[27]

THE ROMANCE OF DESIRE—THE BLONDE VENUS AND HER LOVES

"Blonde Venus the movie" was not the only *Blonde Venus* story released by the studios in September 1932. *Screenland,* a fan magazine that published short-story versions of the movies, issued the official printed "The Blonde Venus."[28] The subtitle of the story is "Can a woman be in love with two men at once? Marlene Dietrich, as 'The Blonde Venus,' gives you a startling new angle on an age-old problem." Publicity stills from the movie adorned the text.

However, the story printed in *Screenland* is not the third, approved version of *Blonde Venus*; it is the second, studio-produced variation. It is difficult to explain this except to assume that someone made a major mistake at Paramount and gave Mortimer Franklin (who did the fictionalizing) the wrong script—and no one caught it! Or that Paramount thought this second version would be better for its magazine audience. This latter explanation makes strong sense, for the fictionalized "Blonde Venus" fits very well into the romance genre enjoyed by women. This "Blonde Venus" is a woman torn with desire for two men and *for the freedom to be permitted that heterogeneity of desire.* This "Blonde Venus" is not confined to monogamy, her existence as desiring subject is validated, and her current love accepts this feature in her. Very radical stuff, indeed!

Here is how the story goes. Helen receives money from Nick for Ned's trip and cure, but she delays a sexual liaison. When Helen and Nick learn that Ned is returning, Nick reveals to Helen that he is in love

with her and so must say goodbye. "Then he had her in his arms, kiss-
ing her as she had never been kissed before." Nick suggests they take a
trip together before parting permanently, and Helen agrees. At the end
of the sojourn, this is the scene:

> Nick took her in his arms. "Helen, I can't bear losing you. Stay with
> me. You can't throw away your happiness out of a sense of duty to a
> man you don't love."
>
> She broke away from his embrace. "No, no. That isn't true. I do love
> Ned."
>
> "Then what about me? You can't deny that you love me. Do you
> mean to say you can love two men at once?"
>
> "Yes—that's quite possible, Nick. What's happened to me is true of
> a great many women. They fall in love, they get married, they're very
> happy with their husbands—perhaps they have a child. And all the
> time there's a side of their nature that's never awakened until they
> meet someone like you. Then they are able to love both."
>
> "I don't know what you are talking about," Nick said harshly. "All
> I know is, if you go back to him, we're through for good. Love two men
> at once! Why stop at two? Why not three, or six, or a dozen?"
>
> "You're right, Nick," Helen replied coldly. "We *are* through. I'm
> going home to Ned."

Subsequent events occur as proposed in the second version of the
film script, including Nick's discovering that Ned has had an affair as
well. The problem with the romance between Nick and Helen needs
to be resolved, however, for the breach between them requires a solution for a happy ending to occur. The solution is not Helen's repent-
ing her love of her husband now that she knows he had an affair. No,
this is the resolution:

> Nick returned to Helen and told her of her husband's sudden
> change of mind. "Thank you, Nick, thank you," was all she could say,
> tears dimming the lustre of her eyes.
>
> "And by the way, you're going to marry me, you know," he
> replied.
>
> "Oh, then you've changed your ideas?"
>
> "No—but you're not in love with two men now!"
>
> "Not now—but possibly—some time—"

Nick was holding her close once more.
"I'll take a chance!"

Although Nick is willing to gamble that he is Helen's "true love," the story permits Helen's desires to be the terms by which the romance is negotiated. The story, aimed at most likely women romance fiction readers, exalts a radically subversive ideology of proliferation and permission of women's desires.

That *Screenland* could print such a story requires recognizing at least two features to early 1930s fandom. One is that fans were sophisticated consumers of entertainment. Matching the film to the short story was not necessary, if each had its use and value within its appropriate venue. That the more radical treatment should be in the magazine is quite obvious. Movies were public, mass entertainment while romance fiction magazines were consumed in private. Thus, the *Screenland* "Blonde Venus" could be the romance of desire.

CONCLUSION

Although the movie *Blonde Venus* may have been ambiguous about Helen's motivations, permitting the regulators to suggest that this fallen woman story was in the category of maternal melodrama with a good progressive ideology, the comedic discourse about Dietrich's "real" life and the romantic story offered motivations for a fan to interpret the film's ambiguities in quite another way: Helen is a desiring subject, likely in love with both men. And from everything occurring both publicly in Dietrich's life and more privately in the short story, Helen-as-desiring-subject is not required to repent or to redeem herself. Her desires are permissible. This may still constitute a progressivist ideology—one of taking care of one's self—but it is an ideology quite out of step with monogamy and patriarchy.

This story of the romances of the blonde Venus permits everyone to have what they want. That the film reviewers read the movie as the regulators wished them to do so is not surprising. They dutifully stuck to the material at hand although they did refuse to ignore the ellipses where Helen receives money from Nick and from other men (in her prostitution). Reviewers generally operate as surrogate consumers for an audience interested in the "least objectionable" material. They write what might be most apparent to the average citizen. For not all movie-goers were fans—devotees of the magazines where Dietrich's personal life spilled into the innuendo columns—nor were all moviegoers ad-mirers of romance fiction.

Yet, the fans and romance fiction readers had their blonde Venus anyway. Their story is of a woman as desiring subject, and their reading may have been resisting or even laughing at the official version. Yet I would caution against overidealizing this event. The blonde Venus story is of a woman who desires and is rewarded, but her reward is an-other man. Serial monogamy is still the outcome. Recall as well that the sources for these fans' fantasies were *Photoplay* and *Screenland*, both published by corporations linked to the culture of consumption and capitalism. It was to their advantage to exploit desire and its represen-tation. The fans did not escape dominant ideologies even as they were fed their comedies and romances.

NOTES

A special thanks to Mary Desjardins for helping me sort out these issues and leading me to valuable sources, and to Christina Lane whose dissertation re-search led me to see new aspects to this event. I also very much appreciate sev-eral audiences who provided good questions and counsel: the Department of Communication, University of Missouri-Kansas City (1995), particularly Gre-gory Black and Thomas Poe—who also inspired me to start looking more closely at industry regulation and who themselves provide outstanding models for institutional and textual analysis of censorship; the American Studies Asso-ciation Conference (1995); the Institute of Drama, Film and Theater, University of Trondheim (Norway) (1995); and the Université de la Sorbonne Nouvelle, Paris III (1996), particularly Roger Odin and Noel Burch; and many others. Fi-nally, I appreciate a Special Research Grant from the University of Texas Re-search Institute which supported part of my research.

1. These rules are summarized in Janet Staiger, *Bad Women: Regulating Sex-uality in Early American Cinema* (Minneapolis: University of Minnesota Press, 1995), 70. I go on to criticize the repressive hypothesis approach to regulation in that book.

2. In this essay, "transgressive" and "subversive" should be understood as "not authorized" rather than as necessarily politically radical. Thus, some transgressive readings might be ideologically conservative.

3. I have argued this previously in "Self-Regulation and the Classical

Hollywood Cinema," *Journal of Dramatic Theory and Criticism* 6, no. 1 (Fall 1991): 221–31.

4. As Michael Budd writes, "Fixing the level of sex and violence [by regulatory boards such as the National Board of Censorship] starts to resemble fixing prices—representing it in quantities and modes that will maximize its exchange value. This means factoring the activities of censorship—and anticensorship—groups into the equation of corporate planning, into the industrial practices which produce signifying texts." "The National Board of Review and the Early Art Cinema in New York," *Cinema Journal* 26, no. 1 (Fall 1986): 11.

5. Amanda Anderson, *Tainted Souls and Painted Faces: The Rhetoric of Fallenness in Victorian Culture* (Ithaca: Cornell University Press, 1993), 15.

6. By progressivist ideology, I am referring to ideologies associated with the Progressive era, dated around 1905 though the end of World War I, although lingering culturally much longer. Progressivist ideology should be distinguished from progressive ideologies: ideologies that in any historical moment look toward social and political change to enhance equity within the social formation.

7. Lea Jacobs, *The Wages of Sin: Censorship and the Fallen Woman Film, 1928–1942* (Madison: University of Wisconsin Press, 1991), 3–11, does not make this distinction between fallen women as victims and fallen women as victimizers. I believe doing so helps us see what happens in the *Blonde Venus* case as well as illuminating important dynamics in the era's films; see below. Problems with Jacobs' general lack of sorting among formulas of the fallen woman are also discussed in Linda Williams, "Negotiating Women's Desire: Censorship, Gender, and Genre," *Quarterly Review of Film and Video* 14, no. 4 (1993): 71–75.

8. 1932 Paramount one-sheet; Clipping File, Blonde Venus, Academy of Motion Picture Arts and Sciences, Los Angeles, California (hereafter AMPAS).

9. Different biographies give different information. Very detailed histories of the production of *Blonde Venus* are in Peter Baxter, "The Birth of Venus," *Wide Angle* 10, no. 1 (1988), 4–15; Lea Jacobs, "The Censorship of *Blonde Venus*: Textual Analysis and Historical Method," *Cinema Journal* 27, no. 3 (Spring 1988): 21–31; Peter Baxter, *Just Watch! Sternberg, Paramount and America* (London: BFI, 1993); and Jacobs, *Wages of Sin*, 86–105. My version relies primarily on the Motion Picture Producers and Distributors Association (MPPDA) files in AMPAS, and secondarily on Baxter and Jacobs. Counting versions of the script is complicated. For simplicity, I am just going to do major rewrites. For more specifics, see Baxter.

10. Memo for files from Jason S. Joy, 29 March 1932, MPPDA Case Files, Blonde Venus, AMPAS.

11. Jason S. Joy to Will H. Hays, 1 April 1932; Lamar Trotti to B. P. Schulberg, 20 April 1932; Jason S. Joy to B. P. Schulberg, 25 May 1932; Jason S. Joy to B. P. Schulberg, 26 May 1932; all in MPPDA Case File, Blonde Venus, AMPAS.

12. Jason S. Joy to Harold Hurley [Paramount], 1 September 1932; Jason S. Joy to John Hammell [Paramount], 16 September 1932; both from MPPDA Case File, Blonde Venus, AMPAS. The second letter is interesting in that Joy gives Paramount executives justifications to use if they have negative publicity over the film's subject matter.

13. "Abel," "*Blonde Venus*," *Variety*, 27 September 1932, n.p.; "The *Blonde Venus*," *Close-Up* 9 (September 1932), 192–95; "*Blonde Venus*," *Film Daily*, 24 September 1932, 6; "*Blonde Venus*," *New Outlook* 161 (November 1932), 47; "'Blonde Venus' Stars," *Daily News*, 24 September 1932, 20; John S. Cohen, Jr., "The New Talkie," *New York Sun*, 24 September 1932, n.p.; Thornton Delehauty, "The New Films," *New York Evening Post*, 24 September 1932, S5; "Dietrich Picture, '*Blonde Venus*,' on Paramount View," *New York American*, 24 September 1932, n.p.; W. G., "Marlene Peripatetica," *New Yorker* 8 (1 October 1932): 54–55; Mordant Hall, "*Blonde Venus*," *New York Times*, 24 September 1932, 18; Fosyth Hardy, "*Blonde Venus*," *Cinema Quarterly* [Edinburgh], 1, no. 2 (Winter 1932): 116; Pare Lorentz, "The Screen," *Vanity Fair* 37 (November 1932): 47, 58; McCarthy, "*Blonde Venus*," *Motion Picture Herald*, 10 September 1932, 38; "The National Guide to Motion Pictures," *Photoplay* 42 (November 1932): 58; "The New Pictures," *Time* 20 (3 October 1932): 36–37; José Rodriguez, "*Blonde Venus*," *Rob Wagner's Script* 8, no. 189 (24 September 1932): 8; Richard Watts, Jr., "On the Screen," *New York Herald Tribune*, 24 September 1932, n.p.

14. Reviews of films can sometimes show how inadequate self-regulation was at controlling meanings; see my "Self-Regulation and the Classical Hollywood Cinema." At other times, reviews are insufficient for illustrating the heterogeneity or nonconformity of responses to films. This is a good case of the failure of reviews as evidence of heterogeneous reception.

15. Jacobs, *Wages of Sin*. Examples of traditional approaches to *Blonde Venus* are Olive Graham, "*Blonde Venus*," *CinemaTexas Program Notes* 21, no. 1 (21 September 1981): 25–30; Gaylyn Studlar, *In the Realm of Pleasure: Von Sternberg, Dietrich, and the Masochistic Aesthetic* (Urbana: University of Illinois Press, 1988).

16. Others prior to Jacobs who also use textual analysis to argue that certain plot or stylistic features produce an auto-critique of the containment plot, and that thus the film becomes transgressive as a consequence of the attempt at regulation, are Robin Wood, "Venus de Marlene," *Film Comment* 14, no. 2 (March–April 1978): 58–63; Bill Nichols, *Ideology and the Cinema* (Bloomington: University of Indiana Press, 1981), 104–32; E. Ann Kaplan, *Women and Film: Both Sides of the Camera* (New York: Methuen, 1983), 49–59.

17. Alexander Walker, *Stardom: The Hollywood Phenomenon* (New York: Stein and Day, 1970), 250–51, writes that in 1928 the studios received 32,250,000 fan letters. In 1934, 535 official fan clubs with 750,000 members existed. Gaylyn Studlar, *This Mad Masquerade: Stardom and Masculinity in the Jazz Age* (New York: Columbia University Press, 1996), 90–93, discusses the significance of female

fans for the 1920s film industry. An outstanding recent survey of movie fans, fan magazines, and audiences from 1910 to the early 1930s is Kathryn H. Fuller, *At the Picture Show: Small-Town Audiences and the Creation of Movie Fan Culture* (Washington, DC: Smithsonian Institution Press, 1996), 115–193.

18. The material below may sound more like post-1950 fan magazine and publicity content. Through the 1920s and early 1930s, fan magazines and publicity machines operated rather freely. With the clamping down of the Production Code in 1934, studios threatened lack of access to the stars if reporters continued to print negative or scandal stories. On this history, besides Fuller, *At the Picture Show*, 115–93, see Richard de Cordova, *Picture Personalities: The Emergence of the Star System in America* (Urbana: University of Illinois Press, 1990), 117–34; Walker, *Stardom*, 200, 246. The public's interest in scandal is discussed in 1930 in Louis E. Bisch, "Why Hollywood Scandal Fascinates Us," *Photoplay* 37, no. 2 (January 1930): 73, 100. Studlar, *This Mad Masquerade*, 2, remarks on the fan's conflation of "textual identities" of stars with the stars' "private identities," and Fuller's work also gives examples of this.

19. Standard biographies of Dietrich are Steven Bach, *Marlene Dietrich: Life and Legend* (New York: Morrow, 1992); Maria Riva, *Marlene Dietrich* (New York: Knopf, 1993); also see Baxter, "The Birth of Venus," and Josef Von Sternberg, *Fun in a Chinese Laundry* [1965] (New York: Collier, 1973). An additional parallel which I will not stress here is that Dietrich's daughter was threatened with kidnapping in May 1932, and several stories appeared during the summer about the measures taken to keep children of stars secure from such dangers.

20. Corinne Lowe, "Marlene Dietrich in Person," *Pictorial Review* 32 (August 1931): 53. For other period versions of Dietrich, see Frank Condon, "Greta and Marlene," *Saturday Evening Post* 203 (30 May 1931): 29, 44; Leonard Hall, "Garbo vs. Dietrich," *Photoplay* 29, no. 3 (February 1931): 50–51, 106; Otto Tolischus, "Dietrich—How She Happened," *Photoplay* 39, no. 5 (April 1931): 28–29, 129; Leonard Hall, "The Perils of Marlene," *Photoplay* 30, no. 6 (May 1931): 37, 104.

21. Tolischus, "Dietrich—How She Happened," 28.

22. Leonard (Old Snoop) Hall, "The Extra-Private Life of Marlene Dietrich," *Photoplay* 40, no. 6 (November 1931): 48.

23. Untitled, *Photoplay* 41, no. 2 (January 1932): 78.

24. Kay Evans, "Will Marlene Break the Spell?" *Photoplay* 41, no. 3 (February 1932): 76.

25. "The Monthly Broadcast of Hollywood Goings-On!" *Photoplay* 42, no. 3 (August 1932): 37.

26. "For the Hollywood Parade," *Photoplay* 42, no. 4 (September 1932): 39.

27. Paramount ad, scrapbook, New York Public Library at MFL/+/n.c./2462, 506–7.

28. Mortimer Franklin, "The Blonde Venus," *Screenland*, September 1932.

6

The Cultural Productions of
A Clockwork Orange

This is Stanley Kubrick. He produced, wrote the screenplay for and directed *A Clockwork Orange*. I'm not sure that Kubrick sees himself as a practitioner of the Ludovico Technique, but I think he comes very close. Has it occurred to anyone that, after having our eyes metaphorically clamped open to witness the horrors that Kubrick parades across the screen, like Alex and his adored 9th, none of us will ever again be able to hear "Singin' in the Rain" without a vague feeling of nausea?

—Susan Rice, 1972

WHAT PRECISELY MIGHT be the effects of watching *A Clockwork Orange* has preoccupied several decades of film scholars. Does the film romanticize and then excuse violence? Could it create a questioning of authorities? Is its effect more devastating, as Susan Rice suggests in the epigraph: the unsettling of a pure pleasure in watching Gene Kelly dance?[1] And why did *A Clockwork Orange* become such a favorite among the cult audiences of the 1970s and later?

This essay will not answer any of these questions. What it will attempt is to place the U.S. public critical reception of *A Clockwork Orange* in parts of its cultural context with the hopes that understanding some of the dynamics and tensions existing within the moment of the film's release will provide a description of some associations available to a film viewer of the era. These contextual associations would have a bearing on eventually answering questions about effect.

The critical reception of *A Clockwork Orange* has been studied with rather more detail than that of most other films. This is undoubtedly because of the public debates it generated within weeks of its U.S. release with an "X" rating and its actual censoring in Britain. A particularly good synopsis of the U.S. reaction occurs in Ernest Parmentier's summary of the criticism of *A Clockwork Orange*. Parmentier describes the initial laudatory praise of director Stanley Kubrick and the film, followed by denunciations of both by Andrew Sarris, Stanley Kauffmann, Pauline Kael, Gary Arnold (of the *Washington Post*), and Roger Ebert. A series of letters in the *New York Times* also debated merits and deficits of *A Clockwork Orange*.[2] I will return to these public arguments below.

In Britain, where methods of self-regulation and state regulation differed from those in the U.S., government review of films occurred, with some films being considered by the regulators as unsuitable viewing fare and then prohibited from public screening. Guy Phelps explains that a conservative turn in the voting of 1970 encouraged a retightening of recent more liberal decisions. Thus, when *A Clockwork Orange* appeared, amid several other taboo-testing films such as Ken Russell's *The Devils* and Sam Peckinpah's *Straw Dogs*, the censoring board had a peculiar problem. Since the film itself criticized government attempts to control or condition youth behavior with the proposition that interference by authorities was more immoral than Alex's original behavior, it might look too self-serving of the board to question the film. More important, however, demands by conservative commentators, requesting that the board act against the increasing number and brutality of representations of violence on the screen, pushed the board in the opposite direction toward acting against the film in some way. Because the controversy seemed potentially damaging in the long run, Kubrick convinced his British distributors to select a narrow release: the film was shown for over a year in only one West End London theater (although to large audiences).[3] When the distributors attempted a wider release at the end of that period, local activities of censoring had intensified. In February 1973, the borough of Hastings banned *A Clockwork Orange* on grounds that "it was 'violence for its own sake' and had 'no moral.'"[4] Other local authorities followed the Hastings decision despite controversy in the public discussions.

That *A Clockwork Orange* presented "violence for its own sake" and that it "had no moral" were also major themes in the U.S. controversy, and in that order. The first negative remarks were about the representations of violence. Sarris' review in the *Village Voice* in December 1971 described *A Clockwork Orange* as a "painless, bloodless and ultimately pointless futuristic fantasy." Kauffmann, Kael, and Richard Schickel also attacked the film for its representations of violence, warning that watching so much brutality could desensitize viewers to violence.[5] Thus, ad hoc theories of effects of representation became one line of argumentation, and *A Clockwork Orange* became a strand of the discussion that had operated for centuries about obscenity and audience effect.

The debates in the *New York Times* were couched in philosophical and political discourses. What was the moral of this film? Was it moral? What were the politics of those praising or condemning the film? What were the responsibilities of a filmmaker? Kubrick and actor Malcolm McDowell participated in these discussions, claiming that "liberals" did not like the film because it was forcing them to face reality.[6] Kubrick was particularly reacting to Fred M. Hechinger, who had charged that an "alert liberal . . . should recognize the voice of fascism" in the film.[7]

By the end of the first year of its release, a third line of attack opened on *A Clockwork Orange*. The film was accused of misogyny. Beverly Walker, writing in an early feminist film journal, charged the film adaptation with "an attitude that is ugly, lewd and brutal toward the female human being: all of the women are portrayed as caricatures; the violence committed upon them is treated comically; the most startling aspects of the decor relate to the female form."[8]

Within the context of the U.S. cultural scene of 1971–72, that these three discursive themes—effects of the representation of violence, morality and politics, and gender relations—would come forth to be debated is easy to explain.[9] That they would be the staging grounds for a cult viewer's attraction to the film is also apparent. Precisely how these themes organized themselves in the debates is important to examine, however, for they take on a flavor peculiar to the circumstances of the era. Each of the three discourses was crossed by discourses related to (1) changing definitions of obscenity and pornography as a consequence of the sexual politics of the 1960s, (2) theories of audience effect, and (3) intertextual comparisons—interpreting the ideology of a film in relation to its source material.[10] In other words, the cultural productions of *A Clockwork Orange* were contextually derived but contradictory, and the lack of an open-and-shut case about the meaning or effect or value of the film has been part of the explanation for the film's availability to so many people in so many ways.

EFFECTS OF THE REPRESENTATION OF VIOLENCE:
TESTING DEFINITIONS OF OBSCENITY

At the time of the release of *A Clockwork Orange* in December 1971, a wave of films with scenes of violence was splashing across U.S. screens. In a preview article for the film, *Time* magazine had pointed to Roman Polanski's *Macbeth, Dirty Harry*, and the recent Bond film, *Diamonds Are Forever*, as part of a trend in which *A Clockwork Orange* was also participating.[11] Although some arguments could be made that these films were fictional responses to the nightly news images of Vietnam, two other, very salient, causal factors for the increasingly violent material were the previous twenty-year history of U.S. film exhibition and the changing laws of obscenity and pornography.

Since the end of World War II, foreign films had been appearing with regularity on screens in larger U.S. cities; they were winning best film awards from U.S. and foreign critics and film festivals. Often, foreign films presented more sexually explicit images or dealt with seamier aspects of modern life, creating a stronger sense of verisimilitude (read "realism"). Finally, breaching the boundaries of subject matter that had been considered off-limits by the Hollywood film industry was thus a competitive move by U.S. filmmakers against the foreign cinema. It was also a move of product differentiation against U.S. television, which had taken up the role of the family entertainer. During the twenty years up to 1971, Hollywood films had steadily penetrated earlier limits on sexual and violent materials. It had finally given up on the old production code's binary system of okay/not-okay, and in 1968 moved to a rating system organized by ages.[12] The G-GP-R-X system opened up possibilities of competition through subject matter in ways hitherto undreamed of. Such a system, however, required that previous definitions of obscenity and liability be changed before Hollywood could believe itself safe from criminal prosecution.

The representation of sexually explicit materials is not to be equated with the representation of violently explicit materials, nor is either to be assumed obscene. However, the confusion of these notions was part of public protests of the 1960s. Those protests had to do with what counted as obscenity, and laws and discourses were in transition on this matter. In his excellent study of the history of pornography, Walter Kendrick traces the distinctions, and then confusions, between the terms "obscenity" and "pornography."[13] Kendrick argues that until the

1800s, Western tradition generally separated literature into serious literature and comedy. Serious literature had decorum, high status, and a public availability; comedy was abusive, low, and, if obscene, segregated into a nonpublic space. Obscenity could occur through use of both sexual and scatological materials.

It was not until the mid-1800s that "pornography" appeared, and at first it meant "a description of prostitutes or of prostitution," but also a "description of the life, manners, etc. of prostitutes and their patrons: hence, the expression or suggestion of obscene or unchaste subjects in literature or art" (p. 2). Obviously, chaste versus lascivious representations of prostitutes could occur, and distinguishing between the two became important.

Now I would note here that although Kendrick suggests that obscenity was traditionally located within the realm of comedy (and outside the field of serious literature), obviously images of eroticism have not always been deployed for a comedic effect; we would be naive to think that the nineteenth century invented representations designed for sexual arousal. What seems to be happening, I think, is that the term "obscenity" is being focused toward the sexual (and scatological), and its semantic field is being redistributed to include not only sexuality explicit materials for comedic effects but also erotic ones which do not fit into traditional norms of serious literature. The project of categorization is being confronted by ambiguous materials.

Moreover, soon theorists of law began to try to make distinctions between intent and effect when asked to rule on the categorization of instances of reputed obscenity or pornography. Here theories of audience effect entered. The distinctions made are, in legal discourse, "tests," and legal tests began to be made on the basis of presumptions that images could have audience effects. Kendrick notes that Lord Chief Justice Cockburn concluded an important mid-1800s British decision, *Regina v. Hicklin* (1868), on obscenity on the basis of a test whether there existed in the materials "the tendency to corrupt the minds and morals of those into whose hands it might come." (p. 122). If the conclusion of the "Hicklin Test" was positive, then one could infer that the author's intentions had been obscene, and the author would be judged guilty.

Now two observations are apparent: one is that the materials are being assumed to be naturally readable as obscene or not; the second is that intent is being determined from presumed effect. The various gaps in reasoning in these two propositions are immense.

Although both British and U.S. law generally operated under the Hicklin Test during the 1800s, by the later years of the century U.S. courts were increasingly sympathetic to claims that if the questionable item were "art," then it was excluded from judgments of obscenity (pp. 174–87). In other words, U.S. law began to rewrite the traditional binary categories of serious literature and comedy, with the opposition becoming serious literature/art versus nonserious (i.e., cheap) literature/not-art, and obscenity was possible only in the instance of the latter. In 1913, Judge Learned Hand undermined the "transparent-reading-of-effect-proves-intent" assumptions of the Hicklin Test by separating audiences: a possible effect on underage individuals should not necessitate the general prohibition of an item. It could be available privately, if not publicly, to mature readers. The effects of the troublesome representation were not universal or necessarily degenerate. In some sense, Judge Hand created a "Selected-Effect Test."

Beyond the separations of art versus not-art and universal versus select (and, hence, public versus private), U.S. law added a third binary: the Part-Versus-Whole Test. The courts decided a 1922 case by the argument that although parts of a book might be lewd, the "whole" book was not; the "whole" book was art. If the whole book were art, then the power of art would override the effects of the segments of obscenity. Again, audience effects were significant in the test, but refinements were being made in how those effects were to be determined.[14]

These U.S. trends in regulating sexual materials explains why the United States ruled *Ulysses* (and *The Well of Loneliness*) could be published long before Britain did. It is also the fact that, as a consequence of these tests, U.S. courts delegated pornography to the category of not-art. In 1957 the Roth Test became the new statement of the evolving semantics and theory of effect: "to the average person using community standards," would the dominant theme of the item appeal to prurient interests? In this test, the work is judged as a whole, and the United States as a whole is the community doing the judging. Moreover, obscenity is reduced to sexual content, although not all sexual content is obscene (it is not obscene if it is in art). Obscenity is not protected by free speech, but obscenity is now "material which deals with sex in a manner appealing to prurient interests."[15] While the Roth Test opened up some types of material—the U.S. Supreme Court cleared physique magazines (which were often used as erotic material by gay men) of obscenity charges in the early 1960s[16]—the test also tacitly reduced obscenity to sexual content (although likely scatological material would also be considered). The 1973 refinement of the Roth Test by the Miller Test included not only the Whole-Item Test, but added the query of whether sexual conduct was represented in a "patently offensive" way.[17]

Joining this stream of shifting semantics about obscenity were the cultural, political, and sexual debates of the 1960s: the anti–Vietnam War crisis pitted free-love flower children against gun-toting war militants. "Make love not war" introduced a binary contrast that paralleled the question, why was it that sexuality was deemed by authority figures offensive enough to be prohibited from view but violence was not? Weren't violence and its representations equally or probably more obscene? If sexual content might have harmful effects by appealing to susceptible minds, so might violent images.

Thus, at a time of increasing leniency toward (or increasing means to justify) the representation of sexuality, political differences turned attention toward other subject matter which had also been increasingly portrayed recently in public sites. Alongside the debates on what constituted obscene materials grew the arguments that representations of dominance by one person over another (rapes, objectification of individuals, and so forth) fit the category of "patently offensive" and had a potential to produce harmful effects (a continuation of the Hicklin Test).[18] Thus, antipornography feminists objected not to sexual content but to content they claimed represented violence, and they argued for its categorization as obscenity and for its removal from the public sphere.

In the midst of the late 1960s debates over redefining obscenity to include not only hard-core pornography but also violence appeared *A Clockwork Orange*. While ultimately legally protected as a work of art, *A Clockwork Orange* was not protected in the sphere of public discourse. Thus, the discussion about the representations of violence in the film echoes the centuries-long debates over sexual obscenity.[19] Moreover, the film's violence was not isolated as in the case of other violent films being released at about the same time: *A Clockwork Orange* had sexual content completely intertwined within its violence.

One of the major themes of the attackers of the representations of violence in *A Clockwork Orange* was that it was not art but exploitation. It failed Judge Hand's Whole-Item Test. "Exploitation" was a film-specific term for cheap, prurient, patently offensive, and—a sure sign it was not art—commercially driven. Examples of these criticisms included remarks such as those in *Films in Review* that the film "sinks to the depths of buck-chasing (sex scribblings on walls; total nudity; sight-gags for perverts)."[20] Schickel agreed, defining the film as "commercial cynicism," and David Denby called it a "grotesque extension of the youth movie" (also not art in 1971). Kael pointed out that in one scene the film opens on the rival gang's attempt to gang-rape a young girl, so that, she underlined, more of the stripping can be shown: "it's the purest exploitation."[21]

In these arguments over what category the film belonged to—art or not-art—operate not only discourses concerned with the changing definitions of obscenity and theories of audience effect, but also discourses of intertextual comparison. In the criticisms of its representations of violence (and in the ones on the film's morality and its gender politics), a major strategy of both attackers and defenders was to compare and contrast the source material with the film. Here the source material is Anthony Burgess's novel *A Clockwork Orange*. With the development of auteurist criticism in the 1960s, the film *A Clockwork Orange* also became Stanley Kubrick's film. Thus, attributions of authorship and intent in these comparisons reduce to how Kubrick changed (or did not change) Burgess's work. In the claim that the film's representations of violence classified it as exploitation, not art, attackers used the intertextual-comparison strategy. For example, Kauffmann noted that Kubrick changed the woman whom Alex assaults with one of her favorite art objects from "an old woman to a sexy broad [*sic*] and [killed] her with a giant ceramic phallus (thus changing sheer heartlessness into sex sensation)."[22] With the tacit proposition that the original novel is art, evidence of Kubrick's sexualization of the content proves that Kubrick's film is exploitation and not-art.

Those criticizing the film for its representations of violence not only tried to define it as not-art, but also argued that the representations had harmful effects and passed the Hicklin Test. Kael probably was relying on contemporary social science theses that individual experiences with violent images were not specifically harmful but repeated exposure to such images would eventually be bad when she rejected the idea that violent images were only reflecting reality; instead, she claimed they were "desensitizing us."[23] Vincent Canby somewhat responded to Kael by writing that although he was not disturbed by the violence, he could believe that this might not be the case for "immature audiences" (the Selected-Effect Test).[24]

Some people, of course, disagreed with those criticizing the film on the basis of its representations of violence. In these cases, the writers were attempting to establish that *A Clockwork Orange* was within the category of art and, consequently, not degenerate or obscene in its depictions of violence. If it was art, then the overall effect of the film was an art effect, which de facto would not harm its viewers.

The ways to defend the film as art were similar to the ways to attack it. Kubrick himself defended the film via the intertextual comparison strategy; he claimed, "It's all in the plot."[25] Others argued that the violence was justified realistically. Hollis Alpert pointed to the film's realistic connections, among them "the growth in youthful violence, the drug cultures, and the extraordinary increase in eroticism." Others took what Paul D. Zimmerman aptly described as a "mythic realism" approach: the characters are caricatures, but of "some more basic essence."[26]

A third strategy to make the film art, beyond the intertextual-comparison approach and the realism argument, was the aesthetically motivated thesis. If a critic examined the images of violence in the film and the critic could discern formal and stylistic patterns, then they were a sure sign the film was "art" and not exploitation. Canby wrote, "the movie shows a lot of aimless violence—the exercise of aimless choice—but it is as formally structured as the music of Alex's 'lovely lovely Ludwig Van,' which inspires in Alex sado-masochistic dreams of hangings, volcanic eruptions and other disasters." Cocks in *Time* claimed the violence was "totally stylized, dreamlike, absurd." Alpert believed, "in lesser hands, this kind of thing could be disgusting or hateful, but curiously, as Kubrick handles it, it isn't. For one thing, the stylization throughout is constant." Mythic realism becomes universality: "Imagery, the kind that mythologizes and endures, is the nucleus of the film experience," claimed *Playboy*'s reviewer.[27]

Thus, in the debates about the representations of violence in *A Clockwork Orange*, both sides of the discussion assumed several points: (1) defining the film as art or not art was important, and (2) determining the effects of the representations of violence had pertinence. Like the legal establishment of the era, these tests would determine how to categorize the film, and evaluation would follow.

MORALITY AND POLITICS: READING THE IDEOLOGY OF A FILM

Although for years U.S. Marxist critics had overtly been reading the ideology of texts, and liberal reviewers had tacitly engaged in the same practice, numerous events of the 1960s increased tendencies to include these questions of content in evaluations of movie fare. These 1960s events included all those factors involved with the issues of representing sexuality and violence discussed above, but they also incorporated the implications of auteurist criticism and the move of film criticism into universities and colleges.

Within Western traditions of criticism, a debate has been waged between advocates who believe that human agency accounts for causality and those who stress the importance of social structures. This is often described as the humanist-structuralist debate. For most conservative and liberal commentators, the more prominent cause of events is human decision making; hence, Western literary tradition has so often stressed determining who created a work of art. This concern was important in film criticism almost immediately at the start of the movies, but it certainly increased during the 1960s with the advent of auteurist criticism. Causes for auteurism include the influences of foreign art cinema and foreign film criticism. Defining films as art also permitted the wide introduction of film courses into colleges and universities. Moreover, studying contemporary culture as art (or at least as a reflection of culture) had relevance at a time when young radicals decried the staleness of the status quo institutions, which were often blamed for the public's lackadaisical attitude toward racism and the ever-deepening U.S. commitment in Vietnam.[28]

Trying to determine the authorship of a film, however, had consequences. Once agency can be pinpointed, so can blame. And, thus, locating in Kubrick (or Burgess) responsibility for representations raised philosophical and political issues of morality. Just what was the ideology the author(s) had presented? What were the implications of that ideology?

Both attackers and defenders of the film spent some space on the project of defining its meaning. Burgess himself thought the novel was about "the power of choice." Kael said the film's point was that "the punk was a free human being," while Schickel summarized the thesis as the "loss of the capacity to do evil is a minor tragedy, for it implies a loss also of the creative capacity to do good." Rice described it as "free choice must prevail/man's nature is perverse."[29]

No matter what the movie's thesis, one major strategy to absolve or blame Kubrick for any potentially morally corrupt subject matter was the intertextual-comparison tactic. Critics who wanted to rescue the film argued that the novel was morally worse or that what Kubrick put in the film was already subtextually in the novel.[30] Critics who disliked the film, of course, found the differences from the novel proof of Kubrick's agency and his ideology. So both camps accepted Kubrick as author, used intertextual comparison to determine Kubrick's authorship, and then evaluated what they believed they had discovered.

One primary site on which this debate over ideology and morality focused was the film's representation of Alex. Both in the abstract and via comparison to the novel, reviewers thought Kubrick had created a central protagonist with whom the audience was to side. Alex "has more energy and style and dash—more humanity—than anyone else in the movie"; Alex might be compared with mass killer Charles Manson, yet Alex is "surprisingly but undeniably engaging"; Alex is "more alive than anyone else in the movie, and younger and more attractive."[31] Those who appreciated this protagonist used Alex's representation to justify their respect for the film and to argue a positive moral message; those who did not appreciate this protagonist could also accuse Kubrick of using audience sympathy to make individuals morally complicit with an amoral message.

Indeed, the claims that the film was corrupt, unfair, and amoral were as many as the criticisms of its representations of violence and sexual attack. Kael was one of the first critics to pursue this line of denunciation. "The trick of making the attacked less human than their attackers, so you feel no sympathy for them, is, I think, symptomatic of a new attitude in movies. This attitude says there's no moral difference." The movie makes it too easy to enjoy and even identify with Alex. He is given too many rationales for his behavior (bad parents, bad friends, bad social workers); he is cleaned up compared with the book's Alex; the victims are "cartoon nasties with upper-class accents a mile wide."[32]

Indeed, many of the criticisms in this range of discourse centered on not only whether Alex was made "too nice" but whether Alex's victims were set up to be destroyed. Schickel's view was that "We are never for a moment allowed even a fleeting suggestion of sympathy for anyone else, never permitted to glimpse any other character of personal magnetism, wit, or sexual attractiveness comparable to Alex's. As a result, the film, though surprisingly faithful to the plot line of the novel, is entirely faithless to its meaning."[33]

It was in this group of responses that the accusation was made that the film was fascist. Hechinger's criticism derived from the series of propositions that if the theme was saying that humanity is inevitably corrupt, then this was authoritarian ideology. Jackson Burgess furthered that line, arguing: "the laughter of *Clockwork Orange* is a mean and cynical snigger at the weakness of our own stomachs. . . . A strong stomach is the first requirement of a storm trooper."[34]

Not only was the protagonist too nice in contrast with the victims and the theme amoral or even fascist, but Kubrick's authorial voice was too distant and detached, making him doubly complicit with the theme. Kubrick was described as something of an amoral "god-figure" or a misanthrope. Kauffmann wrote, "But the worst flaw in the film is its air of cool intelligence and ruthless moral inquiry because those elements are least fulfilled." Kael believed that the authorial voice was "a leering, portentous style," while Clayton Riley accused Kubrick of "offer[ing] no cogent or meaningful commentary on [the violence]." Kubrick's authorship could have been redeemed, Denby thought, had values been articulated by the end of the film, but "the mask of the ironist and savage parodist has fallen off, and behind it is revealed the fact of a thoroughgoing misanthrope." "How bored and destructive Kubrick seemed," concluded Seth Feldman.[35]

The conclusions about authorial viewpoint were largely derived from two aspects of the film. One was the adaptational differences between the novel and the film, charged to Kubrick's decision making; the other was technical style. Part and parcel of auteurist criticism was a careful reading of stylistic choices, for, it was often claimed, the authorial voice of a director might be traced through style even if the director was compelled by studio or production circumstances to present a specific plotline. Here auteurist criticism provoked reviewers to attribute nonnormative choices in mise-en-scène, camerawork, editing, and sound to Kubrick's agency and to read them as meaningful expressions of his position vis-à-vis to the plotline he was, so to speak, given. Examples of such defenses have been provided above in relation to justifying the representations of violence as aesthetically motivated, including the classic auteurist praise of "consistency" of aesthetic design. The distance such an aesthetic choice produced could also be read as a protective device for the audience: the coolness provided for the audience a "resilience" needed to view the "multiple horrors."[36]

Critics of the film, however, connected Kubrick's stylistic choices with exploitation cinema (not art). Jackson Burgess pointed out that "the stylization shifts your attention, in a sense, away from the simple physical reality of a rape or a murder and focuses it upon the quality of feeling: cold, mindless, brutality." Kauffmann wrote that the camerawork was "banal and reminiscent" of many other recent films. Kael concluded, "Is there anything sadder—and ultimately more repellent—than a clean-minded pornographer? The numerous rapes and beatings have no ferocity and no sensuality; they're frigidly, pedantically calculated."[37] Kubrick's misanthropy, moreover, was also a misogyny.

GENDER RELATIONS: REVEALING SEXUAL POLITICS

The sexual revolution of the 1960s and the concurrent social and political upheaval had coalesced by the late 1960s. On the national scene feminists were criticizing canonical serious literature from perspectives of gender discrimination: Kate Millett's groundbreaking *Sexual Politics* appeared in 1969, and by the early 1970s feminist film critics and academics were starting to read films ideologically for not only their moral or political politics but also their sexual representations. Joan Mellen's *Women and Their Sexuality in the New Film* was published in 1973, Marjorie Rosen's *Popcorn Venus: Women, Movies and the American Dream* also in 1973, Molly Haskell's *From Reverence to Rape* in 1974, and Laura Mulvey's "Visual Pleasure and Narrative Cinema" in 1975.

In the second volume (1972) of an early feminist journal, Beverly Walker took on *A Clockwork Orange.*[38] Her strategy was the same as that of the traditional auteur critic: she used intertextual comparison with the novel and stylistic choices to conclude that Kubrick "has made an intellectual's pornographic film" (p. 4). Such a claim in 1972 needs to be recognized as a very powerful statement, given the debates about pornography and obscenity described above, and the militancy of feminists of the era. It should also, like the charge of "fascism," be understood as a rhetorical device aggressively arguing for significant social and political change. Its communicative function was not only descriptive but also attention-getting.

Walker's essay pinpointed numerous differences between the novel and the film, for the purpose, Walker argued, of making sex and genitalia more central to the film. The changes she described included ones of mise-en-scène and plot. In the film, the outfits worn by Alex's droogs deemphasize the shoulders (as opposed to the costumes worn by the gang in the novel) and instead call attention to the male genitals, as the action shifts to include not only violence (as in the novel) but *sexual* violence. The Korova Bar is not described in the book; hence, the set design is Kubrick's fantasy. The characteristics of the women are changed from the novel. The novel's cat lady is older and lives in a house with antiques. When Kubrick introduces his cat woman, she is shown in a grotesque yoga position, has a "phony, hard voice," and is surrounded by phallic and sexual decor—to invite, one might claim, sexual thoughts in the observers of the art objects. Such a decor and woman provide the classic excuse that the victim asked for the rape.

Not only is the cat woman redesigned, but Alex's mother is visualized. Walker believed that she was not dressed as befitting her age, although Alex's father seems traditionally clothed. The woman to be raped by the rival gang is clothed in the novel and also only a child (age ten), rather than stripped naked and well endowed. Walker asked, "Why is it the women change radically in this Orwellian world, but not the men?" (p. 9).

The sexual design of the film's mise-en-scène does seem to have excited most of the reviewers (or their layout supervisors). The Korova milk bar and Alex's close-up headshot were the favorite publicity stills to reproduce in articles about the film. Another favorite image was the scene of Alex's rectal examination by the prison guard, featured on the cover of *Films and Filming* for the issue that reviewed the film.[39] That *Films and Filming* took such delight in the film seems to confirm Walker's claim of a "homosexual motif" running through the film, since *Films and Filming* had a covert (or not so covert!) address to gay men. Its review and selection of accompanying photos provide ample evidence of another potential reading of the text, a point to which I will return below.

In conclusion, Walker suggested that the film was "woman-hating." As mentioned above, she believed it had "an attitude that is ugly, lewd and brutal toward the female human being: all of the women are portrayed as caricatures; the violence committed upon them is treated comically; the most startling aspects of the decor relate to the female form" (p. 4). The film was, again, exploitation: "all the naked ladies Kubrick has astutely used as commercial window dressing" (p. 4).

My review of the critical response to the film has focused to a large degree on the negative criticism; yet the film has become a cult favorite. Unfortunately, details of the fans' responses to the film could not be found. Still, speculation from the circumstances of the period and what became the focus of the critical response can give us some glimpse into what might have mattered to the early lovers of the movie.

Kubrick's authorial style was viewed by both supporters and critics as an aloof criticism of the social scene. Where one might put that authorial point of view in a range of political categories was debated, but without doubt that point of view was considered iconoclastic. Such a nontraditional position appeals to most subcultural groups with which cult viewers often align themselves. Kubrick's earlier work had already positioned him as out of the mainstream anyway: *Dr. Strangelove* was critical of every authority figure; *2001* immediately became a head movie. So when Kubrick's next film came out, anti-authoritarian adolescents were ready to take up the film no matter what. The movie's representations of violence, sexuality, and sexual violence could be rationalized as realism or mythic realism, and also enjoyed for their flouting of recent obscenity and pornography taboos.

Additionally, in the late 1960s, film-viewing audiences were well versed in several nontraditional strategies for watching films. One major viewing strategy had been the mainstream, "disposable" strategy in which seeing a film once was the norm. However, the concept and practice of repeat viewings of some movies had already become normative for two types of audiences: art-house devotees and underground/trash-cinema filmgoers. Both types of audiences rewatched films for several reasons: to find authorial signatures, to seek hidden messages, and to participate in a group audience experience.[40] While art-house and underground audiences often overlapped, differences in their makeup did exist and can be used to hypothesize their attraction to *A Clockwork Orange*. Art-house audiences had been typed as "eggheads," and were generally an intellectual crowd. Kubrick's work, with its complicated mise-en-scène and ambiguous message, fits well with the characteristics of an art-house film.

Underground cinema had a more eclectic audience, and because of the places and times where underground cinema was shown in the

1960s (run-down, large-city theaters; midnight screenings), underground cinema's audiences were mostly urban, male, and gay or gay-friendly. Out of the rebel underground cinema of the 1960s, the mid-1970s cult classic *The Rocky Horror Picture Show* developed, with, at least initially, a strong gay participation. Now, I would not go so far as to suggest that more than a few audience aficionados of *A Clockwork Orange* read the film as camp, but that reading is, I believe, available from the sexual politics of the context and parts of evidence remaining (the *Films and Filming* "reading"). Moreover, the exaggeration of the mise-en-scène has echoes in 1960s classic underground films such as *Flaming Creatures* (1963) and *Blonde Cobra* (1963). It is worth noting that Andy Warhol purchased the screenplay rights to Burgess's novel in the mid-1960s and produced his own adaptation of *A Clockwork Orange*: *Vinyl* (1965). Not surprisingly, *Vinyl* exceeds Kubrick's film in terms of the explicit sado-masochistic possibilities of the plot, but the general line of development is remarkably close to that of the novel, which lends more credibility to Walker's thesis of the availability of a homosexual motif subtending the action.

Whatever the causes for the cult following of *A Clockwork Orange*, the density of reactions has perhaps also provided more avenues for speculating about violence, sexuality, morality, and gender politics. If Kubrick unwittingly participated with the authorities in his own version of the Ludovico technique, perhaps this was not the least valuable set of issues on which to inflict scholars and critics of cinema.

NOTES

1. Susan Rice, "Stanley Klockwork's 'Cubrick Orange,'" *Media and Methods* 8, no. 7 (March 1972): 39–43.

2. Ernest Parmentier, "*A Clockwork Orange*," *Filmfacts* 14, no. 24 (15 July 1971): 649–55. Also see Norman Kagan, *The Cinema of Stanley Kubrick* (New York: Grove Press, 1972), 182; Robert Philip Kolker, "Oranges, Dogs, and Ultra-violence," *Journal of Popular Film* 1, no. 3 (Summer 1972): 159–72; and Wallace Coyle, *Stanley Kubrick: A Guide to References and Resources* (Boston: G. K. Hall, 1980), 26–27.

3. Guy Phelps, *Film Censorship* (London: Victor Gollancz, 1975), 69–87. Also see Charles Barr, "*Straw Dogs, A Clockwork Orange* and the Critics," *Screen* 13, no. 2 (Summer 1972): 17–31.

4. Phelps, *Film Censorship*, 169.

5. Andrew Sarris, "Films in Focus," *Village Voice* 16, no. 52 (30 December 1971): 49; Stanley Kauffmann, "*A Clockwork Orange*," *New Republic*, 1 and 8 January 1972, 22 and 32; Pauline Kael, "Stanley Strangelove," *New Yorker* 48 (1 January 1972): 50–53; Richard Schickel, "Future Shock and Family Affairs," *Life* 72, no. 4 (4 February 1972): 14.

6. Tom Burke, "Malcolm McDowell: The Liberals, They Hate 'Clockwork,'" *New York Times*, 30 January 1972, sect. 2, 13.

7. Stanley Kubrick, "Now Kubrick Fights Back," *New York Times*, 27 February 1972, sect. 2, 1.

8. Beverly Walker, "From Novel to Film: Kubrick's *A Clockwork Orange*," *Women and Film* 2 (1972): 4.

9. I am restricting this essay to the U.S. reception of the film. Phelps and Barr provide a valuable explanation of part of the British reception, although more work could be done.

10. This observation has been stimulated by the recent reading of Walter Metz, "Webs of Significance: Intertextual and Cultural Historical Approaches to Cold War American Film Adaptations," Ph.D. dss., University of Texas at Austin, 1996.

11. Jay Cocks, "Season's Greetings: Bang! Kubrick: Degrees of Madness," *Time*, 20 December 1971, 80.

12. A good synopsis of this is in Garth Jowett, "'A Significant Medium for the Communication of Ideas': The Miracle Decision and the Decline of Motion Picture Censorship, 1952–1986," in *Movie Censorship and American Culture*, ed. Francis G. Couvares (Washington, DC: Smithsonian Institution Press, 1996), 258–76.

13. Walter Kendrick, *The Secret Museum: Pornography in Modern Culture* (New York: Viking Press, 1987).

14. The events described here seem part of a larger trend in U.S. culture in dealing with regulating images. It parallels what I earlier observed happening with sexual images in the movies between 1895 and 1915. See Janet Staiger, *Bad Women: Regulating Sexuality in Early American Cinema* (Minneapolis: University of Minnesota Press, 1995).

15. Kendrick, *Secret Museum*, 201.

16. Martin Duberman, *Stonewall* (New York: Plume, 1993), 97. Also see Richard Ellis, "Disseminating Desire: Grove Press and 'The End[s] of Obscenity,'" in *Perspectives on Pornography: Sexuality in Film and Literature*, ed. Gary Day and Clive Bloom (New York: St. Martin's Press, 1988), 26–43.

17. Linda Williams, "Second Thoughts on *Hard Core*," in *Dirty Looks: Women, Pornography, Power*, ed. Pamela Church Gibson and Roma Gibson (London: British Film Institute, 1993), 48.

18. These strands of argumentation reproduce themselves today with the new V-chip and television ratings systems.

19. These criticisms were directed not solely toward *A Clockwork Orange* but against the whole wave of violent movies appearing after 1967. See for example the reception of *Bonnie and Clyde*.

20. In researching the reception of *A Clockwork Orange*, I secured fifty-seven reviews and articles published during the first two years of the film's U.S. release. In these notes, I shall cite only those items from which I quote or significantly paraphrase. H[arry] H[art], "*A Clockwork Orange*," *Films in Review* 23, no. 1 (January 1972): 51.

21. Richard Schickel, "Future Shock and Family Affairs," *Life* 72, no. 4 (4 February 1972): 14; David Denby, "Pop Nihilism at the Movies," *Atlantic* 229, no. 3 (March 1972): 102; Kael, "Stanley Strangelove," 52.

22. Stanley Kauffmann, "*A Clockwork Orange*," *New Republic*, 1 and 8 January 1972, 22.

23. Kael, "Stanley Strangelove," 53.

24. Vincent Canby, "'Orange'—'Disorienting but Human Comedy,'" *New York Times*, 9 January 1972, sect. 2, 7.

25. Stanley Kubrick quoted in Craig McGregor, "Nice Boy from the Bronx?" *New York Times*, 30 January 1972, sect. 2, 13.

26. Hollis Alpert, "Milk-Plus and Ultra-Violence," *Saturday Review* 54 (25 December 1971): 40; Paul D. Zimmerman, "Kubrick's Brilliant Vision," *Newsweek* 79, no. 1 (3 January 1972): 29; Robert Boyers, "Kubrick's *A Clockwork Orange*: Some Observations," *Film Heritage* 7, no. 4 (Summer 1972): 3.

27. Vincent Canby, "'A Clockwork Orange' Dazzles the Senses and Mind," *New York Times*, 20 December 1971, 44; Cocks, "Season's Greetings," 80; Alpert, "Milk-Plus and Ultra-Violence," 40; "Kubrick's 'A Clockwork Orange,'" *Playboy* 19, no. 1 (January 1972): 200.

28. Janet Staiger, "The Politics of Film Canons," *Cinema Journal* 24, no. 3 (Spring 1985): 4–23; David Bordwell, *Making Meaning: Inference and Rhetoric in the Interpretation of Cinema* (Cambridge: Harvard University Press, 1989); Janet Staiger, "With the Compliments of the Auteur: Art Cinema and the Complexities of Its Reading Strategies," in *Interpreting Films: Studies in the Historical Reception of American Cinema* (Princeton: Princeton University Press, 1992), 178–95.

29. Anthony Burgess, "Clockwork Marmalade," *Listener* 87, no. 2238 (7 February 1972): 198; Kael, "Stanley Strangelove," 50; Schickel, "Future Shock and Family Affairs," 14; Rice, "Stanley Klockwork's 'Cubrick Orange,'" 40. Ironically, some of the debate over the film's meaning reproduces issues in the humanist-structuralist debates which were, in fact, beginning to rage in academia at that time.

30. Arthur Gumenik, "'A Clockwork Orange': Novel into Film," *Film Heritage* 7, no. 4 (Summer 1972): 7–18+.

31. Craig Fisher, "Stanley Kubrick Produces, Directs 'Clockwork Or-

ange,'" *Hollywood Reporter,* 14 December 1971, 10; Cocks, "Season's Greetings," 80; Kael, "Stanley Strangelove," 50.

32. Kael, "Stanley Strangelove," 50–51.

33. Schickel, "Future Shock and Family Affairs," 14.

34. Hechinger paraphrased in Kubrick, "Now Kubrick Fights Back," 11; Jackson Burgess, "*A Clockwork Orange,*" *Film Quarterly* 25, no. 3 (Spring 1972): 35–36.

35. Kauffmann, "*A Clockwork Orange,*" 22; Kael, "Stanley Strangelove," 52; Clayton Riley, ". . . Or 'A *Dangerous, Criminally Irresponsible Horror Show*'?" *New York Times,* 9 January 1972, sect. 2, 1; Denby, "Pop Nihilism at the Movies," 102; Seth Feldman, "*A Clockwork Orange,*" *Take One* 3, no. 3 (April 1972): 21.

36. Boyers, "Kubrick's *A Clockwork Orange,*" 2. Also see Stephen Mamber, "*A Clockwork Orange,*" *Cinema* [Los Angeles, CA], 7, no. 3 (Winter 1973): 48–57.

37. Burgess, "*A Clockwork Orange,*" 35; Kauffmann, "*A Clockwork Orange,*" 32; Kael, "Stanley Strangelove," 50.

38. Walker, "From Novel to Film," 4–10.

39. *Films and Filming* 18, no. 5 (February 1972).

40. Staiger, "With the Compliments of the Auteur," 178–95; Janet Staiger, "Finding Community in the Early 1960s Underground Cinema," in *Swinging Single: Representing Sexuality in the 1960s,* ed. Hilary Radner and Moya Luckett (Minneapolis: University of Minnesota Press, 1999), 38–74 [Chapter 8 here].

PART III

INTERPRETATION AND IDENTITY THEORY

7

The Places of Empirical Subjects
in the Event of Mass Culture

Jeanie Bueller and Ideology

DURING THE 1990 U.S. presidential campaign, various contenders were asked their favorite movie, perhaps, as one columnist explained, just in case everything else evened out for the undecided voter. Youthful forty-two-year-old Dan Quayle picked *Ferris Bueller's Day Off*, explaining: "it reminded me of my time in school."[1]

For a critical theorist, such a choice would seem to indicate something worth considering, but the question is, just what does Quayle's choice mean? Why was he so perfectly the subject addressed by that film? What was its production of meaning for him? Or rather, how can we use a film such as *Ferris Bueller's Day Off* to consider and reconsider Louis Althusser's theories of ideology, aesthetics, institutions such as schools and families, and mass culture?

A fine essay by Chip Rhodes (to which this essay initially responded) details both the limitations and the possibilities of revised Althusserian Marxism for use by those interested in the theory and practice of historical change. Althusser's privileging of some aesthetics to the denigration of others has troubled many cultural critics, but, in my opinion, unjustly. As Rhodes suggests, it may be possible to recognize the overdetermined, contradictory, and uneven nature of even popular texts, opening sites for resistance without necessarily resorting to a return to a humanist representation of the subject.

What does concern me, however, is how Rhodes describes where the possibilities exist for his revision of Althusserian theory. Specifically, he contrasts "a strict Althusserian approach [which] should conceive of texts and subjects as both the bearers of structures" with a humanist approach that "affirms the existence of a subject that can be distinguished from its social context." Rhodes claims this opposition is an erroneous one. Instead, we need to understand that the dominant ideological apparatus has changed from the school to mass culture. What the humanists do not realize, according to Rhodes, is that their favored textual modes are complicit with this new dominant ideological apparatus, in fact *are* the new dominant ideological apparatus.

According to Rhodes, when Althusser wrote in 1968, he considered the production of subjects for capitalism to be primarily performed in the ideological state apparatuses (ISAs) by schools (and, to a lesser extent, the family). Rhodes argues that today mass culture has replaced these older ISAs as the primary producer of subjects in capitalism, because now it is more valuable for capitalism to produce subjects who will be good consumers. What Rhodes is doing is arguing that once we shift from a culture of production to a culture of consumption, the dominant ISAs need to shift from schools (and family) to mass culture with its pleasure aesthetics. Thus, mass culture may appear to empower or provide use value to individual subjects (as in Rhodes's version of the theories of humanists such as John Fiske and Fredric Jameson),[2] but mass culture does this just as the older ISAs did, by falsely constituting subjects. Mass culture texts, like the older hegemonic ISAs, must be read symptomatically.

Thus, Rhodes argues for reading recent popular texts in a revised Althusserian mode by elucidating how the texts provide subject positions for pleasurable consumption. This new mode would, he thinks, thus include the aesthetics ignored in Althusser's original presentation. Rhodes concludes by arguing that even the popular text offers only a contradictory opportunity for the subject because the dialectic is inevitable, a simple, irrefutable outcome of a Marxist theory of history.

In attempting to make his argument, with which I agree for the most part, Rhodes does, however, neglect one aspect to Althusser's theory which might be valuable in finding a way to mediate the apparent opposition between a strict structuralism and a retrogressive pure humanism. The neglected aspect is the interpellation process. Althusser specifically distinguishes between the individual and the subject. This distinction might allow us to consider the possibility of the historical change in dominant ISAs that Rhodes discusses without reverting, once again, to the text as producer of the fully, if unevenly, interpellated subject.

Althusser stresses that the function of ideology is to hail the individual to take up a subject position in a structural relation. Both the terms "individual" and "subject" are theoretical—humans are never individuals in the abstract. Rather humans are always in process, moving from subject position to subject position. Yet simultaneously, subject positions are also theoretical. They are sites of structural relations, but Althusser's formulation suggests the possibility of refusal to take up a proffered position, of not recognizing the ritual of a handshake or a calling by name. He writes,

> I say: the category of the subject is constitutive of all ideology, but at the same time and immediately I add *that the category of the subject is only constitutive of all ideology insofar as all ideology has the function (which defines it) of "constituting" concrete individuals as subjects.*[3]

Consequently, Althusser creates the problematic (because of its Lacanian foundations) description of "hailing" individuals: "*all ideology hails or interpellates concrete individuals as concrete subjects*. . . . I shall then suggest that ideology 'acts' or 'functions' in such a way that it 'recruits' subjects among the individuals (it recruits them all), or 'transforms' the individuals into subjects (it transforms them all)" (pp. 173–74).

As these passages continue, Althusser may not suggest any free will or unlimited agency on the part of individuals in connection with which hailings they recognize to be addressed to them, but it seems to me that this is the place for a meeting between a "strict Althusserian" approach and a "humanist" one. Much of the work of cultural studies has been to understand how identities (also to be thought of as subject positions) are constructed for individuals. Althusser even provides the explanation for the variety of identities/subject positions available. The ISAs are private, they are plural, and they function by ideology. They are, for Althusser, "the *site* of class struggle, and often of bitter forms of class struggle" (p. 147).

Like some other writers, I prefer to think of ideologies as having progressive and reactionary potentials, depending upon how they are transformed through their encounters with subjects in historical contexts.[4] This is because I believe that while individuals are constituted as subjects, they are also capable of recognizing contradiction and structured oppression to the point of (at least) resisting. Yet as Jonathan Dollimore writes, it would also be a mistake to consider history as so unstable as to be at every moment capable of revolution: "So the critique of ideology identifies the contingency of the social (it could always be otherwise), and its potential instability (ruling groups doubly contested from without and within), but does not underestimate the difficulty of change (existing social arrangements are powerfully invested and are not easily made otherwise)."[5]

How is this awareness possible? It is possible because of two features built into the Althusserian model. One is the contradictory nature of any specific ideology that will attempt to hail concrete individuals to take up specific subject positions; the second is that individuals may not recognize that ideology or may reject being hailed as those subjects. While people are always already subjects, as a "feminist," for instance, I am inclined by being the bearer of the meaning of that structure to resist evidences of patriarchy. I reject being interpellated as a "woman" into standard patriarchal addresses because that is contrary to my subject position as feminist. I am not, however, "free," nor do I have unlimited agency to be something else, since it is through opposition that I refuse that patriarchal subject position.

Let me illustrate this by using *Ferris Bueller's Day Off* as the example. Rhodes provides a fine ideological analysis of the film in relation to a "consuming" ideology and subject, but he presumes a (fully) interpellated subject. Moreover, for subject positioning to work in *Ferris Bueller's Day Off*, this subject seems to be an adolescent Anglo middle- or upper-class heterosexual male—Quayle, for example.

Studying the responses of empirical subjects is a very complex process, full of historiographical and theoretical problems. I can rehearse here only two of these difficulties.[6] One is to find traces of the relations between individuals and texts, since the words of peoples without dominant voices are seldom recorded permanently for the researcher to locate later. Moreover, determining what identities in the interaction with a specific text are at stake for the individual would be very significant in understanding the interpellation or resistance, but, again, this is a difficult task. What the researcher must often do is resort to very contaminated evidence or convoluted and speculative analysis.

Here, it would be quite valuable to find evidence of subjects other than adolescent, Anglo, middle-/upper-class, heterosexual males. And, in fact, some such material traces are available for *Ferris Bueller's Day Off*. These are reviews and commentary about the film printed in national papers and periodicals. In a survey of thirteen such instances, several surprising results emerge.

Of the thirteen writers, only two seem to have taken up the apparent subject position offered.[7] One of these was nationally syndicated columnist George Will. Will declared, "the greatest movie of all time is showing now at fine theaters everywhere. . . . By 'greatest movie' I mean the moviest movie, the one most true to the general spirit of movies, the spirit of effortless escapism." Will acknowledged in anticipation of his critics that *Ferris Bueller's Day Off* could be read as a cultural symptom "of the self-absorption of youth corrupted by the complacency of the Reagan years." But he countered, "Such Zeitgeist-mongering is punctured by Epstein's question: When, other than periods of war or economic calamity, have people not been self-absorbed?" That is, Ferris is the essential human: "as should happen in a teen-ager liberationist movie, Ferris reduces a ferret-faced school administrator to rubble, bamboozles his soggy-headed parents and lives out every teen-ager's fantasy of subverting authority at every turn. Ferris is, as the saying goes, 'into' fun."

Although Ronald Reagan was president in 1986, Democrats ran Congress. Without too much of a stretch, it seems plausible to argue that Will was reading into *Ferris Bueller* an oppositional politics to a conservative's view of what dominated the United States in 1986—schools run without prayers, liberal family (non-)values. Indeed, as Rhodes suggests, the ideal interpellated subject seems to be one that accepts an ideology of capitalist and patriarchal pleasure and consumption.

In opposition to Will (and the second critic, to whom I will return below) were eleven other writers: apparently nine men, one woman, and one unknown (initials only). The identity taken up by these eleven writers were not Republican/insurgent but member of the dominant *adult* population. In review after review, the critics and columnists described the adolescent character of Ferris and the film in unflattering terms. David Ansen in *Newsweek* declared *Ferris Bueller* was "basically a mindless paean to goofing off." "S. H." in *People* wrote that "watching *Ferris Bueller* is like going to a party given by a pushy, over-zealous host." Patrick Goldstein noted in the *Los Angeles Times* that while Ferris was "the mythic teen-ager," the "hero [is] so smug and invincible that he doesn't give us any chance to root for him. . . . This is the new teen banality in all its spoiled splendor." Gene Siskel for the *Chicago Tribune* concluded the film might have been better "if Ferris and his friends had more fun along the way, or if [director John] Hughes had done away

with the most juvenile element of the film, the pathetic, low-comedy attempt of the school principal to catch Ferris in the act of ditching."
David Sterritt in the *Christian Science Monitor* observed, "Ferris Bueller
is no more complex or compelling than other Hughes heroes, and his
'day off' is just another frivolous episode." James K. Glassman in the
New Republic actually called for real revolution rather than this artificial
one: "The triumph of teenagers over adult authority is an old theme,
but there used to be a point to the struggle. Today we have suburban
(usually North Shore Chicago) kids faking out their parents so that they
can throw a big party (*Risky Business* again) or go swimming. Bring back
Sal Mineo. He was cutting-edge."[8]

Accounts of the audience for this film relate that, indeed, teens enjoyed it, and given that the Hollywood film industry is interested in cul-
tivating that demographic group, the film's address seems to have been
quite successful. That a bunch of adults, except for Quayle and Will,
didn't find it appealing is not surprising.

What is perhaps a bit intriguing, then, is the fact that the second
critic who enjoyed the movie was a woman. Rita Kempley of the *Washington Post* began her review, "I wish Ferris Bueller were a friend of
mine. He's the kind of pal who talks you into cutting classes, into grab-
bing a summer day before it gets away."

> Ferris is the archetypal all-American boy, a direct descendant of Tom
> Sawyer and Joel ("Risky Business") Goodsen with a lot of Andy Hardy
> mixed in. Everybody loves Ferris, to the supreme irritation of his jeal-
> ous sister (Jennifer Grey smolders with sibling indignation) and the
> suspicious dean of students (Jeffrey Jones, whose pursuit of the truant
> Ferris recalls a prim Clouseau).

Kempley concluded, "'Day Off' transports you. It takes you out of
yourself for a while—like a Ferris-wheel ride, if you'll pardon the pun.
It takes you higher, gives you an overview, and helps you appreciate the
carnival."

A couple of ways exist to consider this response to the film. One is
to argue that Kempley is succumbing, as Rhodes predicts, to the mass-
culture consumption ideology. Another version is to perceive her as
perceiving the text as a critique of authority. Coming as it does from a
nondominant member of society, Kempley's response needs to be evaluated differently than Quayle's and Will's reactions. Quayle and Will

are privileged white males who can afford to support this dominant ideology; Kempley may be privileged and probably is white, but not all of her identities provide her with simple access to the potential blessings of the consumer society.

Indeed, as I suggested above, what identities are mobilized for what real humans in the interaction with this mass culture text matter for considering any interpretation of the ideological effects. Rhodes's reading of this film is one that does well to describe how it is complicit with consumer ideology. However, the reading and evaluation might look different if the analysis considered the subject hailed to be an adolescent female, a gay male, a Hispanic, or a working-class youth. For Rhodes focuses upon the main plotline and not the moments of contradiction or "discoherence" (an "incongruity verging on a meaningful contradiction," to use Dollimore's term) that might work alternatively for individuals taking up those subject positions.

In the case of contradiction, I speak specifically, for example, about the subplot in which Ferris' behavior forces his sister Jeanie to confront her presumption that by abiding by normative behavior she will succeed in winning approval of authority figures or peers. What she learns (or the individual interpellated into a subject position that focuses on the character's structural relation learns) is that neither her parents nor her schoolmates recognize her obedience as meaningful in opposition to Ferris' charm and charisma. If one were to foreground Jeanie's conflicts through the day's sequence of events, one might well find a contradiction between the film's ideological insistence on occasional rebellion against authority and its structural lack of payoff for the woman. Ferris and his friend Cameron become individuals, i.e., men; Jeanie gets a speeding ticket. And the final scene indicates that she will only be happy when she capitulates to Ferris' or another boy's (such as the James Dean impostor in the police station) covert systems of rebellion and massive ego—built on artificial or superficial pleasures.

Where Jeanie is moderately effective is in her unintended battle with the scapegoat authority figure—the school principal. Yet, for a woman in patriarchy, the dominant ISAs have not necessarily altered totally and remain school and the family. The displacement from the original oppressors (social norms and relations constructed for women in patriarchy and inscribed in family relations from the day of birth) to external figures (embodied in the institution of the school system and specifically the substitute male authority figure) may give solace to

individuals taking up subject positions to consume this movie with
pleasure.

Thus, this is hardly a progressive text from a woman's subject position. While the film's ideological operations are not the same for adolescent women as for adolescent men, its relation to a woman's real position vis-à-vis gender relations in the United States is still imaginary, if
contradictory. Securing victory over the school principal is an empty triumph for Jeanie compared with her failure relative to patriarchy as a
whole. Yet this hollow victory may be an instance of a discoherence—
an incongruity verging on a meaningful contradiction should the subject sense that *as a woman* she is rewarded neither for normative behavior nor for "individualism,"as her brother and Cameron surely are. The
constructed opposition works only for men. As the critic Kempley
wrote, the film is a potential allegory about the *carnival* of life—a telling,
if not actually resisting, reading for a woman interacting with this film.

Besides identifying with one of the boys or with Jeanie, readers may
be hailed to take up a subject position identifying with the two ethnic
minorities, who oddly enough seem to come out with the only successful (unproblematized) consuming act of the day. Given the Ferrari
owned by Cameron's father to park in the garage, the Hispanic atten-
dant and his African American buddy get a free ride and the day off.
From the point of view of this text, this strikes me as another instance of
discoherence—a textual gesture motivating Cameron's illusionary
break with production and patriarchy which still also suggests some
distorted reflection of the structuring absence motivating this film.
Class is (nearly) absent. Ferris whips out cash as though its productive
source is inexhaustible. Of course it is, for these are rich kids from the
Chicago suburbs. An abundant source of cash surely does not exist,
however, for the parking attendants, who ignore property rights and do
what is "natural"—appropriate the car for a day-long drive in the coun-
try. This display of the real relations of individuals in our social formation is surely unintended by the ideological address of *Ferris Bueller's
Day Off*, especially if the film is about an ideology of pleasurable consumerism within capitalism's property system. But it is there anyway,
to be read by the individual taking up the subject position of Althusserian cultural critic.

I would agree with Rhodes that it would be theoretically and practically dangerous to conceive of popular culture as necessarily empowering. However, simultaneously, it seems important to think how Al-

THE PLACES OF EMPIRICAL SUBJECTS 123

thusserian Marxism might illuminate the possibilities for subjects sensing the contradictory aspects of specific ideologies (such as patriarchy, racism, heterosexualism) that might lead to resistance. Additionally, I can conceive of the possibility of limited conscious agency by individuals who take up subject positions in ideologies that might address them in progressive or regressive ways. Thus, Rhodes's call for "hard empirical work to determine the balance of class forces and the structural features of capitalist society at any given historical moment" also should be a call for work on how and when individuals are and are not interpellated as specific subjects in relation to the contradictory ideologies now under contestation. Then we will be able to understand better the dialectical process of humans in history.

NOTES

1. Maureen Dowd, "The Education of Dan Quayle," *New York Times*, 25 June 1989, sect. 6, 18; Eleanor Ringel, "Undecided Voter? Add The Film Factor to Presidential Race," *Atlanta Constitution*, 1 November 1992, sect. N, 1. Bill Clinton picked *High Noon*; George Bush chose *The Longest Day*; Al Gore nominated *National Lampoon's Vacation*. I guess presidents require male melodrama; vice-presidents, comedies about loafing around.

2. I phrase it this way because I am not convinced that that is what Fiske and Jameson propose.

3. Louis Althusser, *Lenin and Philosophy*, trans. Ben Brewster (New York: Random House, 1971), 171. Italics in original.

4. Althusser makes a major distinction between Ideology in general (which has no history) and specific ideologies which do transform historically.

5. Jonathan Dollimore, *Sexual Dissidence: Augustine to Wilde, Freud to Foucault* (Oxford: Clarendon Press, 1991), 87.

6. For a detailed discussion, see Janet Staiger, *Interpreting Films: Studies in the Historical Reception of American Cinema* (Princeton NJ: Princeton University Press, 1992).

7. I do not contest Rhodes's reading of the film. These essays were culled from a Lexus/Nexus search for the period following the film's release. The thirteen in alphabetical order are: David Ansen, "Goofing Off in Grand Style," *Newsweek*, 16 June 1986, 75; Paul Attanasio, "Movies 'Ferris': More Teen Tedium," *Washington Post*, 12 June 1986, Style section, D4; Nina Darnton, "A Youth's Day Off," *New York Times*, 11 June 1986, sect. C, 24; S. H., "*Ferris Bueller's Day Off*," *People*, 23 June 1986, 8; James K. Glassman, "Cutting Edge," *New Republic*, 195 (28 July 1986), 43; Patrick Goldstein, "A Director's Off Day in His Su-

perteen's 'Day Off,'" *Los Angeles Times,* 11 June 1986, Calendar section, 1; Rita Kempley, "'Day Off' Is Right On," *Washington Post,* 13 June 1986, weekend section, 29; Jack Nicholson cited in William C. Trott, "Nicholson Lost at 'Ferris,'" *United Press International,* 14 July 1986; Richard Schickel, *"Ferris Bueller's Day Off," Time,* 23 June 1986, 74; Gene Siskel, "'Ferris Bueller'—An Off Day for Fun," *Chicago Tribune,* 11 June 1986, Tempo section, 3; David Sterritt, "A Film Going Along for the Ride, Tracking Teens Playing Hooky," *Christian Science Monitor,* 18 June 1986, Arts and Leisure section, 23; George F. Will, "The Greatest Movie," *Washington Post,* 26 June 1986, editorial section, A25; Jeffrey Yorke, "Film Talk," *Washington Post,* 18 July 1986, Weekend section, N31.

8. The last reference to Sal Mineo is textually motivated. For me, one of the most pleasant moments (to which I will return below) is the sister Jeanie's encounter with a James Dean character in the police station, bringing into the film the intertext of *Rebel Without a Cause.*

8

Finding Community in the Early 1960s

Underground Cinema and Sexual Politics

IN AN ESSAY about finding evidence of communities among peoples who believe themselves to be alone,[1] Joan Scott focuses on science fiction writer Samuel Delany's experience of a St. Mark's bathhouse in 1963: "Watching the scene establishes for Delany a 'fact that flew in the face' of the prevailing representation of homosexuals in the 1950s as 'isolated perverts,' as subjects 'gone awry.'" Rather, "he emphasizes not the discovery of an identity, but a participation in a movement."[2]

It is this same potential of finding others like oneself not only for identity but for community building that I believe the space of the underground cinema of the early 1960s provided. Moreover, the Otherness that seemed so threatening in oneself was, as it was for the St. Mark's bathhouses, a sexual Otherness that did not neatly fit the dominant images of these Others as traditionally conveyed in print, television, and mainstream film. The experience of going to the underground cinema contradicted impressions of isolation as it also elevated images of perverts and subjects gone awry. It vaunted sexual Otherness as an avant-garde aesthetic. It posed sexual Otherness as even a popular culture, as play and laughter, set in a complicated difference against a serious bourgeois art culture. The underground cinema of the early 1960s was a space for validation, empowerment, and often ironic resistance that used sexuality, politics, popular cultural iconography, and humor to establish community among subcultures.

What I wish to emphasize in this essay, then, are three points. One is the clarity with which at least New York intellectuals associated this cinema with the emergence of tacit, if not aggressive, gay sexual liberation activities and with a critique of traditional gendered, heterosexual, same-race/ethnicity sexual norms.[3] Not merely an identity crisis *but a movement* was at stake in the American underground cinema explosion of the early to mid 1960s. The second point is that going to these films after midnight was a declaration of where one stood in these debates. The midnight cinema was—like the St. Mark's bathhouse—an expression of community and a site for community building, which would eventually have its culmination, at least for the mainstream press and for gay men, in the Stonewall events of 1969. Thus I will contribute to refining debates about the history of gay liberation. Third, the ironic appropriations of popular culture were stylistic tactics directed against bourgeois culture but also assertive rhetorical strategies for creating these subcultural community connections. Critical debates about aesthetics and taste were part of this politics of sexual and personal freedom. It was in these years that feminist, civil rights, and gay/lesbian/transgendered/bisexual movements (hereafter *sexual rights movements*) realized that the personal is political. My argument in this essay, then, is that events do not come from nowhere. While Marxist warnings against teleological historiography need to be respected, simultaneously it is still the case that prior events prepare the conditions for radical transformations. The subtext for my essay is the emergence, or rather reemergence, of a visible gay culture in New York City in the mid-1960s that paralleled its existence in the 1910s and 1920s.[4] I need to stress, however, that the gay culture was not homogeneous. Rather, hierarchies existed within it that required toppling for Stonewall to have the meaning it has now.

Several scholars have studied various parts of these events, noting some of these connections. In particular, David E. James writes: "Contemporary accounts of underground film in the popular press tended, more or less sensationally, to stress the coincidence of formal infractions of orthodox film grammar and parallel moral and social transgressions, interpreting the latter either as evidence of the filmmakers' degeneracy or as their social criticism."[5] I will take up James's remarks by looking at some of the dialogue among various members of the New York and mass media as they discussed and evaluated the events around the underground cinema from 1959 to about 1966.[6] I will extend his remarks by emphasizing the functions of popular culture and humor in these discussions, although the opposition James finds is not so definitely resistant when camp and sexual desire enter into the complex.

THE SCENE

What was the contextual scene for the emergence of the underground cinema? New moviegoing behavior, the live theater scene, "beat culture," and politics all influenced the configuration and meaning of the underground cinema.

Mainstream American moviegoing and movie marketing were in a transitional stage. While historical epics, male melodramas, and musicals that harbored homosexual themes as subtexts commanded the venues of first-run theaters,[7] by necessity subsequent-run theaters catered to various subgroups or "niche" markets that opened up taboo areas of content and sometimes violated taste cultures of high art. Art cinemas and 16-mm film societies had been flourishing for the full decade of the 1950s and remained committed to a highbrow approach to contemporary themes. But another clientele was being exploited: the teenager.

Thomas Doherty describes the impact of a rather innocent B movie—*Rock around the Clock* (1956). The physical response in the theaters to hearing "our" music included "screaming, foot-stomping, and the occasional scuffle."[8] The in-house fun could spill into the streets, and even staid children of the Midwest were reported to have "snake-danced downtown and broken store windows" (p. 82). The enthusiasm of teens for the less reputable genres of the teen-pix and science fiction and horror films provoked film companies to exploit those passions.

Besides using color and widescreen technologies to draw audiences out of their living rooms and into theaters and drive-ins, film firms also returned to the old ploys of showmen. Gimmicks that relied on being at a theater made a comeback. When coupled with the fantastic genres of the horror film and science fiction, a play space was created. William Castle's work provides some outstanding examples. In a series of films produced from 1958 through the early 1960s, Castle constructed novel in-house experiences as part of his movies' marketing strategies: a Lloyd's of London insurance policy against death from the shock of watching *Macabre* (1958), reinforced by the stationing of ambulances and nurses near the theaters; a skeleton rigged to fly across an auditorium at the climax of *House on Haunted Hill* (1958); an electric current to buzz the bottoms of patrons during *The Tingler* (1959).[9] Moviegoing for youth in the late 1950s could be serious (reserved seats for major openings of Hollywood films), but often it was fantasy and play in a physically lively environment such as a neighborhood theater that was showing some movie for the teen market or the drive-in that catered to moving around inside and outside the car. Moreover, in these places the space was usually away from adults. It was the teens' grounds for group exchange, just as certain streets were for cruising and drugstore soda fountains were for shakes and fries.

Both the subject matter of these movies and the theater scene became important contexts for the underground cinema. Sexual themes and problems were commonly explicit in the horror films and other favorite teen-pix of the era. The most obvious, and probably most influential, horror-genre example is *Psycho* (1960). Norman Bates is not just a serial killer; his behavior is connected to his mother's sexual choices and his own sexual ambivalences. *Psycho*, of course, does not support Norman's cross-dressing choice, and it places the blame on mother— both sexuality and bad mothers being common 1950s discourse. Two aspects of moviegoing behavior set the stage for the underground cinema, however: the tendency of the teenager movie market to form an isolated community away from adults, and the introduction of sexually explicit themes in fantasy form.[10]

A second salient predecessor for underground movies was the live theater scene, which also introduced sexual topics and a renewed sense of the physical environment. As Parker Tyler notes, underground cinema had as one of its contexts the "happenings" of the late 1950s.[11] The cinema had just as immediately the theatrical context of off-off-Broadway. Historians of American theater date the beginning of off-off-Broadway "somewhat arbitrarily as September 27, 1960."[12] That was when the revival of Alfred Jarry's *King Ubu* opened at Take 3, a Greenwich Village coffeehouse. Following this production came many more café-theater productions.

Off-off-Broadway had multiple connotations for the early 1960s New York scene. It was promoted as nonprofit (as opposed to the increasing commercialization and capital-intensive Broadway and even off-Broadway). It confronted a tacit boundary between the public and the private by intermingling audience and performer and by putting theater into the hands of anyone. Although cafés were the initial sites for the theater troupes of off-off-Broadway, some of the most important groups found homes in friendly local churches, such as the Judson Memorial Baptist-Congregationalist Church on Washington Square and St. Mark's Church-in-the-Bouwerie on the Lower East Side.[13] Off-off-Broadway also produced cutting-edge sexual dramas. Edward

Albee's work started within this community, and, as I shall indicate, some of the early underground cinema was exhibited in off-off-Broadway venues.

Albee's work, like that of the underground filmmakers, provoked attacks for its sexual rights representations. In an early 1960 review of *The Zoo Story*, Robert Brustein of the *New Republic* wrote:

> On the other hand, I am deeply depressed by the uses to which [Albee's] talent has been put. In its implicit assumption that the psychotic, the criminal, and the invert [homosexual] are closer to God than anyone else, "The Zoo Story" embodies the same kind of sexual-religious claptrap we are accustomed to from Allen Ginsberg. . . . I will not bore you with a discussion of the masochistic-homosexual perfume which hangs so heavily over "The Zoo Story" except to say that Mr. Albee's love-death, like Mr. Ginsberg's poetry, yields more readily to clinical than theological analysis.[14]

Indeed, the "beat" culture (led by Allen Ginsberg) and its currents of homosexuality are a third contextual predecessor for the underground cinema, as James and Richard Dyer point out.[15] Dyer writes than many of the beat poets (Ginsberg, Robert Duncan, Jack Spicer) were gay and others (Jack Kerouac and Neal Cassady) thought it "cool." For Dyer, Ginsberg's publication of *Howl* in 1956 associated beatness with "homosexuality with revolt against bourgeois convention" (p. 138). James explains the logical dynamic: "Since sex was the sign of social and aesthetic values suppressed in straight society, it could signify deviance and resistance in general, and so social repression of all kinds could be contested via the codes of sexual representation" (pp. 315–316). As early as 1960, one *Village Voice* writer was arguing that an even more radical break was necessary: although "being spokesman for a kind of literary homosexuality" had been valuable, that action was now only a "romanticism."[16] But the *Voice* also continued to describe the doings of the beat culture. In a front-page article in summer 1962, the pilgrimage of beats to Ibiza was detailed, including the fact that "Domino's steam-bath intimacy is probably an important reason for its success."[17]

The beat's appreciation of alternative sexualities was not, however, as liberated as it might seem. The beat's privileged sexuality was of a particular type. As Catharine R. Stimpson argues, "in the late 1940s and

1950s, the Beats prized candor and honesty, energy and rage," not a homosexuality of "concealment and camp, parody and irony."[18] Their homosexual hero was a "rebel who seizes freedom and proclaims the legitimacy of individual desire" (p. 375), who was "'fucked in the ass by saintly motorcyclists' and screamed 'with joy'" (quoting *Howl*, p. 388). The underground cinema would not take up such a distinction, blurring the various styles and politics of sexual liberation—beat and camp—into one general manifesto of desire.

Indeed, much of this was about politics, a politics of anticonsensus and pro-individual freedoms—my fourth contextual predecessor. Although the fight was fought out in every arena, one important battle site was civil rights for blacks. Another was the critique of restrictions on subject matter and words on the screen and in the theater. Obscenity laws were under attack as perfect examples of the attempt by Republican conservatives to mold everyone into conformists, thinking the same thing and saying nothing. The early 1960s were the years of the arrests of Lenny Bruce in Greenwich Village and Los Angeles cafés. In the specific area of film, parts of even the mainstream film industry worked to loosen up remnants of the Production Code, while more legal forms of restriction were challenged as aftermaths of the Roth case (1957). In 1959, the California State Supreme Court reviewed a case involving Raymond Rohauer's theatrical screening of Kenneth Anger's *Fireworks* (1947) in 1957.[19]

Throughout this scene of context, I have perhaps somewhat reductively, but fairly I believe, characterized a series of oppositions providing at least cultural equivalencies, if not models, for the underground cinema. Alternatives to the dominant modes of the 1950s were showing up all over the cultural map. (1) Modes of human interaction in a cultural space, (2) modes of producing cultural texts, (3) modes of representation, (4) subject matter, and (5) political agendas are lining up in a series of "either/ors." Peter Stallybrass and Allon White offer the important observation that hierarchically constructed binary oppositions that are linked with one another are often similarly evaluated.[20] In one of their examples, the top parts of the human body, like upper parts of geographical maps, are presumed better than the lower halves. Or, if heads are associated with the rational and the good, genitalia are connected to the emotional and the bad.

In the case that I am developing, the following dichotomies are being aligned in a map of oppositions: (1) passive, private involvement with a text versus active, communal participation with a text; (2) capitalist alienated labor versus cooperative group labor; (3) smooth, seamless modes of mass-produced representation (i.e., dramatic Hollywood movies) versus rough, reflexive modes of popularly produced representations; (4) repressed (or monogamous, same-race hetero-)sexuality versus sexual exploration and confrontation; and (5) conservative consensus politics that restricts individual rights versus libertarian and liberation politics.

In his excellent analysis of the decade of the 1960s, Fredric Jameson places the start of the era in the late 1950s. In a general methodological statement, he argues that periods are theoretically knowable by their "sharing of a common objective situation, to which a whole range of varied responses and creative innovations is then possible, but always within that situation's structural limits."[21] The underground cinema was one such response to the common situation of the conformist 1950s, but one that would be resisted in certain quarters in part because the quintet of oppositions became "too much" for certain people. As I shall detail in the cases below, whereas some people could invest in all parts of the map, others could not. Specifically, when rough, reflexive popular culture is replaced by sex play and camp humor, some people draw the line. Of course, for others that last taboo is liberating for its creation of community jokes and pleasure.

THE CONNECTION

The underground cinema of the early 1960s, like every other cultural phenomenon, was more a transformation of earlier possibilities than some original act of invention. Although I restrict my use of the term underground cinema to films that explicitly displayed nondominant sexualities in nonnarrative form and style and were created for the midnight urban movie scene in the early 1960s, underground cinema was part of the larger movement of the New American Cinema, which also met with varied responses to its cultural and political allegiances.

"Created" by manifesto in the summer of 1961 (but also a transformation of earlier activities), the New American Cinema was, as Patricia Mellencamp notes, not so much antinarrative as anticommercial and anti-Hollywood.[22] She writes, "the initial impetus was to create alternative narrative features expressive of personal style and link up with the tradition of European art cinema" and its U.S. exhibition circuit.[23] The New American Cinema Group's statement of principles noted the development of a "movement . . . reaching significant proportions." It rejected censorship and called for new forms of financing, labor arrangements, distribution, and exhibition, and for new forms of appreciation for low-budget films from artists. Finally, the group claimed that "we are not joining together to make money. We are joining together to make films. . . . we have had enough of the Big Lie in life and in the arts. . . . We don't want false, polished, slick films—we prefer them rough, unpolished, but alive; we don't want rosy films—we want them the color of blood."[24]

This manifesto was fairly successful publicity. By June 1962, Harris Dienstfrey in *Commentary* was able to write a review of "the New American Cinema" that faithfully reproduced its goals, including its common subject-matter concerns about race relations.[25] Among the original filmmaker signers of the 1961 manifesto were Robert Frank and Alfred Leslie (*Pull My Daisy*, 1959) and Shirley Clarke (*The Connection*, 1959). Named as an ally was John Cassavetes, who had recently completed *Shadows* (1959). What all three of these films (as well as others) had in common were direct public associations with beat culture or off-off-Broadway theater. Thus they had implicit connections to sexual liberation politics. Moreover, Clarke's and Cassavetes' films also directly addressed black civil rights issues.

Pull My Daisy stars beats Ginsberg, Gregory Corso, and Peter Orlovsky and features a witty voice-over narration by Kerouac. Some drugs are shared and jazz is played. Peter (played by Orlovsky) asks a visitor who is proselytizing for an Eastern religion if baseball is holy. Eventually the boys go out together, leaving the wife and child at home.[26] *Shadows* begins with a group listening to rock 'n' roll.[27] Events revolve around a black family with an older brother who is a jazz musician and has a couple of white friends, a sister who dates and then has sex with a white man who doesn't realize until later that she is black, and a younger brother. Issues of interracial sex and prejudice are a major part of the film.

The Connection is perhaps a useful example in this group to study further. In the late 1950s, one of the major off-off-Broadway theater groups was the Living Theater, led by Julian Beck and Judith Malina. As Lauren Rabinovitz notes, the Living Theater had a "symbolic allegiance to marginalized and oppressed groups."[28] In 1959, it produced *The Con-*

nection, written by Jack Gelber, about drug addiction. Despite initially bad reviews in the *New Yorker*, *New York Times*, and *Village Voice*, the play won praise in other quarters. A paid advertisement in the *Village Voice* in August 1959 illustrates the intensity with which supporters viewed *The Connection* as socially significant. After suggesting that critics who disliked the play likely would have also misunderstood James Joyce, D. H. Lawrence, and Henry Miller,[29] the author wrote, "This is not one of the regular Broadway, county-fair-type, spun-sugar musicals that both the expense-account trade and the critics find such good 'summer entertainment.' And it is not one of those expanded soap operas (next week East Lynne), alleged 'serious' dramas, in which the hero (emasculated to begin with) is threatened by the tired old buzz-saw dressed and disguised as castration."[30] This assertion of a masculine treatment of the topic of drug addiction is important for understanding the nature of the discursive debates around the film version. The assertion of masculinity also aligns with the general beat attitude against a bourgeoisie that beats accused of being soft.

At the same time as the appearance of the play version of *The Connection*, the Living Theater had been showing films as part of a film society run by experimental filmmaker Stan VanDerBeek. Clarke and others shot in 1959 a film version of *The Connection* which Clarke took to the spring 1961 Cannes Film Festival, accompanied by Ginsberg, Corso, and Orlovsky. The film was a success. Back home, however, *The Connection* had been determined obscene in New York State because it used the word "shit" as a slang term for heroin. During the appeals process, and rejecting the notion the film was obscene, the leadership of an important off-off-Broadway site, the Judson Memorial Church, screened the film without admission charges in October 1962.[31]

New York critics were as unfriendly to the film as they had been to the play. In his weekly column for the *Village Voice*, Jonas Mekas defended the film against criticisms that its content was "'drab,' 'offensive,' 'odd,' 'crude,' 'sick,' 'vulgar,' 'shoddy,' 'sordid,' 'disagreeable,' etc."[32] He countered: "Why don't you admit that you are washed out, that you can't cope with modern cinema?" Mekas' response, of course, had no effect, but over the years the film version of *The Connection* has achieved respect for its tough subject matter and participation in a general opposition to censorship.

Before the film was shown in New York City, the play version altered. It traveled to London in spring 1961, to less than an ecstatic response. And when it was revived in fall 1961 back in New York City, its lead and some textual material had changed, producing a different effect, according to the *Village Voice* reviewer:

> There are many other changes. . . . I am not sure they are all for the best. On the other hand, they seem to feed directly into the desires of the audience. Certainly this is not for the best. "The Connection" is today being played as a comedy, at least as "camped up" at the late show for the tourist trade on Saturday nights, and as busy as Judith Malina is with newer commitments, I feel that she herself might be well advised to revisit it.[33]

If in fall 1961 some late-night versions of *The Connection* had turned to camp, why would that be? The answer has to do, I think, with the overall midnight scene in New York.

FLAMING CREATURES

As a branch of the New American Cinema, underground cinema was in content sexually explicit and in location "underground"—primarily New York City but also Los Angeles and San Francisco. In the early 1960s, the term underground had specific connotations. One *Village Voice* headline on January 25, 1962, declared, "The Bourgeois Mothers' Underground, On the Rise."[34] The story described a group of seventy-five Village housewives who traveled to Washington, D.C., as a public protest about the dangers of nuclear war. Labeled as part of "the peace movement," the group's members had not known each other until they gathered on the train ride.

The repeated phenomenon of individuals taking resistant political action against the norm and then finding others who were like themselves seems an important recurring event in this period. Similar revelations were operating in civil and sexual rights. In these same years, the *Village Voice* published several articles indicating a different stance by some gays toward social and civil repression of homosexuals. In March 1959, Seymour Krim published a "Press of Freedom" column titled "Revolt of the Homosexual."[35] Krim did not take the common 1950s view of homosexuality as an aberration or illness, then even the official view of the Mattachine Society. Instead, he asserted the naturalness and acceptability of homosexuality. Turning to Donald Webster Cory's *The Homosexual in America* to justify his views, Krim claimed:

> We want recognition for our simple human rights, just like Negroes, Jews, and women. . . . Courageous gay people are now beginning to realize that they are human beings who must fight to gain acceptance for what they are—not what others want them to be. . . . In the future you'll see the equally suave acknowledgment of different standards, including the right of the homosexual to fully express himself as a "healthy" individual in terms of his tradition. . . . When this movement becomes powerful enough—and gay people refuse either to hide or flaunt themselves—it will be openly accepted.[36]

Krim was answered the following week in an essay titled "The Gay Underground—A Reply to Mr. Krim."[37] The author discounted Krim's assertion that a movement was possible, but, again, underground refers to the association of minorities not just in resistance against the dominant but also in a common cause unified by a political agenda for change. In fact, several months later, another *Voice* article reported that one gay rights advocate had proposed a third political party for a homosexual voting bloc.[38] Other articles surveying sexual politics for gays continued to appear throughout the period.[39] Thus, for New Yorkers in the early 1960s, the term underground had connotations not of the hidden but of alternative communities and political activism. Additionally, discourse by homosexual men about their rights was beginning to take a different rhetorical tactic than commonly existed in the 1950s.

The movement effect of the underground cinema was partially propelled by the community associations developed through earlier filmgoing connections. As scholars have noted, the post–World War II efforts of Maya Deren, Amos Vogel, and Mekas to create film distribution organizations, venues, and journals for filmmakers helped instill the sense that numerous individuals were involved in nontraditional film work. They also created various alliances and conflicts.[40] Rabinovitz describes several of these; another is mentioned in Calvin Tomkins' 1973 essay on the scene. Tomkins notes that in 1961 Vogel decided not to show Stan Brakhage's *Anticipation of the Night* at his Cinema 16 society. Mekas accepted the piece for his programming, and later with friends began a competitive film distribution system,

Film-Makers' Cooperative, in 1962. For various reasons, Cinema 16 went out of business in 1963, and Vogel, with Richard Roud, co-founded the New York Film Festival.

Meanwhile, Mekas was championing much more offbeat work in the late-night shows at various small film theaters. The term "underground" was applied to movies throughout this period in several ways, but eventually it took on a meaning similar to the wider cultural definition—a liberal or radical agenda with overt demonstrations of involvement by groups of individuals. In a summer 1960 *Film Culture* essay, Mekas wrote about the movies he was championing: "The underground is beginning to boil, to open up, to shoot out."[41] (The masculine eroticism of this image is hard to miss!)

The screenings organized by Mekas and others led to festivals and awards, all of which did not go without their own troubles as the underground cinema began bubbling. Andrew Sarris, asked to judge at the September 1962 Film-Makers' Festival at the Charles Theater, reported his general disgust with the whole lot of films:

> I am aware that Parker Tyler has disassociated himself from the deliberations of a jury which merely wanted to get the hell out of the theatre as quickly as possible. I will go Mr. Tyler one better. I wish to disassociate myself from a primitive movement which fancies itself the moral guardian of cinema. I can take the ineptness, but not the cynical exploitation of the ineptness.[42]

From the context, I am not sure what Sarris meant by "cynical exploitation of the ineptness," although he did express gratitude "for little favors like clearly focused images, audible sound tracks, an occasional glimpse of a pretty girl, an infrequent glimmer of intelligence, and most rarely of all, a friendly gesture to the audience" (p. 13).

Indeed, the underground cinema of the early 1960s was different from the first wave of the New American Cinema. What Sarris was likely complaining about are films such as *The Flower Thief* (Ron Rice, 1960), *Little Stabs at Happiness* (Ken Jacobs, 1959–63), *Blonde Cobra* (Jacobs, Jack Smith, and Bob Fleischner, 1959–63), and, to come, *Flaming Creatures* (Smith, 1963), *The Queen of Sheba Meets the Atom Man* (Rice, 1963), *Scorpio Rising* (Kenneth Anger, 1963), and *Christmas on Earth* (a.k.a. *Cocks and Cunts*; Barbara Rubin, 1963). All of these are now regarded as the canonical exemplars of the underground cinema.

What is wrong with these films beyond Sarris' general accusation of technical ineptness? I would argue that, along with all of the other stylistic, production, and political connotations, these films' representations of nonheterosexual sex and interracial sex and their playful, humorous, sometimes campy approach to sex proved hard to take for some people, even devotees of art and experimental cinema. Although Andrew Ross implies that camp became a way for New York intellectuals to deal with popular culture, this was not possible immediately or for all New Yorkers.[43]

Let me begin with a brief counterexample. In the late 1950s, Brakhage had been exploring the "everyday," including sexuality. *Window Water Baby Moving*—the documentary of the birth of his and his wife's child—showed private body parts. As Tyler would note in 1969, "the emergent message of such films is their novelty in terms of according public exhibition to what has been considered strictly domestic and private."[44] Even earlier, Brakhage had recorded his own masturbation in *Flesh of Morning*.

Tyler connects the sources of Brakhage's work to cinema verité and a longer tradition of highbrow aesthetics, but I wish to stress the effects. Once one creates the binary opposition quintet that I have described above, a series of consequences develops: the verisimilitude of the shooting style of cinema verité is contrasted with the artificiality of Hollywood fiction filmmaking; the obvious explosion of hidden sexual acts is contrasted with the obvious representational repression of those acts; the privileging of the everyday and the popular is contrasted with high culture; the seriousness of Hollywood and even some experimental and art cinema is parodied. These oppositions then become a rallying point for a rebellion from the underground. Recall the metaphors above—the New American Cinema wanted a cinema "the color of blood"; Mekas noted that the underground was "beginning to boil, to open up, to shoot out." Brakhage's films were the indication of change, the place for some potential transformations, but Brakhage's alliances with high art, normative sexuality,[45] seriousness, and masculinity provided only a launching pad for the revolution.

The rebellion would come from a new set of filmmakers supported by the underground theatrical scene both as movement and play space, described so well by J. Hoberman and Jonathan Rosenbaum in *Midnight Movies*. Mekas' share in this venture, despite allegations that his motives were not pure, needs to be recognized as well. These screenings were much like those for the teen-pix of the era but with a Village beat cast: audiences smoked marijuana and very vocally responded to the films. As one critic of *The Flower Thief* acknowledged, "One of the really delightful aspects of the Charles Theatre is that booing, hissing, and applause are all permitted equally, so that one can express one's feelings on the spot." Andy Warhol described these screenings as "a lot like a party."[46]

Beyond the exuberant screening scene, what has not been stressed in the analyses of these films is how linked were nontraditional sexuality, racial civil rights issues, and the fun of popular culture. Each of the canonical films employs variants of these representational materials. *The Flower Thief*'s main character (played by Taylor Mead) wanders through San Francisco accompanied not only by classical music but by progressive jazz and gospel music. Beat poetry provides part of the sound track. Americana in the form of the flag, sparklers, and amusement parks are part of the flower thief's environment. *Little Stabs at Happiness* associates old popular music with scenes of Jack Smith dressed as a clown with balloons and a mirror. In the opening section, Smith performs oral sex on a doll. *Blonde Cobra* is a homage to the 1944 Hollywood film *Cobra Woman*, starring Maria Montez, but Ken Jacobs and Smith's version does not have the reverence and fetishization of Montez that Joseph Cornell brings to Rose Hobart in his *Rose Hobart* (1939).[47] Instead, Smith camps a performance of Montez. Smith's cross-dressing and erotic storytelling follow the nostalgic opening music, "Let's Call the Whole Thing Off."

The notorious *Flaming Creatures* also uses older popular music as background to stylized images of masturbation, cross-dressing, seduction, and rape. Here advertising is employed as commentary in a fabulous second movement that describes the benefits of a new lipstick, which is then liberally applied to lips and penises. Performance is doubly stressed throughout: the characters almost perform performers. Fake noses on "females" gesture toward an obvious ironic use of Freudian symbolism, especially in retrospect after the "women" lift their skirts to reveal their own penises. Hollywood genres are travestied to exaggeration: *Flaming Creatures* references melodrama but also the horror film. As a woman rises out of a coffin, carrying lilies in her hands (a classic image of the femme fatale), the sound track is of the country-and-western "Wasn't It God Who Made Honky Tonk Angels?" Characters appear not only in strange genders but also in odd races. One of the dancers is in blackface. The film closes to an apparent homage to some (to me unknown) classical painting while "Be Bop a Lula, She's My Baby" trails away.[48]

Christmas on Earth explores dynamics of couplings in a more serious but equally provocative way. Dated around 1963, the two reels of film are now supposed to be projected one on top of the other (another sexual congress?). Reel A, to be shown at full size, displays close-ups of heterosexuality: penises, anuses, mouths, vaginas. Reel B, to be projected at half of reel A's size and in the middle of the screen over reel A, represents 1960s tabooed sex: interracial and homosexual. These images are partially performances. For instance, a white woman appears not only in blackface but in black body (her breasts and stomach remain white, providing a second "face"). At the end of the film, all of the participants wave toward the camera.[49]

Scorpio Rising is another excellent instance of the combination of homosexuality, popular culture, and camp satire, with Anger's appropriation of images of male buddies from Hollywood movies, television, and comic strips. *The Queen of Sheba Meets the Atom Man* pairs a black woman with Taylor Mead, invokes several trashy Hollywood genres, and again uses popular music and jazz.

Although many people appreciated this new cinema, others did not. One recurrent theme is how badly shot by Hollywood standards these films are: out-of-focus and overexposed images, lack of establishing shots, and panning too fast, which prevents the viewer's seeing what is likely (or hopefully) there. These were obviously studied effects by underground filmmakers, and easily justified as that.[50] It is also clear that many people missed or resisted the jokes in the films because other things stood in the way.

An obvious problem was the nontraditional sexuality. It was even nontraditional pornography! Stag movies had been a part of a homosocial scene for males since the 1910s, and exploitation cinema began developing during the late 1950s, but both were still quite nonpublic and unavailable to "innocents" unless they were initiated into them at smokers, lodges, or fraternity parties—in scenes with a strong resemblance to underground cinema events as Warhol and others recall them.[51] As Thomas Waugh has discovered, some male same-sex scenes exist in traditional pornography, but they are extremely rare.[52] These male same-sex scenes are used as preludes to heterosexual sex and are treated without much emphasis. Beyond these rare images of male same-sex actions, traditional stag films also have some instances of cross-dressing, but mostly as drag performances with the humorous "surprise" of revealing the performer's penis at the end of the act. This humor, and the general treatment of the rare male same-sex scene, might appeal to an individual gay man, but the general structure of heterosexual stag-film pornography works to disavow a homoerotic address to the male spectator(pp. 14–15).

If this representation of male same-sex sexuality differed from traditional hard-core pornography, it was even nontraditional for the rare examples of early 1960s gay-addressed erotica! Waugh writes that he has found no evidence of any organized gay audience for gay pornography prior to 1960: it was too illegal and taboo (pp. 6–8). However, gay soft-core erotica was being produced by film companies such as Apollo and Zenith in the 1940s and 1950s. This erotica consisted of short narratives justifying nearly complete male nudity (occasionally genitals were displayed). Promises of sexual activities to occur offscreen or after the film's narrative ends may be implicit, but most onscreen same-sex bodily contact was limited to physical sport such as playful wrestling, swimming, or bodybuilding.[53] Thus the rare instances of male same-sex scenes found in heterosexual-addressed stag films were about all the hard-core images of male same-sex sexuality that appear to have existed before 1960.

Thus the underground cinema was multiply confounding in its representation of male same-sex sexuality. It addressed not only heterosexual devotees of avant-garde cinema but gay audiences in a new way. Significantly, it was not using the conventions of a heterosexual stag reel or even standard gay erotica for that audience. Arthur Knight, reviewing *Flaming Creatures* for *Saturday Review* in autumn 1963, objected: "A faggoty stag-reel, it comes as close to hardcore pornography as anything ever presented in a theater. . . . Everything is shown in sickening detail, defiling at once both sex and cinema."[54] Although it would take almost a year from its initial screening for *Flaming Creatures* to be seized by the police for obscenity, when it was and, two weeks later, Jean Genet's *Un Chant d'Amour* was seized as well, *Variety* proclaimed in its March 18, 1964, headline: "Cops Raid Homo Films Again."[55] *Variety* described *Flaming Creatures* as "a 58–minute montage of a transvestite orgy." In a formal statement, Mekas argued that the films were art and thus deserved unrestricted availability for viewing. As Tomkins notes, the March 1964 publicity brought the underground out of Greenwich

Village: "The public, which had been largely oblivious of the underground's existence, assumed that 'underground' was synonymous with dirty pictures."[56]

Prior to *Flaming Creatures'* obscenity charges, one way to appreciate the underground cinema had been to associate it with art, which was part of the pre–March 1964 public discourse. In his *New York Times* review of *The Flower Thief* in July 1962, Eugene Archer analyzed the film by finding associations with beat culture, but, more significantly, he uncovered highbrow allusions. Among the intertextual references he discovered were *The Seventh Seal*, the "pose of marines planting the flag on Iwo Jima," and "films by Sergei Eisenstein, Charlie Chaplin, Luis Bunuel and Alain Resnais."[57]

Another pre-obscenity-charge response was to treat the films with amused paternalism. A July 1963 *New Yorker* essay considered Mekas, Ken Jacobs, the Film-Makers' Cooperative, and "underground cinema" as diverting New York-iana: "The results range from 'poetic' color and motion studies to blunt documentary denunciations of Society and the Bomb, but most share a total disdain for the traditional manner of storytelling on film, and also for the 'self-consciously art' experimental films of the twenties and thirties."[58] Pete Hamill in the *Saturday Evening Post* in September 1963 also gave an overall positive representation of all of the New American films, and quoted Jacobs as indicating that what he was producing was "art," although Hamill described *Flaming Creatures* as "a sophomoric exercise in the kind of sex that Henry Miller dealt with 30 years ago" and *Blonde Cobra* as "accompanied by Smith's voice telling fraternity-house stories that presumably are meant to be shocking." Yet the antipathy found in some writers' remarks about these films was not present in Hamill's essay. His conclusion was that by encouraging the filmmakers to be "bad," a new cinema might develop, one that "at least . . . won't be Debbie Reynolds or Doris Day, sailing into a saccharine sunset."[59]

After the charges of obscenity, the descriptions shifted from art or bemusement to a serious debate because now the underground cinema represented a political cause, connected to its representations of sex acts and display of parts of the human anatomy. In an editorial, the *Nation* called for an end to censorship: "even the banning of hard-core commercial pornography invites trouble." Several weeks later the *Nation* published a critical defense of *Flaming Creatures* by Susan Sontag, who ended up calling the film an example of "pop art" in anticipation of within this same year including the film in her essay on camp. Sontag declaimed, "Smith's film has the sloppiness, the arbitrariness, the looseness of pop art. It also has pop art's gaiety, its ingenuousness, its exhilarating freedom from moralism."[60] As Ross suggests, Sontag's move to justify this cinema as pop art and camp was a break with "the style and legitimacy of the old liberal intelligentsia, whose puritanism had always set it apart from the frivolous excesses of the ruling class."[61] Sontag would, however, back off from equating camp with homosexuality in her "Notes on 'Camp.'"

The question of whether the underground cinema's presentations of play and sexual diversity promoted moralism or amoralism was where the film community divided. By mid-1964, two important supporters of experimental and art cinema openly criticized this part of the New American Cinema. In May 1964, Vogel published in the *Village Voice* a statement accusing Mekas and his supporters of inflating the significance of these films and "disregarding even the most advanced and adventurous contemporary artists of the international cinema, such as Antonioni, Resnais, Godard." By promoting only this cinema, Vogel asserted,

> Jonas [Mekas] has become more dogmatic, more extremist, more publicity-conscious. While the flamboyancy and provocative extravagance of the positions taken has [sic] undoubtedly served to make at least one segment of the independent film movement more visible . . . it has also been accompanied by an absence of style and seriousness, a lack of concern for film form, rhythm, and theory which leads many people to view the existing works and pretensions with an indulgent, amused air, smiling at the antics of the movement or somewhat repelled by the "camp" atmosphere of its screenings.[62]

Vogel continued by arguing that Mekas was anticipating and perhaps hurting the possibilities of a true revolution in the American cinema: "however justified an objective, the question of timing and tactics is a crucial one." Moreover, *Flaming Creatures*, "despite flashes of brilliance and moments of perverse, tortured beauty, remains a tragically sad film noir, replete with limp genitalia and limp art" (p. 18). Vogel was clearly supporting repeals of obscenity laws and the promotion of expression. What Vogel objected to was the use of what he considered to be a less than high art, less than serious film, an unmasculine cinema as the test case for obscenity, for fear the masses would not support the cause.

Predictably, letters to the *Village Voice* divided over Vogel's remarks. Two letters supported Vogel, even calling for the *Voice* to drop Mekas' column; a third argued that Vogel was blind to an important evaluative prejudice: "The reason why Genet's film 'Un Chant d'Amour' has been praised by those who cannot stomach 'Flaming Creatures' is not that it is a smoother construction but that it evokes pity: a nice, warm, serious, recognizable emotion. Homosexual love on the screen, yes; a comic conception of human sex, no."[63] "Brooks Brothers" gayness, yes; drag queens, no.

Dwight Macdonald was another critic of the purported tone of this cinema. In July 1964, he called *Flaming Creatures* and *Un Chant d'Amour* "two sexually explicit, and perverse, movies."[64] However, his view of the problem was opposite that of Vogel: "Like the Beat littérateurs, the movie-makers of the New American Cinema are moralists rather than artists" (p. 361). Macdonald's widely known attacks against mass culture and in defense of high art and his concern for the social threats of mass culture as standardization informed his opinion. Here Macdonald was responding to many aspects of the underground cinema, but the pop art features were likely highly influential in his evaluation, as much as the representation of the "perverse."[65]

These debates continued through the summer of 1964, as Macdonald and other leftist colleagues, including Lewis Jacobs, Edouard de Laurot, and Peter Goldfarb, issued a statement:

> The New American Cinema is a movement much vaster in quantity and quality than its restricted and distorted image insistently publicized throughout the world by the New York Village Group of filmmakers (Joanas [*sic*] Mekas, Adam [*sic*] Sitney, et al.).
>
> This misrepresentation is all the more regrettable since the films of the New York Group are on the whole characterized by (a) in their content a solipsistic alienation from reality and society (b) in their form by a lack of originality and professional level (c) in their documentation . . . by a specious or superficial realism—justifying these inadequacies with a mystique of spontaneity which in fact hides creative impotence, more often than not.[66]

This split continued through the 1966 New York Film Festival, run by Vogel, Sarris, and others. Sarris justified not showing some of the New American films that were connected to this trend by claiming many people and critics were opposed to it: Warhol was "pointedly excluded from the proceedings so as not to offend the regular reviewers."[67]

Vogel, Macdonald, Lewis Jacobs, and many others were supporters of cinema and radical politics. Yet how cinema might produce radical change was constantly debated among these people. Indications in the rhetoric and discourse of these writers are that part of their difficulties with the underground cinema had to do with its representations—as not serious enough; as pop art and camp; as perverse.[68] Thus to the set of oppositions, in opposition to high art play and laughter need to be added in a new category of "attitude," an attitude that was too gay—in the double sense of that term. Some of the antagonisms were probably also personal, against Mekas. The debates over *Flaming Creatures* did not end underground cinema; however, the movement took an interesting permutation when the movies of Warhol, excluded from the 1966 New York Film Festival, began to receive national acclaim.

THE CHELSEA GIRLS

Andy Warhol's films provide the break from the underground as political movement to aboveground—even general—cinema. It may be a bit too much to claim that his films permitted the acceptance by a counterculture generation of soft-core and hard-core pornography. Yet the play with sexual desire explicit in *Blow Job, My Hustler, The Chelsea Girls, Lonesome Cowboys,* and so many others of his films took away some of the threat that nontraditional sexuality presented to the middle class. When even *Newsweek* and *Life* could report on this cinema in a somewhat enthusiastic way, a sexual liberation seemed tolerable, maybe even fashionable.

Warhol's early involvement with the Mekas underground screenings has been detailed by Hoberman and Rosenbaum, among others.[69] Warhol liked to play with his affection for this cinema as he played with his love of dominant Hollywood and consumer culture. In an interview published in spring 1966 in *Film Culture*, David Ehrenstein asked Warhol:

DE: Who in the New American Cinema do you admire?

AW: Jaaaacck Smiiiitttth.

DE: You really like Jack Smith?

AW: When I was little, I always . . . . . . thought he was my best director. . . . . I mean, just the only person I would ever try to copy, and
just . . . . so terrific and now since I'm grown up, I just think that he
makes the best movies.[70] [Ellipses are Warhol's pauses, not dele-
tions of the text.]

By the time Sontag defended *Flaming Creatures*, pop art had become the next New York art fashion, so her stance was a smart tactic
for justifying the film. *Film Culture* was also promoting pop art as an
iconography worth considering within the New American film scene.
In fact, it could even find pop art in the old enemy Hollywood. In
Film Culture's summer 1963 issue, Charles Boultenhouse published
what I take to be a partially ironic essay, "The Camera as a God," in
which he declared that "Hollywood is the Original Pop Art and is
GREAT because IT IS WHAT IT IS. Gorgeous flesh and mostly terrible
acting! Divine! Campy dialogue and preposterous plots! Divine! Sexy
fantasy and unorgasmic tedium! Divine!"[71] Three issues later,
Michael McClure did a tribute to Jayne Mansfield in something of the
same tone and much like Smith's earlier homage to Maria Montez.[72]
Warhol's first films for the underground were *Kiss*, shown weekly
as the "serial" at the Gramercy Arts Theater. *Kiss* was three-minute
kisses with variant pairings, some heterosexual, others homosexual.[73]
The Kuchar brothers rapidly learned the discourse of Hollywood advertising, and their promotions of their forthcoming films are among
the most amusing documents of the cinema.[74]

The pop art and camp inflections of the underground and trends in
the New York art scene were—although different—connected,[75] and
suspiciously incorporated old Hollywood as part of their subject matter
rather than the subject matter many New York intellectuals privileged:
the foreign art film and the auteur cinema promoted by Sarris. This
makes sense. If foreign art films, auteurs who transcend the mundane
of Hollywood, and segments of the New American Cinema were
praised for realism and seriousness, then in this binary inversion,
grade-B Hollywood could become a "good" object again, albeit inflected by camp humor or exaggerated as commodity by pop art.

Aligned with the foreign art film was also high modernism—the American abstract expressionism that Warhol discusses as a "macho" world from which he was excluded as "too swish."[76]

Pop art and camp were contextually associated by opposition to the dominant, and so too were pop art and sexual diversity. In fact, in their cases, a dangerous subversion was occurring. In April 1966, Vivian Gornick published in the *Village Voice* an article, "It's Queer Hand Stoking the Campfire," arguing a homosexual control over pop art: "Popular culture is now in the hands of the homosexuals. It is homosexual taste that determines largely style, story, statement in painting, literature, dance, amusements, and acquisitions for a goodly proportion of the intellectual middle class. It is the homosexual temperament which is guiding the progress of Pop Art."[77] Gornick outlined this influence in a bitter essay, deriving her authority from earlier *Voice* discussions of gay rights and gay sensibilities. Moreover, she declared that camp was not, as Sontag described it, "tender" but rather a "raging put-on of the middle classes," "a malicious fairy's joke" (p. 1). Thus, whether praised or condemned, the connections of pop art, play, and a camp gay aesthetic were explicitly being made.

Although the exhibition of Warhol's *The Chelsea Girls* in a midtown theater in December 1966 is a good marker of public acceptance of underground cinema, the way was paved earlier. Two years before, in December 1964, *Newsweek* did a long story on Warhol as pop painter and described his unconventional work in film.[78] Then in January 1965, Shana Alexander described for mass circulation *Life* readers what it was like to watch *Flaming Creatures, Scorpio Rising,* and other such films underground. She began:

> The other night I infiltrated a crowd of 350 cultivated New York sophisticates who were squeezed into a dark cellar staring at a wrinkled bedsheet. The occasion was the world premiere of *Harlot* [Warhol], yet another in the rash of "underground movies" which have become the current passion of New York's avant garde. . . . if a bunch of intelligent people will spend two solid hours and $2.50 apiece to see a single, grainy, wobbly shot projected onto a bedsheet of a man dressed up as Jean Harlow eating a banana (that's what we saw in the cellar), then the movie business must be in worse shape than anyone has any idea.[79]

Alexander noted the value of Warhol's paintings, retrospectives occurring at the Metropolitan and Carnegie Museums, and Ford Foundation grants to underground filmmakers, although she concluded with some expressions of concern, not about possible effects of pornography, but about "fake artists, phony art, and pompous, pretentious critics" (p. 23). Mekas and his "cinematheque" made the *New York Times Sunday Magazine* later in 1965.[80]

By this time "expanded cinema" was beginning to replace "underground cinema" as the mid-1960s transition to hippie and acid drug countercultures developed. In late 1965, Mekas did a two-week, mixed media show; in February 1966, Warhol staged "Andy Warhol, Up-Tight," with the Velvet Underground and with multiple images projected on walls and ceilings. Simultaneously on the West Coast, Ken Kesey, the Merry Pranksters, and the Grateful Dead conducted a series of "acid tests," and Bill Graham staged a large public one at the Fillmore. In April 1966, the famous "Erupting-Exploding-Plastic Inevitable" production with a revolving mirrored ballroom globe and multimedia marked a high point in pop history.

The expanded cinema maintained the tradition of mixed responses. Howard Junker in the *Nation* complained, "How many ill-conceived, half-baked, technically incompetent, faggoty, poetic films can anyone see before announcing: 'I've made that scene. And never mind about the art form of the age.'" Stanley Kauffmann, reviewer for the *New Republic* opined, "many of [the underground filmmakers] equate radicalism with personal gesture and style—revolt consummated by bizarre hair and dress, unconventional sexual behavior, flirtations with drugs."[81]

It was in September 1966 that *The Chelsea Girls* debuted at Mekas' cinematheque.[82] In a real sense, the praise by *Newsweek* reviewer Jack Kroll marked a mass-media acceptance of these films as potentially art, despite all the other connotations: "it is a fascinating and significant movie event."[83] Warhol's characters were compared with Gelber's, Albee's, and John Updike's—all icons of 1960s contemporary aesthetics, and Kroll encouraged the distribution of the film to film societies and universities.[84]

Several months later, *Newsweek* published another long essay by Kroll, "Up from Underground," that also brought these films positive recognition as an "'official' avant-garde movement" as in other arts.

Kroll declared, "the underground has at last surfaced and is moving into public consciousness with a vengeance."[85] Likewise, *Time* in the same month produced an extended examination of the scene. After describing images from an underground film, the writer indicated that the filmmaker "calls it a work of art. The startling thing is that a great many Americans now agree with him." Pop art, camp art was, finally, Art.[86]

In the history of underground cinema, the commercial success of *The Chelsea Girls* indicates at least a growing toleration of these types of images and attitudes. The success also provided sufficient hopes for packaging underground films and distributing them on a routine basis, first attempted by Mike Getz in late 1966 and then in mid-1967 in London by Raymond Durgnat.[87] The most obvious legacy of this distribution of cinema was the late-1960s explosion of feature-length soft-core and hard-core pornography, eventually crossing many prior lines of sexual prohibition, and more generally the commercialization of the sexual revolution in mainstream cinema. Some stylistic tactics of the underground cinema also found their way into mainstream film, particularly the head movies of the late sixties and other "independent" films such as *Easy Rider*.[88]

The critical and commercial success of underground cinema also marked the conclusion of the most lively time for underground cinema as a community film exhibition movement. In 1969, Brakhage filmed *Love Making*; Tyler calmly wrote:

> the second part of the new film, showing two hippie-type males making standardized love (one active, one passive) and featuring unmistakable fellatio, does supply some human interest. . . . For the strictly built-in audience at this premiere, the routine homosexual acts passed with no more than a few semisilent gloats, some scattered, suppressed gasps. So far as stirring up articulate moral or emotional reflexes could be observed, they passed like the eight hours Warhol devoted to looking at the Empire State building.[89]

Admittedly, Tyler's fellow viewers were a "built-in" audience, but something significant had happened in the decade between *The Flower Thief* and *Love Making* to allow Tyler to compare an explicit representation of homosexuality with *Empire*.[90]

The emergence of underground cinema was decisively tied to, and I believe participatory in, sexual liberation politics. That is not to suggest that underground cinema was totally liberated itself. As scholars have pointed out, the representation of women fared badly at times. James notes that Carolee Schneemann was moved to create her own representation of lovemaking after being dissatisfied with Brakhage's images, and Mellencamp argues rightly that this avant-garde provides little or no place for the female spectator.[91] Moreover, the degree to which camp reverence for and homages to Hollywood, stars, and popular culture in general was truly resistant and oppositional is worth reflection, as is the commercialization to which this pop/camp culture was put. This is why I initially labeled this a complex situation.

Yet that the underground cinema was able to so penetrate American culture still deserves notice. Obviously the social conditions of a counterculture and the appropriation of pop culture and comedy made many of the films palatable to people who might otherwise have turned away from them. In fact, the joy and play overrunning the seriousness underpinning the representations likely helped to bind the community and spread it to a larger scene. Although some people may have thought the middle class was unaware of the joke being played on them, I'm not so sure that at least the youth of the middle class were not ready to participate in that joke. All those laughing together at the underground scene created a gay community across sexual orientations.

Waugh argues that the gay address of these films was obvious by 1967. Roger McNiven notes that underground movie "camp" was a "pretext for pornography."[92] I believe this study of New York's reception of its underground cinema indicates that the gay address—at least among Villagers—was apparent right away. Moreover, and however, this gay address set up the events at Stonewall in two significant ways. For one thing, these films were not embarrassed by their sexual deviance. They flaunted it and played with it. For another, the sexual deviance was, within its contemporary gay hierarchies, the most underprivileged—it was directed toward fairies and drag queens, not respectable middle-class gay men.

Studies of Stonewall seek to explain that 1969 event. In one of the major historical contributions, John D'Emilio suggests that two conditions created the "fairy revolt": a new discourse on gay life, replacing the 1950s pathological rhetoric, and a new militancy.[93] The militancy, led by individuals such as Franklin Kameny, derived from increasing general resentment of government interference in personal lives. In 1961, Kameny formed a branch of the Mattachine Society and argued for a civil rights approach (marches, sit-ins) to securing rights for gays and preventing persecution (such as being fired for supposed security reasons). In New York City in 1962, Randy Wicker founded the Homosexual League of New York, with some good publicity in *Newsweek*, the *New York Times*, and the *Village Voice*. The spring 1965 much publicized abuse of homosexuals in Cuba also set up a valuable contrast for U.S. citizens.

These actions and related court petitions, as valuable as they were, were conducted by a small number of people in fairly respectable ways. As Elizabeth Lapovsky Kennedy and Madeline D. Davis argue, this homophile movement was still "accommodationist."[94] Kennedy and Davis suggest that the movement needed to incorporate the wide variety of gays and lesbians—men from leather bars, drag queens, butches and femmes—and to refuse "to deny their difference" in order, finally, to achieve the gay pride symbolized by the events at Stonewall. Most historians of Stonewall stress that it was the transvestites and drag queens who finally fought back, creating the transformation known as the gay liberation movement.

I believe that part of this flaunting of difference derives from the self-identities created in the space of underground cinema in the early 1960s. Several times, screenings flowed into the streets, and confrontations with police or censors at screenings were part of the possible evening events. But most significantly, this underground cinema took up the repressed—even by some homosexuals—images and played with them, had fun, and threw them into the public arena for common consumption. Recognition of this cinema and its makers—from Jack Smith and Andy Warhol to Kenneth Anger—set the stage for validating camp as high style, and gays by association. The underground cinema was not the only early-1960s space for gay play, but it was one that endorsed and even rewarded resistance. It was a scene that "'flew in the face' of the prevailing representation of homosexuals in the 1950s as 'isolated perverts,' as subjects 'gone awry'"—or at least the subjects gone awry were having fun going there! Watching underground movies in New York City in the early 1960s was the beginning of a "participation in a movement"; it was building a community that would later erupt into a revolution.

NOTES

This essay is dedicated to Roger McNiven, who introduced me in the mid-1980s to some of these ideas and who died too early of AIDs. I would also like to thank the audience at the 1996 Conference of the Society for Cinema Studies, Allan Campbell, and Anne Morey for helpful comments, and David Gerstner for his continuing support and friendship.

1. Cindy Patton discusses the problems with using *community* to describe groups of gays, but chooses to use the term in lieu of a better one. I do as well. See her "Safe Sex and the Pornographic Vernacular," in *How Do I Look? Queer Film and Video,* ed. Bad Object-Choices (Seattle: Bay Press, 1991), 32n.

2. Samuel Delany in *Motion of Light in Water,* described in Joan Scott, "The Evidence of Experience," *Critical Inquiry* 17, no. 4 (Summer 1991): 773–74.

3. The claims I make in this essay apply only to the reception of this cinema in New York City. I do not assume that people outside of New York were as cognizant as those around the Greenwich Village scene of these connotations. It is the case, however, as Thomas Poe pointed out at the 1996 Society for Cinema Studies conference, that some gay men outside of New York City were aware of these events and took them as signposts for themselves and their future

4. See the groundbreaking work of George Chauncey, *Gay New York: Gender, Urban Culture, and the Making of the Gay Male World, 1890–1940* (New York: Basic Books, 1994).

5. David E. James, *Allegories of Cinema: American Film in the Sixties* (Princeton: Princeton University Press, 1989), 95 n.7. Also published recently with a similar argument is Juan A. Suarez, *Bike Boys, Drag Queens, and Superstars: Avant-Garde, Mass Culture, and Gay Identities in the 1960s Underground Cinema* (Bloomington: Indiana University Press, 1996).

6. As I indicate below, I use the term "New American Cinema" to describe the widest range of non-Hollywood film practices being produced at this time. I reserve the term underground cinema for a specific subset of films that explicitly displayed nondominant sexualities in nonnarrative form and style. To count as underground cinema for the purposes of this essay, a film needs to contain some sexually explicit material and not look like a narrative Hollywood film.

7. The obvious reference is Vito Russo, *The Celluloid Closet: Homosexuality in the Movies* (New York: Harper & Row, 1981), especially 76–77, 108.

8. Thomas Doherty, *Teenagers and Teenpics: The Juvenilization of American Movies in the 1950s* (Boston: Unwin Hyman, 1988), 82.

9. William Castle, *Step Right Up! . . . I'm Gonna Scare the Pants off America* (New York: G. P. Putnam's Sons, 1976), 136–59. I am indebted to Alison Macor's

research for this information. Castle's activities need to be used to contextualize Alfred Hitchcock's *Psycho* (1960) gimmick of preventing people from entering the theater after the movie started.

10. I shall discuss stag movies and gay erotica of the period below.

11. Parker Tyler, *Underground Film: A Critical History* (New York: Grove Press, 1969), 11.

12. Nick Orzel and Michael Smith, Introduction, in *Eight Plays from Off-Off Broadway*, ed. Orzel and Smith (New York: Bobbs-Merrill, 1966), 6.

13. The fact that the troupes' mode of production was often cooperative and communal is important. These were groups of people organizing to produce many plays together, which also marks an alternative politics from that of commercial theater.

14. Robert Brustein, quoted in Nat Hentoff, "No Paul Whiteman?" *Village Voice* 5, no. 21 (9 March 1960), 6.

15. James, *Allegories of Cinema*, 120, 315–16; Richard Dyer, *Now You See It: Studies on Lesbian and Gay Film* (London: Routledge, 1990), 138.

16. John Fles, "The End of the Affair, or Beyond the Beat Generation," *Village Voice* 6, no. 8 (15 December 1960), 4.

17. Louise Levitas, "Beats Meet at Ibiza," *Village Voice* 7, no. 34 (14 June 1962), 1.

18. Catharine R. Stimpson, "The Beat Generation and the Trials of Homosexual Liberation," *Salmagundi*, nos. 58–59 (Fall 1982–Winter 1983): 375.

19. Russo, *Celluloid Closet*, 118.

20. Peter Stallybrass and Allon White, *The Politics and Poetics of Transgression* (London: Methuen, 1986), 2–3.

21. Fredric Jameson, "Periodizing the 60s," in *The 60s without Apology*, ed. Sohnya Sayres, Anders Stephanson, Stanley Aronowitz, and Fredric Jameson (Minneapolis: University of Minnesota Press, 1984), 178.

22. New American Cinema Group, "The First Statement of the New American Cinema Group," *Film Culture*, nos. 22–23 (Summer 1961), rpt. in *Film Culture Reader*, ed. P. Adams Sitney (New York: Praeger, 1970), 79–83; Patricia Mellencamp, *Indiscretions: Avant-Garde Film, Video, and Feminism* (Bloomington: Indiana University Press, 1990), 1. Also see Lauren Rabinovitz, *Points of Resistance: Women, Power and Politics in the New York Avant-Garde Cinema, 1943–1971* (Urbana: University of Illinois Press, 1991), 108–9.

23. Mellencamp, *Indiscretions*, 2

24. New American Cinema Group, "First Statement of the New American Cinema Group," 82–83.

25. Harris Dienstfrey, "The New American Cinema," *Commentary* 33, no. 6 (June 1962): 495–504.

26. *Pull My Daisy* is not the first film to show beat culture sympathetically. Parker Tyler describes Stan Brakhage's *Desistfilm* (1955) as "the first important

beatnik film with the air of a spontaneous Happening. Disarmingly candid in depicting youth in the simple occupation of getting high, being tricksy, and then running harmlessly wild." *Underground Film,* 26. Robert Hatch of the *Nation* liked *Pull My Daisy,* suggesting that the filmmakers "are what we have been needing since Hal Roach left us." "Films," *Nation* 190, no. 25 (18 June 1960): 540.

27. This is not the first version of the film, but the one Cassavetes reshot and recut. See Jonas Mekas, "Cinema of the New Generation," *Film Culture,* no. 21 (Summer 1960): 11.

28. Rabinovitz, *Points of Resistance,* 117.

29. Not coincidentally, these are all writers whose publications earned them obscenity charges.

30. H. B. Lutz, "Some Words on 'The Connection,'" *Village Voice* 4, no. 41 (5 August 1959), 9.

31. J. Hoberman and Jonathan Rosenbaum, *Midnight Movies* (New York: Harper & Row, 1983), 40; Rabinovitz, *Points of Resistance,* 118; "'Connection' Film at Judson Church," *Village Voice* 7, no. 52 (18 October 1962), 1, 10.

32. Jonas Mekas, [11 October 1962], *Movie Journal: The Rise of a New American Cinema, 1959–1971* (New York: Collier Books, 1972), 71.

33. J. T., "*The Connection* Revisited," *Village Voice* 7, no. 1 (26 October 1961), 10.

34. "The Bourgeois Mothers' Underground, On the Rise," *Village Voice* 7, no. 14 (25 January 1962), 3.

35. Seymour Krim, "Revolt of the Homosexual," *Village Voice* 4, no. 21 (18 March 1959), 12, 16. Also see Dyer, *Now You See It,* 134–38.

36. Krim, "Revolt of the Homosexual," 12, 16, also remarks, "The old categories of a man being Mars and a woman Venus are artificial: only insensitive people or poseurs pretend to a cartoon image of masculinity vs. femininity" (16).

37. "The Gay Underground—A Reply to Mr. Krim," *Village Voice* 4, no. 22 (25 March 1959), 4–5.

38. Stephanie Garvis, "Politics: A Third Party for the Third Sex?" *Village Voice* 7, no. 49 (27 September 1962), 3. For more context for this proposition, see my conclusion.

39. See, most immediately, Stephanie Garvis, "The Homosexual's Labyrinth Of Law and Social Custom," *Village Voice* 7, no. 51 (11 October 1962), 7, 20; Soren Agenoux, "City of Night," *Village Voice* 8, no. 41 (1 August 1963), 5, 15.

40. Rabinovitz, *Points of Resistance,* 80–84; J. R. Goddard, "'I Step on Toes from Time to Time,'" *Village Voice* 7, no. 8 (14 December 1961), 1, 18 [on Amos Vogel and Cinema 16]; Hoberman and Rosenbaum, *Midnight Movies,* 39; Calvin Tomkins, "All Pockets Open," *New Yorker* 48, no. 46 (6 January 1973), 36–37.

41. Tomkins, "All Pockets Open," 37; Nat Hentoff, "Last Call for Cinema

16," *Village Voice* 8, no.18 (21 February 1963), 4; "Cinema of the New Generation," *Film Culture,* no. 21 (Summer 1960): 9. Stan VanDerBeek used "underground" a year later likewise to describe a filmmaking trend; his discussion
concerned many experimental filmmakers who eventually were not catego-
rized in quite this way. Stan VanDerBeek, "The Cinema Delimina: Films from
the Underground," *Film Quarterly* 14, no. 4 (Summer 1961): 5–15. Also see
Hoberman and Rosenbaum, *Midnight Movies,* 40n; James, *Allegories of Cinema,*
94–95; Mellencamp, *Indiscretions,* 3–4. James captures the revolutionary connotations of the term better than VanDerBeek.

42. Andrew Sarris, "Movie Journal: Hello and Goodbye to the New American Cinema," *Village Voice* 7, no. 48 (20 September 1962), 13. Sarris continued to
voice his displeasure over this cinema, including an oration at the 1966 New
York Film Festival; see below.

43. Andrew Ross, *No Respect: Intellectuals and Popular Culture* (New York:
Routledge, 1989), 135–36.

44. Tyler, *Underground Film,* 37. Tyler notes that Deren objected to the films
as an invasion: "woman's privacy had been deliberately, tactlessly invaded."

45. Although masturbation may not have been publicly approved, it was
on the way to being considered normal. It was certainly masculine. Brakhage's
heterosexuality was also not in doubt.

46. Tomkins, "All Pockets Open," 31–35; Hoberman and Rosenbaum, *Midnight Movies,* 40–43; David McReynolds, "'The Flower Thief'—Invalid or Incompetent," [Letters to the Editor], *Village Voice,* 7, no. 40 (26 July 1962), 13;
Andy Warhol and Pat Hackett, *POPism: The Warhol '60s* (New York: Harper &
Row, 1980), 49. Tomkins notes, as others have, that Mekas started out his career
with a different aesthetic. In 1955, Mekas attacked experimental cinema as permeated by "the conspiracy of homosexuality that is becoming one of the most
persistent and shocking characteristics of American Film poetry today"; Jonas
Mekas, "The Experimental Film in America," *Film Culture,* no. 3 (May-June
1955), rpt. in *Film Culture Reader,* ed. Sitney, 23. Also see Rabinovitz, *Points of Resistance,* 84; Dyer, *Now You See It,* 102.

47. By 1960, the Cornell film was a recognized masterpiece in the American avant-garde. Thus *Blonde Cobra* seems a camp version of *Rose Hobart.* This is
reinforced by Smith's homage to Maria Montez in *Film Culture,* which might be
read as a parody of auteur/high art criticism; for example, "Don't slander her
[Montez's] beautiful womanliness that took joy in her own beauty and all
beauty—or whatever in her that turned plaster cornball sets to beauty" (28).
Jack Smith, "The Perfect Filmic Appositeness of Maria Montez," *Film Culture,*
no. 27 (Winter 1962/63): 28–32+.

48. Smith apparently created *Flaming Creatures* to be a comedy, an effect
that works for me. However, as J. Hoberman reports, "Smith himself felt
burned, bitterly complaining that his film, 'designed as a comedy,' was trans-

formed into 'a sex issue of the Cocktail World'"; J. Hoberman, "The Big Heat," *Village Voice*, 12 November 1991, 61. Also see Michael Moon, "Flaming Closets," *October*, no. 51 (1989): 19–54.

49. For background on the director, Barbara Rubin, see J. Hoberman, *Vulgar Modernism: Writing on Movies and Other Media* (Philadelphia: Temple University Press, 1991), 141–42.

50. For criticisms of competence, see George Dowden, "'The Flower Thief'—Invalid or Incompetent," [Letters to the Editor], *Village Voice*, 7, no. 40 (26 July 1962), 11; Pete Hamill, "Explosion in the Movie Underground," *Saturday Evening Post* 236, no. 33 (28 September 1963), 82, 84. For arguments that this is an intentional choice, see Ron Rice, "Foundation for the Invention and Creation of Absurd Movies," *Film Culture*, no. 24 (Spring 1962): 19; P. Adams Sitney, "'The Sin of Jesus' and 'The Flower Thief,'" *Film Culture*, no. 25 (Summer 1962): 32–33.

51. Linda Williams, *Hard Core: Power, Pleasure, and the "Frenzy of the Visible"* (Berkeley: University of California Press, 1989), 58–152.

52. Thomas Waugh, "Homoerotic Representation in the Stag Film, 1920–40," *Wide Angle* 14, no. 2 (1992): 14–15. Female same-sex scenes are quite common and, like male same-sex scenes, are usually preludes to heterosexual couplings. See Williams, *Hard Core*.

53. My special thanks to David Gerstner for alerting me to this cinema. I have viewed a compilation of these films under the general title *Gay Erotica from the 1940s and 1950s: One to Many* (Apollo), *The Beach Bar Nightmare* (Apollo), *Auntie's African Paradise* (Zenith), *Cellmates* (Zenith), *The Cyclist* (Apollo), *Cocktails* (unknown), *Ben-Hurry* (Zenith), *The Captive* (Zenith), and *Fanny's Hill* (Pat Rocco for Bizarre).

54. Arthur Knight, quoted in Hoberman, "Big Heat," 61.

55. "Avant-Garde Movie Seized as Obscene," *New York Times*, 4 March 1964; Stephanie Gervis Harrington, "City Sleuths Douse 'Flaming Creatures,'" *Village Voice* 9, no. 21 (12 March 1964), 3, 13; "Mekas Gaoled Again, Genet Film Does It," *Village Voice* 9, no. 22 (19 March 1964), 13; "Cops Raid Homo Films Again," *Variety* 234, no. 4 (18 March 1964), 5. *Variety*'s labeling of these films as "homo" was not without cause: Mekas had previously publicly represented the underground cinema as connected to homosexuality. See his *Village Voice* columns reprinted in *Movie Journal*: "*Flaming Creatures* and the Ecstatic Beauty of the New Cinema" (18 April 1963), 82–83; "On the Baudelairean Cinema" (2 May 1963), 85–86; "On *Blonde Cobra* and *Flaming Creatures*" (24 October 1963), 101–3. *Flaming Creatures* premiered on 29 April 1963. Its seizure occurred on 3 March 1964 as part of a New York City cleanup for the 1964 World's Fair; see Hoberman, "Big Heat," 61, and Hoberman and Rosenbaum, *Midnight Movies*, 59–60, for excellent accounts of the film's legal history. Also see Dyer, *Now You See It*, 145–49; Tomkins, "All Pockets Open," 38–39; and, of course, Mekas in

Movie Journal. Tomkins notes that when Mekas brought *Flaming Creatures* to the December 1963 Knokke-le-Zoute International Experimental Film Competition, he showed it privately to Jean-Luc Godard, Roman Polanski, and others. Mekas' version is in *"Flaming Creatures* at Knokke-le Zoute," *Village Voice,* 16 January 1964, rpt. in *Movie Journal,* 111–115.

56. Tomkins, "All Pockets Open," 40. These films were also being seen and seized in Los Angeles. Arthur Knight had viewed the film there, and Mike Getz was found guilty on 13 March 1964 of screening "the obscene film" *Scorpio Rising* on 7 March at the Cinema Theater in Hollywood; Hoberman and Rosenbaum, *Midnight Movies,* 59–60. Mekas' versions are in "On Obscenity," *Village Voice,* 12 March 1964; "Underground Manifesto on Censorship," *Village Voice,* 12 March 1964; "Report from Jail," *Village Voice,* 19 March 1964, rpt. in *Movie Journal,* 126–130; "On the Misery of Community Standards," *Village Voice,* 18 June 1964, rpt. in *Movie Journal,* 141–44.

57. Eugene Archer, *"The Flower Thief," New York Times,* 14 July 1962, 11.

58. "Cinema Underground," *New Yorker* 39 (13 July 1963), 17.

59. Pete Hamill, "Explosion in the Movie Underground," *Saturday Evening Post* 236, no. 33 (28 September 1963), 82, 84.

60. "Flaming Censorship," *Nation* 198, no. 14 (30 March 1964), 311; Susan Sontag, "A Feast for Open Eyes," *Nation* 198, no. 16 (13 April 1964), 374–76; Susan Sontag, "Notes on 'Camp,'" [*Partisan Review,* 1964], rpt. in *Against Interpretation* (New York: Delta, 1978). Hoberman and Rosenbaum state that the editor who assigned Sontag the *Nation* piece was fired for doing so; *Midnight Movies,* 61. It is not clear to me why this would occur, but the decision may have had to do with the subsequent debates over morality. Do note that the *Nation* published filmmaker Ken Kelman's positive views on New American Cinema within the month: Ken Kelman, "Anticipations of the Light," *Nation* 198, no. 20 (11 May 1964), 490–94. An excellent later analysis of *Flaming Creatures* is in Grandin Conover, "'Flaming Creatures': Rhapsodic Asexuality," *Village Voice* 9, no. 40 (28 July 1964): 9 and 15.

61. Ross, *No Respect,* 147–65. Sontag was not the first to make the connection between this cinema and pop art; see Mekas, *Movie Journal:* "On Andy Warhol" (5 December 1963), 109–10; "On Andy Warhol's *Sleep*" (30 January 1964), 116.

62. Amos Vogel, *"Flaming Creatures* Cannot Carry Freedom's Torch," *Village Voice* 9, no. 29 (7 May 1964), 9. See Mekas' response, "Movie Journal," *Village Voice* 9, no. 30 (14 May 1964), 15.

63. Elizabeth Sutherland, "Flaming Cause," *Village Voice* 9, no. 30 (14 May 1964), 4. Dwight Macdonald, *On Movies* (New York: Berkeley Medallion Books, 1969), 341.

64. Dwight Macdonald, *On Movies* (New York: Berkeley Medallion Books, 1969), 341.

65. Also see Dwight Macdonald, "A Theory of Mass Culture," *Diogenes*, no. 3 (Summer 1953): 1–17; Dwight Macdonald, "Objections to the New American Cinema" in *The New American Cinema*, ed. Gregory Battcock (New York: Dutton, 1967), 197–204. On Macdonald and taste, see Ross, *No Respect*, 42–64.

66. "In Camera," *Films and Filming* 11, no. 2 (November 1964): 37.

67. Andrew Sarris, "The Independent Cinema" [1966], rpt. in *The New American Cinema*, ed. Battcock, 51. Also see Fred Wellington, "Liberalism, Subversion, and Evangelism: Toward the Definition of a Problem," in *The New American Cinema*, ed. Battcock, 38–47. Annette Michelson did not take the festival's prevailing position, siding with Sontag; see her festival address, "Film and the Radical Persuasion" [1966] rpt. in *The New American Cinema*, ed. Battcock, 83–102.

68. It is perhaps difficult to return to this time for film scholars who are now so familiar with representations of sexuality. Consider that the defense for the 1964 Los Angeles obscenity trial concerning Getz's screening of *Scorpio Rising* was pleased with an all-woman jury: "he feared that a male juror with anxieties about his masculinity might respond hysterically to the homoerotic undertones of Anger's film." Fred Haines, "Art in Court: 1. *City of Angels vs. Scorpio Rising*," *Nation* 199, no. 6 (14 September 1964), 123. The women found Getz guilty.

69. On Warhol's involvement, see Stephen Koch, *Stargazer: Andy Warhol's World and His Films* (New York: Praeger, 1973); Dyer, *Now You See It*, 149–62; Calvin Tomkins, *The Scene: Reports on Post-Modern Art* (New York: Viking Press, 1976), 35–53; Hoberman and Rosenbaum, *Midnight Movies*, 58–75; Matthew Tinkcom, "Camp and the Question of Value," Ph.D. diss., University of Pittsburgh, 1995. Warhol's version is in Warhol and Hackett, *POPism*, 25–35 and throughout.

70. David Ehrenstein, "Interview with Andy Warhol," *Film Culture*, no. 40 (Spring 1966): 41.

71. Charles Boultenhouse, "The Camera as a God," *Film Culture*, no. 29 (Summer 1963), rpt. in *Film Culture Reader*, ed. Sitney, 137.

72. Michael McClure, "Defense of Jayne Mansfield," *Film Culture*, no. 32 (Spring 1964), rpt. in *Film Culture Reader*, ed. Sitney, 160–67.

73. Hoberman, *Vulgar Modernism*, 181. And an echo of the famous 1896 film *The Kiss*.

74. "An Interview with Kuchar Brothers" (5 March 1964) in Mekas, *Movie Journal*, 122–26.

75. Ken Jacobs was later to indicate that he and Smith "hated" pop art. Distinguishing between pop art and camp, or, as Jacobs put it, his and Smith's "'Human Wreckage' aesthetic," is important for a finer discussion of these features. See Jacobs' 1971 interview quoted in Carel Rowe, *The Baudelairean Cinema: A Trend within the American Avant-Garde* (Ann Arbor, MI: UMI Research Press,

1982), 39. Also see Sasha Torres, "The Caped Crusader of Camp: Pop, Camp, and the *Batman* Television Series," in *Pop Out: Queer Warhol,* ed. Jennifer Doyle, Jonathan Flatley, and José Esteban Muñoz (Durham: Duke University Press, 1996), 238–55. Torres writes that although pop, camp, and gay sensibilities were by 1966 linked, they were not equivalents. She argues that camp was going through a "de-gaying" in the mid 1960s by Sontag and others, a de-gaying that permitted the potentially suspect *Batman* series to be considered "camp" but not gay.

76. Warhol and Hackett, *POPism,* 12–15. Ironically, American abstract expressionism, while perhaps macho, was not immune to attacks by conservatives. In the early 1950s, some right-wingers accused creators of these paintings of hiding information in them to pass on to U.S. enemies. William Hauptman, "The Suppression of Art in the McCarthy Decade," *Artforum* 12, no. 2 (October 1973): 48–52.

77. Vivian Gornick, "It's a Queer Hand Stoking the Campfire," *Village Voice* 9, no. 25 (7 April 1966), 1, 20.

78. "Saint Andrew," *Newsweek,* 7 December 1964, 102–4.

79. Shana Alexander, "Report from Underground," *Life* 58 (28 January 1965), 23. See Mekas' reaction, "On the Establishment and the Boobs of the Shana Alexanders," *Village Voice,* 11 February 1965, rpt. in *Movie Journal,* 176–78.

80. Alan Levy, "Voice of the 'Underground Cinema,'" *New York Times Sunday Magazine,* 19 September 1965. Also see Eugene Boe, "Lights! Camera! But Where's the Action?" *Status,* March 1966, 71–74; Elenore Lester, "So He Stopped Painting Brillo Boxes and Bought a Movie Camera," *New York Times,* 11 December 1966.

81. Howard Junker, "The Underground Renaissance," *Nation* 201, no. 22 (27 December 1965), 539; Stanley Kauffmann, *A World on Film* (New York: Dell, 1966), 424. Also see Robert Hatch, "Media-Mix," *Nation* 202, no. 5 (31 January 1966), 139.

82. Hoberman and Rosenbaum, *Midnight Movies,* 68–69; Koch, *Stargazer,* 70–71.

83. Jack Kroll, "Underground in Hell," *Newsweek,* 14 November 1966, n.p. This preparation goes through an interest in pornography by mass media in 1965. See "On Perverts and Art," *Village Voice,* 22 April 1965, rpt. in Mekas, *Movie Journal,* 183–84.

84. But see the review by Dan Sullivan, "*The Chelsea Girls,*" *New York Times,* 2 December 1966, 46.

85. Jack Kroll, "Up from Underground," *Newsweek,* 13 February 1967, 117–19.

86. "The New Underground Films," *Time,* 17 February 1967, 94–99. Bosley Crowther continued to disagree; see his review of *My Hustler, New York Times,*

11 July 1967, 29, in which he pointed out that the Cinematheque had moved to a new theater that used to show burlesque and nudie films. This was fitting for another "homosexual strip-tease." Also see Rosalyn Regelson, "Where Are 'The Chelsea Girls' Taking Us?" *New York Times,* 24 September 1967. These reviewers were a bit late in noticing this trend. In 1962, Rudy M. Franchi, discussing X-rated movies, predicted the underground cinema would be "art" and "exhibited widely in art houses, playing with quality foreign and American films." "The Coming of Age in the X-Film," *Cavalier* (July 1962), 85.

87. Hoberman and Rosenbaum, *Midnight Movies,* 73; "In Camera," *Films and Filming* 13, no. 10 (July 1967), 38.

88. The late 1960s also was the beginning of the development of erotic films for gay audiences, in part because of changing obscenity laws. See Paul Alcuin Siebenand, *The Beginnings of Gay Cinema in Los Angeles: The Industry and the Audience* (Ann Arbor: UMI Press, 1980). On connections between these events and the development of hard-core pornographic exhibition, both hetero and homo, see Hoberman and Rosenbaum, *Midnight Movies,* 76; Tomkins, "All Pockets Open," 45.

89. Tyler, *Underground Film,* 224.

90. Critics of Warhol suggest that *Empire* was a camp joke: eight hours of a hard-on.

91. James, *Allegories of Cinema,* 317; Mellencamp, *Indiscretions,* 21 and throughout.

92. Thomas Waugh, "Cockteaser," in *Pop Out,* ed. Doyle et al., 59–73; Roger McNiven, Ph.D. comprehensive exam, New York University, April 1987.

93. John D'Emilio, *Sexual Politics, Sexual Communities: The Making of a Homosexual Minority in the United States, 1940–1970* (Chicago: University of Chicago Press, 1983), 129–75. Also see Neil Miller, *Out of the Past: Gay and Lesbian History from 1869 to the Present* (New York: Vintage Books, 1995), 340–54.

94. Elizabeth Lapovsky Kennedy and Madeline D. Davis, *Boots of Leather, Slippers of Gold: The History of a Lesbian Community* (New York: Routledge, 1993), 372–73.

FILMOGRAPHY: SOURCES FOR FILMS VIEWED FOR THIS ESSAY

Blonde Cobra (Ken Jacobs, Jack Smith, and Bob Fleischner, 1959–63). Film-Makers' Cooperative, viewed 19 September 1995.

Christmas on Earth (a.k.a. *Cocks and Cunts;* Barbara Rubin, 1963). Film-Maker's Cooperative, viewed 17 July 1995.

Flaming Creatures (Jack Smith, 1963). Film-Makers' Cooperative, viewed 24 July 1995.

The Flower Thief (Ron Rice, 1960). Film-Makers' Cooperative, viewed 18 July 1995.

Gay Erotica from the 1940s and 1950s (Apollo, Zenith, and Bizarre Productions). Videotape purchased December 1996 from Little Rickie, New York, NY.

Little Stabs at Happiness (Ken Jacobs, 1959–63). Film-Makers' Cooperative, viewed 18 July 1995.

Pull My Daisy (Robert Frank and Alfred Leslie, 1959). Library of Congress, viewed 11 July 1995.

The Queen of Sheba Meets the Atom Man (Ron Rice, 1963). Film-Makers' Cooperative, viewed 24 July 1995.

Scorpio Rising (Kenneth Anger, 1963). Museum of Modern Art, viewed 19 September 1995.

Shadows (John Cassavetes, 1959). Bravo television transmission [transmission date unknown].

9

Taboos and Totems

Cultural Meanings of The Silence of the Lambs

BY THE FIFTH week of the release of *The Silence of the Lambs* (1991), the debates over the film had solidified into a set of propositions: (1) that whether or not Jonathan Demme had intended to create a homophobic film, the character of the serial murderer had attributes associated with stereotypes of gay men; (2) that in a time of paranoia over AIDS and increased violence directed toward gays in the United States, even suggesting connections between homosexuals and serial murderers was irresponsible; but (3) that the character of Clarice Starling played by Jodie Foster was a positive image of a woman working in a patriarchal society and, thus, empowering for women viewers. The diversion in views produced a consequent division: two nondominant groups, some gay men and some feminists (both straight and lesbian), found themselves at odds over evaluating the film.

The controversy further escalated when several activists "outed" Jodie Foster. "Outing" is the recent practice by some people to declare publicly that certain individuals are homosexual or bisexual[1] even though those people have not chosen to make their sexual preferences known. The argument for doing this is that it is hypocritical for famous people to remain private about such preferences if they participate in public activities which perpetuate homophobia. Rather, they should help promote gay rights.

Foster's outing produced in the most vitriolic counteranalysis the claim that Foster was being outed because she was a strong woman and that she was being "offer[ed] up [by gay activists] as a sacrifice in the furtherance of gay visibility."[2] "You don't have to look far," the woman argued, "to find a reason why a culture with screen idols such as Marilyn Monroe and Judy Garland would object so vociferously to an actress like Jodie Foster. Like their straight brothers, the gay men who condemn Jodie Foster and *Lambs* are out to destroy a woman who doesn't put male interests first and doesn't conform to their ideas of what a woman should be. Under the guise of promoting gay consciousness, they're falling back on the same reliable weapon that men have used for centuries against women who claim a little too much for themselves—they're calling her a dyke."

Although other women were not so strong in their condemnation of Foster's outing, all thirteen of those women whose views of the movie, *The Silence of the Lambs*, I had available to me expressed praise for the film. These included at least two lesbians, one of whom criticized Larry Kramer of ACT UP for his "patronizing" attitude toward Foster, trying to treat her as a "disobedient daughter."[3]

Whether Foster is or is not a lesbian or bisexual "in real life" is not the point of this essay. Whether the character she plays in *The Silence of the Lambs* is or is not a lesbian is also not at issue here. What I shall be pursuing instead is the ultimate stitching together of gay and woman that became the "climax" of the discussion. I shall argue that this possibility, while not inevitable, is grounded in its reception context and process. What I shall be doing here is what I call historical reception studies. This research attempts to illuminate the cultural meanings of texts in specific times and social circumstances to specific viewers, and it attempts to contribute to discussions about the spectatorial effects of films by moving beyond text-centered analyses.

Because I wish to present an application of this rather than an extended theoretical argument, I will simply lay out several hypotheses informing my research:

1. Immanent meaning in a text is denied.

2. "Free readers" do not exist either.

3. Instead, contexts of social formations and constructed identities of the self in relation to historical conditions explain the interpretative strategies and affective responses of readers. Thus, receptions need to be related to specific historical conditions as events.

4. Furthermore, because the historical context's discursive formation is contradictory and heterogeneous, no reading is unified.

5. The best means currently available for analyzing cultural meanings exist in poststructuralist and ideological textual analyses. These methods, of necessity, draw upon multiple theoretical frameworks and perspectives such as deconstructionism, psychoanalysis, cognitive psychology, linguistics, anthropology, cultural studies Marxism, and feminist, ethnic and minority, and lesbian and gay studies. They do so with

a clear understanding that the connections and differences among the frameworks and perspectives must be theorized.

Consequently, historical reception studies work combines contemporary critical and cultural studies to understand why distinct interpretative and affective experiences circulate historically in specific social formations. In a case study, the following steps might occur:

1. An object of analysis is determined. This object is an event, not a text: that is, it is a set of interpretations or affective experiences produced by individuals from an encounter with a text or set of texts within a social situation. It is not an analysis of the text, although it might include an analysis of what textually might be facilitating the reading.

2. Traces of that event are located. Here I shall be using primarily traces in the form of printed prose and images, but when available, oral accounts would be very good sites of additional evidence. The print and images include about twenty reviews, news articles, letters to newspapers, advertisements, illustrations, and publicity which circulated in the major mass media.

3. The traces are analyzed textually and culturally. That is, just as new historians elucidate causal processes to explain conjunctions called "events" and then characterize the social significance of these events in relation to specific groups of people, so too does this research. Furthermore, the analyses avoid categorizing receptions into preferred, negotiated, or resistant readings. Rather, the processes of interpretation are described since more richness in explanation can be achieved by describing the readings than by reducing them to three specific generalizations.

4. Finally, the range of readings is surveyed not only for what seems possible at that moment but also for what the readings did not consider. That is, structuring absences are important as well.

My project will be to work toward explicating the event of the "sacrificial" outing of Jodie Foster. I shall argue that, although this event might be attributed simply to contemporary U.S. stereotypes of lesbians—i.e., a strong woman must be a lesbian—or even to informal oral communication circulated by gays and lesbians about Foster's sexual preferences, it was facilitated by the critical response *The Silence of the Lambs* received. Furthermore, Foster's outing is symptomatic of current cultural taboos and totems. Thus, calling Foster a lesbian is more overdetermined linguistically, psychoanalytically, and culturally than it might appear.

In this initial study of the event, three specific reading strategies occur.[4] These are: (1) the construction of binary oppositions with deployments of high and low, good and bad attributions; (2) the use of metaphor and analogy; and (3), most pertinent to the event, the hybridization or grafting of incompatible terms together. This third practice is activated from the prior two strategies and even finds its motivation from one of the dominant metaphors in the discourse.

TABOOS

Perhaps because many writers have gone to film school or because thinking in oppositions so colors our everyday lives, reviewers of *The Silence of the Lambs* often structured their plot analyses around a central binary opposition. The most obvious opposition was between Hannibal "The Cannibal" Lecter and Jame "Buffalo Bill" Gumb. One reviewer noticed that Lecter is upperclass and witty while Gumb is a "working-class lout."[5] The reviewer even emphasized how this sets up an audience to sympathize with the "good" Lecter and to find disgusting the "bad" Gumb. He critically summarized, "Lecter: rich, wise, clever, helpful, and funny. Gumb: working-class, stupid, dense, and dull. Lecter: straight. Gumb: gay. Lecter: abstract evil; Gumb: evil incarnate." David Denby characterized the Lecter/Gumb opposition as between "an unimaginable vicious genius; the other merely rabid and weird."[6] Another reviewer wrote that the film had "two villains who represent quite different incarnations of evil. Buffalo Bill, a grotesque enigma, has absolutely no redeeming virtues. But Lecter is strangely sympathetic, a symbol of muzzled rage."[7]

Important to this evaluation is that Lecter's victims are bureaucrats and authority figures, such as the census taker whose liver he ate with a nice Chianti. Meanwhile, Gumb goes after young, overweight women. Additionally, of course, Gumb is played as effeminate—something remarked upon by several reviewers who also acknowledged the gay community's concern about the film.

Binary oppositions are commonly deployed in ways such that the two terms in the opposition are not equal. Peter Stallybrass and Allon White in *The Politics and Poetics of Transgression* argue that cultural oppositions often duplicate themselves in various discursive realms.[8] That is, hierarchies reproduce themselves across various symbolic systems such as psychic forms, the human body, geographical spaces, and social orders. One symbolic system will then refer to the other to warrant its ordering. An obvious example would be the equation commonly made between the head as exalted and the lower anatomy as base; the physical body is written over by a metaphysical discourse.[9]

This hierarchization of binary oppositions functions analogically to legitimate Lecter's cannibalism. Thus, the class attributions, choice of victims, and socialized behavior patterns are read not merely as oppositions but ones with values attached which reinforce each other. Viewers routinely enjoyed Lecter, particularly as played by Anthony Hopkins. *Variety*'s reviewer symptomatically joked: the "juiciest part is Hopkins."[10] Lecter, of course, offers an interesting problem since he breaks a taboo which would normally be described as the horror for a film.

Can we explain the spectators' acceptance of this transgression beyond attributing it to the functioning of the textual array of values attached to the binary oppositions? Freud writes in *Totem and Taboo* that taboos are occasionally breached only to reassert the boundaries authenticating them. One instance of such a breach is the ritual eating of something considered taboo. Such a thing might even be the plant or animal which the tribe considers to be its totem. Totems stand as symbols for the group.

But according to Freud, they are also causal explanations. The totem is the tribe's origin, the "father" of the tribe. Thus, Freud links the ritual eating of totems to the oedipal story and argues that what has been established as out-of-bounds (e.g., killing one's father) is in the ritual the symbolic consumption of the totem's character. A current example of such a ritual act, Freud writes, is the Christian Communion. Drinking wine and eating bread is devouring one's own kind. Lecter, of course, forgoes the more oblique symbolism: he actually eats members of the tribe, but for the same purpose.[11] Lecter's ingestion of his own kind, authorized as the incorporation of the bodies of authority figures and legitimated through socially originated hierarchies of binary oppositions, provides both textual and contextual determinations for spectators to accept, and even find pleasure in, his destruction of boundaries.

Consequently, and as part of the weirdly disconcerting pleasure of the event, the reviewers made all sorts of jokes about accepting the broken taboo as if they too wished to participate in the ritual. These jokes occurred in the form of puns, and were thus doubly validated, since puns are a lawful disruption of traditional meanings. For example, Denby wrote: "The horrors of the scene are brought off with, well, taste."[12] Another reviewer noted, "Buffalo Bill is famous for killing women, skinning them and leaving the cocoon of an exotic moth in their mouths. Lecter made his name by eating the flesh of his victims raw. All of that may sound a little hard to swallow."[13] One columnist gave Demme a "C- in Mise-en-Scène 101 for the way he fleshes out (so to speak) the villainous Jame Gumb on screen."[14] Notice that all of these wisecracks were made apologetically, because they do, indeed, open fissures in social categorizing. Headlines are particularly susceptible to wordplay, and the discursive motif continued there. Examples include: "Overcooked Lambs," "Skin Deep: Jonathan Demme's Chatter of the Hams," and "Gluttons for Punishment."[15]

Thus, a very powerful and significant binary opposition between Lecter and Gumb was constructed and circulated by viewers of the film. A second structuring binary opposition was proposed by Denby and J. Hoberman, who pointed out that Clarice Starling has several fathers with which to contend.[16] Hoberman expanded the comparison: Crawford, the FBI agent, is her daytime dad who is rational; Lecter, her nighttime father, is a "charismatic suitor."[17] This reading of the film as an incest story was transformed in other reviews. As one writer suggested, *The Silence of the Lambs* can be seen as about Starling, who is "changing, trying to formulate an identity."[18] Interpreting the film as an oedipal passage for Starling was reinforced visually by iconographic materials published with the reviews. Most illustrations were supplied by Orion in its publicity kit. These featured Lecter standing behind Starling with Crawford behind both of them. Some illustrations cut out Crawford; others left him in. All three people face forward so that Crawford and Lecter seem to be peering over Starling's shoulder.

Reading *The Silence of the Lambs* as an initiation/oedipal story fits in an eerie way a discussion of the slasher genre by Carol Clover. She argues that in this genre women are victimized by psychopathic killers. However, she continues, it would be an error to assume that slasher pictures are simple cases of misogyny. For one thing, we ought not to imagine that gender characteristics determine viewer identification.[19] This is particularly important with cinematic representation, in which the physical body is often so powerful as an immediate signifier of gender. Furthermore, viewer identification does not necessarily remain stably located in a single character throughout a film. For instance, Clover believes that in slasher movies identification seems to alter during the course of the picture from sympathizing with the killer to identifying with the woman-hero. Clover also argues that the (apparently male) monster is usually characterized as bisexual while the woman-hero is not so simply a "woman." She is often "unfeminine," even tracking the killer into "his underground labyrinth."[20]

The ultimate confrontation in the slasher film, Clover believes, is between a "shared femininity" and a "shared masculinity" in which the monster is castrated. Thus, the woman-hero is able to appropriate (here Clover refers to Linda Williams' work) "'all those phallic symbols'" of the killer's. Moreover, and important to our discussion of *The Silence of the Lambs*, the woman-hero is "a congenial double for the adolescent male," who is now negotiating sexual identity. The woman-hero is a safe identificatory substitute for a male, with the repressed plot about male-to-male relations. The woman-hero is thus a "homoerotic stand-in."

Psychoanalytical discourse is widespread, and Hoberman, among others, was familiar with it. Thus, the historical discourse of psychoanalysis may have abetted his reading of the film as an oedipal crisis for Starling, one that ends "happily." Starling is permitted to join the FBI; Lecter rewards her with unfettered independence from threats by him. Furthermore, and most significantly, Starling kills Gumb, symbol of aberrant sexual behavior, thus overtly denying homoeroticism while permitting it to exist in the apparently heterosexual Crawford-Starling pair.

Thus, one way some reviewers seem to have read the film is Starling-as-Masquerading-Woman who accedes to patriarchy. However, another way exists to understand parts of the interpretative reception of *The Silence of the Lambs*. To explore that I need to draw out further the second interpretative strategy: the use of metaphor and analogy.

TOTEMS

We can assume that some reviewers of the movie read the original novel, which is thus part of the potential context for interpreting the film. The novel employs a rather hackneyed device: the various characters are linked to animals, with a theme of natural preying.[21] At the first meeting between Crawford and Starling, Crawford describes Lecter's behavior: "It's the kind of curiosity that makes a snake look in a bird's nest" (p. 6). Starling, of course, is thus forewarned. Later, added to Lecter's attributes is the classic connection between the snake and the devil: "Dr. Lecter's eyes are maroon and they reflect the light in pinpoints of red" (p. 16); his tongue flickers in and out of his face (p. 144). Thus, the metaphor builds a set of parallelisms: body attributes equal snake equals devil; therefore, evil.

The animal motif as metaphor and category for social cognition, perhaps prompted by the novel, Starling's name, or the title of the film, perhaps from force of habit, permeated reception discourse about *The Silence of the Lambs.* Lecter was a "cobra"[22] who lived in a "snake pit of an asylum."[23] He made "hissing, vile, intimate remarks to women."[24]

The initiation theme crisscrosses with this motif. Starling was described as "molelike" for her penetration of the killers' habitats. She descended into the "dungeon-like bowels" of the prison;[25] she raided the "basement of death."[26] Stuart Klawans pointed out that Starling must overcome all sorts of obstacles: the initial course in the opening shots, a "labyrinth of offices," "a mazelike dungeon."[27]

But Starling was not always, or usually, the one doing the preying. "Lecter plays cat and mouse with Clarice."[28] For viewers, Starling could become the totem animal with whom she identifies: she was the "lamb in wolves' territory."[29] Also crossing was the devil association. Starling "must defend herself at all times, lest [Lecter] eat her soul."[30]

Social discourses are never uniform or logical even as they try to map hierarchies across semantic categories. In the reception of *The Silence of the Lambs,* Lecter's meaning was mobile; sometimes on the top, other times on the bottom. This inversion is most obvious when he is positioned not to counsel but to threaten Starling. The photographs of the series of father figures with Starling could be read another way. Some men reviewers took Starling to be a woman-victim. Could readers perceive Starling as a woman in danger?

In a discussion of the representation of the naked female body, Margaret R. Miles points out that by the fifteenth century, a common visual motif was the positioning of a woman in a frontal pose with the figure of Adam, her lover, standing behind her.[31] Or Adam is transformed into the figure of Death and the woman dances with him. Or in even more threatening and troubling images, Death copulates with the woman in sadomasochistic brutalism. These images are reminiscent of representations of vampirism, a later connection of animals, eating, sexuality,

and death. Miles argues that their significance is the patriarchal connection of woman with sin, sex, and death. But she also notes that "Julia
Kristeva has stated that [while] 'significance is inherent in the human
body,' . . . little more can be said about what is signified until one examines the meanings of bodies in their particular religious and social
contexts."[32]

Hauntingly, then, another theme in the critical reception of the film
is the ambiguous threat of Lecter to Starling as woman-victim. When
they discussed it, many reviewers did take the threat to be sexual in
some way. Added to this was the suggestion of pandering by Crawford,
who sends Starling to Lecter hoping, as Vincent Canby puts it, "to
arouse his interest."[33] This reading, however, does not mean that Starling was necessarily being read psychically as female, with the sexuality as heterosexual. In fact it could be repressed polymorphous sexuality, but the space was opened for the former reception. This leads to another feature in the array of interpretations.

MINOTAURS AND MOTHS

Women who discussed the film in the public discourse that I surveyed
liked *The Silence of the Lambs* and seemed especially to sympathize with
Starling. Julie Salamon described Starling as "an attractive woman of
unexceptional size doing what used to be thought of as a man's job. . . .
She is a rare heroine, a woman who goes about her work the way men
do in movies, without seeming less a woman."[34] Amy Taubin praised
the movie as a "feminist film" which "suggests that [sexuality and sexual role] fantasies can be exhumed and examined, and that their meanings can be shifted." Taubin went on to invert traditional mythology:
after describing Starling's discussions with Lecter as "the meeting of
Oedipus and the Sphinx," she claimed that the pleasure of the film was
"the two-hour spectacle of a woman solving the perverse riddles of patriarchy—all by herself."[35]

Again, Starling was being placed in the narrative position traditionally given to a male. However, in Taubin's scenario, Lecter is not the
patriarchal father. Rather, Lecter must fit in the slot of the Sphinx, the
monstrous hybrid with the upper torso of a woman and the lower torso
an amalgamation of animal body parts. Although symptomatically its
gender is unknown, the Sphinx has traditionally been associated with

the "maternal." Interestingly, however, no other reviewer surveyed suggested that Lecter had any feminine traits, perhaps because by contrast he seemed masculine compared with Gumb.[36]

Another monstrous hybrid was also mentioned in the reviews. Hoberman retitled the movie "Nancy Drew Meets the Minotaur." The Minotaur is a double inversion of the Sphinx, for its lower body is that of a human male while its head is that of a bull.[37] Thus, the human body halves that define the two beasts are reversed as well as the genders. Furthermore, the Minotaur is absolutely knowable as male, since the lower portion of its body is entirely visible—the area legitimated by medical discourse as that which defines and describes sexual difference.[38] This Minotaur association is reinforced through the labyrinth metaphors mentioned earlier.

The third reading strategy is hybridization, the grafting together of irreconcilables. The associations with these particular mythical beasts are some evidence of this. Note, in particular, that what is grotesque is not the blurring of boundaries or even their transgression, as in Lecter's cannibalism in which he ingests another and takes on its attributes. Rather, what is disturbing is the all too apparent, seeable combination of disparate semantical categories: human/animal. Again, Hoberman's discourse is particularly insightful. About Gumb, he wrote, "[Buffalo Bill] is a jarring billboard of discordant signs—a figure stitched together like the Frankenstein monster."[39]

Hoberman's vocabulary, then, gives us the thread to another pattern of interpretation motivated by the text and mobilized by the historical context. Gumb received his nickname because he skins his victims and sews those skins together to make himself an outfit. Literally stripping the women of their outer raiment, Gumb tries to fashion himself into the woman he desires to be. All of the reviewers decided he was the ultimate monster.

Working from Kristeva's thoughts about the abject, Barbara Creed has recently argued that the horror to be confronted in some films is not just the phallic mother but, finally, the archaic mother of the imaginary, pre-oedipal experience.[40] The monstrous horror is not the castrated female but the maternal authority which threatens the "obliteration of the self."

Many of the reviewers observed that Gumb's behavior is readable as effeminate, leading to the inference, despite lines of dialogue, that he is homosexual. As the reviewer for the *Los Angeles Reader* put it, Gumb has a "swishy stage-homosexual posturing."[41] This association seems to be emphasized and commented upon by a sketch accompanying a *Village Voice* article in which Gumb holds a needle and thread while Starling has a pencil and paper. Again, Starling is face forward in the foreground with the threat behind her, looking toward her. No matter Starling's gender, Gumb's is by cultural categories feminized.

Also reinforcing this threat of the engulfing maternal monster is Gumb's totem: the death's-head moth, so named because the markings on its back resemble those of a skull. It is this animal which he wishes to imitate in its transformation into beauty; it is this totem which he shoves down his victims' throats. Klawans observed that Jack the Ripper is considered to be the first serial killer, who Klawans noted arrives when women start living on their own in the city.[42] Furthermore, to make his self apparent, to construct his own identity, the serial killer will repeat his signature at each crime scene. By "pattern, [the killer] writes in code with his victims' bodies."[43] The film, then, meticulously follows common lore about such behavior. The death's-head moth functions symbolically to write "Gumb" on the bodies of women. According to the movie plot, Gumb did this as well to forecast his forthcoming transformation and new link to the identity "woman." With a moth in their mouths, the women's interiors are now exteriorized—their skins gone but their bodies the cocoon for a new beauty.

This association of moth, maternity, and monster is strongly prepared for extratextually, so the fact that the viewers responded to it is not surprising. For *The Silence of the Lambs*, the moth was a major motif in the advertising campaign through the posters of it covering Starling's mouth.[44] But the ad's image does not have the moth *in* Starling's throat. It would not be visible. It covers her mouth, hiding an orifice. In this film, and in symptomatic displacement, inversions exist all over the interpretational landscape. Outsides become insides both in Lecter's cannibalism and in Gumb's scripting his forthcoming transformation.

Furthermore, the moth is stitched across Starling's mouth. Starling is figured and readable as a hybrid monster as well. If she is easily thought of as an individual in search of her identity, she, like Gumb, can be associated with the moth. She is interpretable as part of his clan. But this stitching is across the mouth, leaving Starling, like so many victims, silenced.

Recall that readers have also equated Starling with the lambs she tried to save from slaughter. After death, lambs have two functions:

they can be eaten; their hides can be worn. In both cases, the sacrifice is incorporated by the killer—internally via swallowing and externally via masquerading as an other. In both cases, difference and identity are threatened. Klawans asked, why is the audience being worked over in *The Silence of the Lambs*? "The best answer . . . and it's a good one—is that the protagonist is a woman. She might even be a lesbian." Other male writers also publicly regarded this as a distinct possibility prior to the outing of Foster.[45] Thus, although Starling is a woman, she may not be a "normal" woman. We thus have a complete quadrant of gender and sexual preferences available in the film: Lecter, heterosexual male; female victims, (heterosexual) females; Gumb, homosexual male; Starling, homosexual female. Reading Starling as a lesbian, however, is not a direct result of textual evidence but an inference from the interpretative strategies and the discursive context of the film.

Mary Douglas writes in *Purity and Danger* that social pollution comes from threats to the political and cultural unity of a group.[46] Social pollution anxieties can be rewritten over the human body in a concern for its orifices, since body openings "are connected symbolically to social pre-occupations about exits and entrances" (p. 126). In my analysis of this public discourse, the most apparent danger was from incorporating or transgressing traditional oppositions. Douglas believes that one way to cancel such social pollution is a confessional rite.

As the release date for *The Silence of the Lambs* neared, Orion and the producers used the Hollywood strategy of attracting attention to it by giving several benefit shows. One party was for the AIDS Project of Los Angeles. In the United States in 1991, this gesture of concern could not be disassociated from the public assumption that AIDS is primarily a disease of gay men and lower-class drug users. Gay activists immediately read the event as a pollution rite: "They [are attempting] to launder the film by using . . . an organization whose clients are mostly gay to offset criticism."[47] To gay activists, the act of trying to imply concern for homosexuals was thus an inverted confession of the homophobia of the film.

This event occurred extratextually and prior to the film's opening. Thus, it determined the reception of the film for many viewers. When the film went on to do good box office, the intensity of the threat increased. For gay activists, an external threat—wide reinforcement of the notion that effeminate men are psychopathic serial killers—was not only being ignored by massive numbers of audience members but likely being, again, incorporated into public mythologies. Thus, some gay activists chose to blur the line which is so often crossed: the difference between fiction and real social life.

Notice that gay activists did not try to argue that Starling was a lesbian. Like Orion, they made the argument that the movie had some (obscure) value to social life. Like Orion, they made the argument extratextually: *Jodie Foster* was a lesbian. In a time in which homo- or bisexuality was threatened as a personal identity—threatened not just by social stereotyping but by real physical threats from homophobic violence—"sacrificing" Foster seemed logical. That is, pointing out the hypocrisy of the filmmakers by arguing that Foster had not yet come to terms with her own identity and sexual preferences was necessary if society was ever to come to terms with its notions of "monsters."

As I have indicated, Foster might well have come under attack simply because of stereotypes of the strong woman as a lesbian as well as informal oral communication about her, but motifs in the advertising and film, combined with reading strategies by its viewers, reinforced the credibility of the accusation by those who chose to out her. Starling's gender is ambiguous. She is easily read as a "son" in a patriarchal identity crisis; she is easily read as "unfeminine," tracking archaic mothers in their lairs; she is easily read as a hybrid—a moth person. And within a structural square of oppositions and inversions, her position is the most "other": not heterosexual, not male. She could be the lamb sacrificed in punishment for the film's expressed homophobia and repressed polymorphous sexuality.

Of course, other people pointed out that those choosing to out her were in an odd way accepting the notion that being called a lesbian would be humiliating. And that, in any case, Foster was being denigrated or patronized just as women so often are in our culture. As I mentioned earlier, women—both straight and lesbian—uniformly defended her and the movie as a positive, powerful representation of a female.

In closing I wish to underline what I have been doing theoretically. This study is an attempt to indicate how contemporary theoretical frameworks can be useful in determining the cultural meanings (with the plural emphasized) of a specific text. What I have not done is to try to unify the text or the readings by asserting that one reading or set of oppositions or displacements is more viable than another. I have tried to provide the range of readings and to give an initial account of what might explain that range.

Additionally, my primary evidence for the cultural meanings of the events was not derived from a textual reading of the film. It came from public discourse. From that discourse, mediated though it is, I determined what textual, extratextual, and social determinants might account for the readings in my sample. I did not, although I might have, discuss significant absences in the discourse, a critical one being "blood," which is obviously significant considering how AIDS is transmitted.

Determining the cultural meaning of a text is full of assumptions and pitfalls. Interpreting interpretations is viciously circular. Additionally, the discourse I used is public and therefore already suspect. It is by no means representative of its culture—although I would be willing to argue that it has some relation to it as well as an effect on it. Given these (and other) problems, however, I still believe that research of this sort is helpful in a project of trying to understand how individuals interpret the world and how they use discourse to shape, or reshape, that world. While I have made no decision about the political gesture of outing, I do believe I need to work toward understanding what acts of resistance such as that one mean in my social formation.

What this investigation has reaffirmed for me, then, is that at this time homosexuality, bisexuality, or ambiguous sexual preference was threatening to a wide range of readers. Gumb's death as an "unnatural" person was met with a sigh of relief. "Sick" though the movie's ending may be, Lecter's continued career as a cannibal of authority figures was met with a shaky laugh of pleasure. Maybe this is because Lecter's act of murder is one that the dominant culture takes to be a normal ritual of incorporation, father to son, and not the hybridizing of monsters such as men who sew rather than model themselves after appropriately masculine authority figures.

NOTES

I would like to thank Eithne Johnson for preparing such an interesting Ph.D. reading list, Beth Wichterich for helping me understand parts of the events and audiences at the 1991 Nordiskt Filmsymposium (Lund, Sweden), the Women's Research Seminars at the University of Texas at Austin, and the University of Wisconsin—Madison for giving me very valuable responses to drafts of this essay.

1. In this chapter I will usually not refer to bisexuality as a sexual preference. However, bisexuality should be considered an implied option throughout.

2. Leslie Larson, "Foster Freeze," [Letter to] *Village Voice,* 2 April 1991, n.p.(from *The Silence of the Lambs* clipping film, Academy of Motion Picture Arts and Sciences Margaret Herrick Library; hereafter SLfile). Background, descriptions, and debates preceding this can be found in David J. Fox, "Gays Decry Benefit Screening of 'Lambs,'" *Los Angeles Times,* 4 February 1991 (SLfile); Michael Musto, "La Dolce Musto," *Village Voice,* 12 February 1991 (SLfile); Amy Taubin, "Demme's Monde," *Village Voice,* 19 February 1991, 64, 76–77; Lisa Kennedy, ed., "Writers on the Lamb," *Village Voice,* 5 March 1991, 49, 56; Michelangelo Signorile, "Lamb Chops," letter to *Village Voice,* 12 March 1991 (SLfile); letters to *Village Voice,* 19 March 1991 (SLfile); Elaine Dutka, "'Silence' Fuels a Loud and Angry Debate," *Los Angeles Times,* 20 March 1991, (SLfile); and Michael Bronski, "Reel Politic," *Z Magazine* 4, no. 5 (May 1991): 80–84.

3. Julie Salamon, "Film: Weirdo Killer Shrink Meets the G-Girl," *Wall Street Journal,* 14 February 1991; Taubin, "Demme's Monde"; Kennedy, "Writers on the Lamb"; Martha Gever in Kennedy, "Writers on the Lamb"; C. Carr in Kennedy, "Writers on the Lamb"; Sheila Benson, "Why Do Critics Love These Repellent Movies?," *Los Angeles Times Calendar,* 17 March 1991; Andrea Kusten, letters to *Village Voice,* 19 March 1991; Anna Hamilton Phelan, Tammy Bruce, and Phyllis Frank, quoted in Dutka, "'Silence' Fuels a Loud and Angry Debate"; Leslie Larson, letter to *Village Voice,* 2 April 1991; B. Ruby Rich, quoted in Bronski, "Reel Politic"; Maria Magenit, quoted in Bronksi, "Reel Politic."

4. If I were explaining something else about the reception of *The Silence of the Lambs*, other features and practices in the discourse might be pertinent.

5. Henry Sheehan, "Overcooked Lambs," *Los Angeles Reader,* 15 February 1991, 29–30. These notes contain only the sources from which I quote; other reviews were part of my sample.

6. David Denby, "Something Wilder," *New York* 24, no. 7 (18 February 1991), 60–61.

7. Brian D. Johnson, "The Evil That Men Do," *Maclean's,* 18 February 1991, 51–52.

8. Peter Stallybrass and Allon White, *The Politics and Poetics of Transgression* (London: Methuen, 1986).

9. "A recurrent pattern emerges: the 'top' attempts to reject and eliminate the 'bottom' for reasons of prestige and status, only to discover, not only that it is in some way frequently dependent upon that low-Other . . . but also that the top includes the low symbolically, as a primary eroticized constituent of its own fantasy life. The result is a mobile, conflictual fusion of power, fear and desire in the construction of subjectivity: a psychological dependence upon precisely those Others which are being rigorously opposed and excluded at the social level. It is for this reason that what is socially peripheral

is so frequently symbolically central (like long hair in the 1960s)." Stallybrass and White, *Politics and Poetics of Transgression*, 5.

10. "Cart," *"The Silence of the Lambs," Variety*, 11 February 1991, 109.

11. Sigmund Freud, *Totem and Taboo: Resemblances between the Psychic Lives of Savages and Neurotics* [1918], trans. A. A. Brill (New York: Vintage Books, 1946). "The cannibalism of primitive races derives its more sublime motivation in a similar manner. By absorbing parts of the body of a person through the act of eating we also come to possess the properties which belonged to that person" (107).

12. Denby, "Something Wilder," 60–61.

13. Johnson, "Evil That Men Do," 51–2.

14. Stephen Harvey, "Writers on the Lamb," *Village Voice*, 5 March 1991, 49.

15. Sheehan, "Overcooked Lambs," 29; John Powers, "Skin Deep: Jonathan Demme's Chatter of the Hams," *L.A. Week*, 15–21 February 1991, 27; Stanley Kauffmann, "Gluttons for Punishment," *New Republic*, 18 February 1991, 48.

16. J. Hoberman, "Skin Flick," *Village Voice*, 19 February 1991, 61.

17. As Hoberman notices, in the original novel, Starling's relation with her mother is a dominant theme. In the film, her mother's death and its meaning to Starling are repressed, with the film concentrating on Starling's need to deal with her father's death.

18. Terrence Rafferty, "The Current Cinema: Moth and Flame," *New Yorker*, 25 February 1991, 87–88.

19. Carol J. Clover, "Her Body, Himself: Gender in the Slasher Film," *Representations*, no. 20 (Fall 1987): 187–228.

20. Starling was widely perceived by the viewers to be unfeminine. She was variously referred to in her role as an FBI recruit. Although Orion's publicity materials described her as "gutsy," repeating verbatim studio handout sheets is taboo among reviewers; equally unsettling might have been the unconscious connection between that adjective and Lecter's idiosyncratic diet. Here, however, Starling was variously relabeled to be "tenacious," "sturdy," "tough," "resourceful," "persistent," "ambitious," "driven." *The Silence of the Lambs* publicity materials, Orion Pictures (SLfile); "Cart," *"Silence of the Lambs,"* 109.

21. Thomas Harris, *The Silence of the Lambs* (New York: St. Martin's, 1988).

22. Rafferty, "Current Cinema," 87–88.

23. Peter Travers, "Snapshots from Hell: *The Silence of the Lambs*," *Rolling Stone*, 7 March 1991, 87–88.

24. Denby, "Something Wilder," 60–61.

25. Chuck Smith, "Hollywood Horror," *Vanguard*, 19 April 1991 (SLfile).

26. Hoberman, "Skin Flick," 61.

27. Stuart Klawans, "Films," *Nation*, 25 February 1991, 246–47.

28. Powers, "Skin Deep," 27.

29. Smith, "Hollywood Horror."

30. Richard A. Blake, "Visions of Evil," *America* 64, no. 10 (16 March 1991): 292. *Commonweal*'s reviewer implied the film was about Faust and Mephisto. The *Rolling Stone* headline said the film had "snapshots from hell."

31. Margaret R. Miles, *Carnal Knowing: Female Nakedness and Religious Meaning in the Christian West* (New York: Vintage Books, 1989).

32. Miles, *Carnal Knowing*, 12 and xi.

33. Vincent Canby, "Methods of Madness in 'Silence of the Lambs,'" *New York Times*, 14 February 1991, C-17.

34. Salamon, "Film."

35. Taubin in Kennedy, "Writers on the Lamb."

36. Reviewers did at times discuss him not only as monstrous but as alien or as an extraterrestrial.

37. In *Alice Doesn't: Feminism, Semiotics, Cinema* (Bloomington: Indiana University Press,1984), Teresa de Lauretis' analysis of narrativity and gender uses the oedipal myth with its stories of the Sphinx and the Minotaur as part of her argument about patriarchy's construction of desire. This odd coincidence is not particularly troublesome to explain since the equation is widely known through feminist discourse, and Taubin and Hoberman both are familiar with that discourse. We do not need to assume anything more than that common social and discursive networks provoked this conjunction of terms.

38. Arnold I. Davidson, "Sex and the Emergence of Sexuality," *Critical Inquiry* 14, no. 1 (Autumn 1987): 16–48, writes that it was through psychiatry that a split was made between anatomical sex and psychological sex. Medicalization takes over, investigating for visual evidence of sex both externally and internally.

39. Hoberman, "Skin Flick," 61.

40. Barbara Creed, "Horror and the Monstrous-Feminine: An Imaginary Abjection," *Screen* 27, no. 1 (January–February 1986): 44–70.

41. Sheehan, "Overcooked Lambs," 29–30.

42. And as psychoanalysis as a discourse begins its dissemination.

43. Klawans, "Films," 246–47.

44. The image was derived from the novel but appeared even during publicity generated while the film was in production. Its potency is obvious from the fact that the ad campaign won an award for the best movie poster of the year. Eithne Johnson informs me that the posters used Dali's "punning" picture of women to create the skull. Furthermore, moths and butterflies have a long-standing association with the vagina. No reviewer, however, made note of either.

45. Klawans, "Films," 246–47; Smith, "Hollywood Horror."

46. Mary Douglas, *Purity and Danger: An Analysis of the Concepts of Pollution and Taboo* (1966; rpt.,London: Ark Paperbacks,1984), 122.

47. Richard Jennings, quoted in David J. Fox, "Gays Decry Benefit Screening of 'Lambs,'" *Los Angeles Times*, 4 February 1991 (SLfile).

10

Hitchcock in Texas

Intertextuality in the Face of Blood and Gore

AT THE UNIVERSITY of Texas at Austin, I teach a course in Cult Movies which is really devoted to introducing my students to various theories of how readers use texts cognitively, sociologically, and psychologically. Since I live in Austin, Texas, I could scarcely avoid teaching *The Texas Chain Saw Massacre* (Tobe Hooper, USA, 1974), although written descriptions and word of mouth had made the prospect of actually watching the film more dreaded than anticipated. Watching a family of men attack four youngsters who happen to stumble into their home, presumably then using their bodies for Texas barbecue, did not excite me.

Indeed, the first viewing of the text affronted my feminist sensibilities. I was outraged by the images of abuse of both men and women, and at that point in my viewing career—raised on art cinema and Hollywood films, with only a few aggressive avant-garde texts as comparable in their onslaughts on the human body—I was, well, shocked! The class discussion was lively, however, and the movie seemed to serve a useful pedagogical purpose of questioning the social effects of cult movie behavior. Moreover, Robin Wood's excellent discussions of it as a comedy about the family worked well with my theoretical concerns.[1] Thus, I kept the film in for the second time I taught the course.

Something strange happened to me that time, however. It has been common for my students to laugh at "inappropriate" places in films, and we often discuss laughter as a cathartic response for viewers. The second time through *The Texas Chain Saw Massacre*, though, I began to see all sorts of intertextual references to Hitchcock's *Psycho*, primed in part no doubt by Wood's essay, which discusses *Psycho* as a predecessor of *The Texas Chain Saw Massacre* in criticisms of the family. These intertextual references included:

1. Both films represent the protagonists keeping their dead and "living dead" ancestors mummified in the house.

2. Both films are structured around a car drive into an isolated area where a house seems to offer protagonists a chance for reestablishing social contact, but eventually the house provides precisely the opposite: a very antisocial contact.

3. Both films imply that the oddness of the children is a result of family relations.

4. Both films suggest serial killing is random and a matter of chance intrusion by unwitting victims.

5. Both films employ the same architecture for the house, in the case of *The Texas Chain Saw Massacre* even playing with the viewers' expectations about the spatial locations from which the murderers will come.

6. Both films use birds as motifs to accompany the serial killers (*Psycho*'s Norman Bates enjoys taxidermy; *Texas Chain Saw*'s family members have a pet chicken they keep in a birdcage).

7. Both films use excessive close-ups of eyes matched to other round objects as stylistic transition points and, upon further analysis, in a symbolic chain of meaning. In the case of *Psycho*, Marion's eye is graphically matched to the shower drain; for *Texas Chain Saw Massacre*, Sally's eye is matched to a perfectly full moon.

These references are probably sufficient to establish my argument that *Psycho* is a *complex* intertextual source for *The Texas Chain Saw Massacre*. However, my reading of the allusions began to go even further. Here are another two comparisons:

8. Both films have the threatening protagonists clean up the women's bodies using a broom, stuff the bodies and brooms in vehicles, nearly drive off, but return to turn out the lights. This occurs in *Psycho* as part of the cleanup of Marion's murder; in *Texas Chain Saw Massacre*, the victim Sally tries to escape one of the sons but unwittingly runs into the Father's barbeque shop, whereupon the Father stuffs her live into a gunnysack to bring back to the house.

9. Both films shoot one of the key attacks from an overhead camera position. In the case of *Psycho* this is during the death of the detective; in *Texas Chain Saw Massacre*, the feeble attempt by Grandpa to whack Sally with the hammer has several overhead shots.

By the time I was seeing these allusions in my second viewing, I was laughing at scenes that had outraged me during my first viewing.

Moreover, I was laughing in places that were not even in the loosest sense likely to have been placed there for comic relief and catharsis. As Michael Goodwin in an early review of *The Texas Chain Saw Massacre* pointed out, this is a film without relief of its horror: "Most horror films work on a cyclical structure in which the 'scare scenes' are separated by neutral sections of exposition. This was a nonstop nightmare in which the moment-to-moment texture is just as loathsome as the big horror scenes. . . . Even the comic relief is dire."[2] Goodwin recounted that when the film was screened in a neighborhood theater in San Francisco in its early months, "people began to emerge from the theatre in a state of shock. Some of them made it to the bathroom before they threw up. Some didn't. The crowd was furious, the manager wasn't there to authorize refunds, and before things got straightened out a few punches were thrown" (p. 115).

This response to the film seems moral and appropriate. But what about mine? Especially since my class had now begun to worry about me. One way to reassure oneself that one is not perverted is to find a community of others—a subculture of like-minded individuals who mirror one's own nature. In my case I needed an interpretative community of fellow scholars who would also have the cultural capital to see the massive intertextual allusions to *Psycho* in *The Texas Chain Saw Massacre*.

I assumed I might find such a community in the reviewers of *The Texas Chain Saw Massacre* or, failing them, the scholarly commentators on the film. I checked the initial reviews of the film, starting in chronological order. The first one was from the *Hollywood Reporter*. Sure enough, John H. Dorr made a connection between the two films. He wrote,

> Made in Austin, Texas, largely by some very talented graduate students of the University of Texas, this Vortex/Henkel/Hooper Production is thoroughly professional, compelling, and gruesome. Squarely within the traditions of the "Psycho" genre, it is a fresh and extreme interpretation that should do for meat-eating what Hitchcock did for shower-taking. . . . "Everything means something I guess" is a throwaway line that nonetheless underscores the raw libidinal anarchy of this story and touches on the sense of humor lurking behind the mayhem.[3]

Good for a start: Dorr connected the film to Hitchcock, *Psycho*, and a humorous subtext, but nothing he wrote indicated that he really saw the array of parallels that I did. Nor did the writer for the next review, which came from the *Los Angeles Times* and whose author, Linda Gross (honestly), saw no humor at all and called the film "despicable."[4] *Variety*'s reviewer, "Mack," always a well-informed critic, made the Hitchcock/*Psycho* connection through *Psycho*'s own original intertext: Robert Bloch's novel about the incident in 1957 in which "Plainfield, Wis. authorities arrested handyman Ed Gein after finding dismembered bodies and disinterred corpses strewn all over his farmhouse."[5]

If my interpretative community was not among the reviewers, perhaps it would be with academics who should be particularly used to looking for such allusions as part of their critical behavior. Within a year, Julian Smith began the serious recital of parallels in an essay for the *Journal of Popular Film*.[6] Remarking on the film's humor, Smith recognized its already canonical place within the midnight movie scene then at its high point in America.[7] Smith also put *The Texas Chain Saw Massacre* into the formula underlying the second parallel I noted: "the introduction of normal individuals into a strange and terrifying environment via an interrupted auto journey. Such films rely on lonely, sinister houses approached by car. The classic example—and a film that may well have inspired *The Texas Chainsaw Massacre*—is Hitchcock's *Psycho*" (pp. 105–6). Although Smith remarked on several of the parallels that I saw, he isolated them from any specific thread of intertextual analysis. Yet, he, like me, could not resist a grudging response of humor. He concluded his essay:

> Before I describe the last image, I should explain that this is a film that tries to be fair and open-handed . . . to both sides—to the travelers and to those who bestill them. Sally escapes, which pleases us, but is there a way to toss a bone, so to speak, to the family we have visited? They are, after all, worthy of our respect. They have responded ingeniously to their culture and environment. They speak for the value of traditional crafts and the sanctity of private property. They have not gone on welfare. They have decorated their home in a way that reflects their personality (grandmother and the family dog have been dried and put on display, their armchairs are armchairs). Besides, anyone who expresses himself with a chainsaw can't be all bad. (P. 108)

In the same year as Smith's critical essay, *The Texas Chain Saw Massacre* appeared in the London Film Festival, elevating it to the status of art object—which might have promoted more readings of intertextual influence. Even before then, it had been put into the Museum of Modern Art's permanent collection, screened at the 1975 Cannes Film Festival with films by Schroeter and Fassbinder, and reviewed favorably by Rex Reed.[8] Guy Phelps in a 1976 essay, "Family Life," in *Sight and Sound* noted *Psycho*'s and *Texas Chain Saw Massacre*'s mutual intertextual debt to Ed Gein's story, but he went no further in detailing intertextual allusions.[9]

Stephen Koch's 1976 diatribe against the film in "Fashions in Pornography" for *Harper's Magazine* described *The Texas Chain Saw Massacre* as "unrelenting sadistic violence as extreme and hideous as a complete lack of imagination can possibly make it."[10] But his greater wrath was directed against any film buff who praised the film for its style and unrelenting form. Although Koch described the classic film buff's strategy of creating intertextual references as justifications for elevating a text to "art" from "trash," since the buffs praising the film were often arguing the film was just that—great trash—Koch was not moved to read it through a *Psycho* filter. Roger Greenspun rebuffed Koch in *Film Comment* in early 1977, but Greenspun spent most of the space of his article on cinematic homages to Hitchcock in Brian De Palma's *Carrie*, not on finding a similar potential in *Texas Chain Saw Massacre*.[11]

However, Wood in his famous and valuable essay "Return of the Repressed" picked out the third parallel in December 1976:[12] blaming the mother (or family) for the psychopathology of the killer. Wood's essay does much to trace a range of motifs in the formulas in which both *Psycho* and *The Texas Chain Saw Massacre* operate. Wood would have it that *Texas Chain Saw Massacre* is a "hideous parody of domesticity" (p. 12). Thus, Wood's primary intertext is to the family and not specifically to *Psycho*.

By 1977, *Texas Chain Saw Massacre* had been connected to other intertexts besides the representation of the family: Mary Mackey in the leftist journal *Jump Cut* read it as having "origins in class difference" and saw the chicken in the birdcage as "symbolizing, perhaps, the female principle trapped and fed on by the family." Sally's leap out the window recalled for Mackey the suicide in *The Birth of a Nation*.[13] Tony

Williams for *Movie* read *Texas Chain Saw Massacre* and other family horror films as part of the American myth of the degeneration of the hunter.[14]

By now, I have come to the end of the 1970s, some five years after the film's release and elevation to the status of an object of intellectual scholarship, and certainly to a time of a devoted interpretative community of scholars of Hitchcock ready to read Hitchcockian influences into films. Somewhere further on in the 1980s, I am sure, all of the intertextual parallels I have seen (and possibly many more) were seen by someone. But I have not found an interpretative community to mirror me and authorize my laughter.

What can I conclude? That I remain a perverted reader? I hope not. I could justify the interpretations I have created by appealing to standing scholarly protocols for making interpretative arguments. These include:

1. *The Authorial Influence Warrant.* After all, Tobe Hooper acknowledges watching *Psycho* when working on *Texas Chain Saw*.[15]
2. *The New Criticism Warrant.* The textual evidence "speaks" for itself.
3. *The Cultural Discursive Structure Warrant. Texas Chain Saw Massacre* is an interesting permutation of a series of discourses operating and transforming around the family and serial killing between 1960 and 1975.[16]

All of those arguments are valuable and would make significant essays. Yet this essay has focused on me, as a perverted reader. Here I am more interested in why I (or any other reader) might make this interpretative move rather than in arguing for some historical or critical validity for the comparison. The issues of real influence—authorial or discursive—are not the point of this essay. The issues of textual and contextual evidence and proof are not the point of this essay.

The surface justification, of course, for my reading is that I have been primed to make this interpretation by the intertexts of the Bloch novel and the direct influence of *Psycho*. But that does not explain why I should find these intertextual references funny. According to Robert Stam, Robert Burgoyne, and Sandy Flitterman-Lewis' reading of Julia Kristeva's interpretation of Mikhail Bakhtin's notion of intertextuality, intertextuality is the "transposition of one or more systems of signs into

another, accompanied by a new articulation of the enunciative and de-
notative position."[17] That rearticulation, however, does not assume
functions of cognition or affect for the reading subject who experiences
or creates the transposition.

Research on intertextuality has focused on types of intertextuality,
but little work has been accomplished on the functions of intertextuality for the reader or why a reader might be primed or cued to take up a
particular function. In the case of *The Texas Chain Saw Massacre*, I would
assert that I have been cognitively primed to make this humorous interpretation by several other contextual/intertextual situations:

1. Humor has long been associated with *The Texas Chain Saw Massacre*, from Wood's remarks about it as a family comedy to numerous
cartoons, jokes, and comic skits. The images of the main characters, especially the brother who wields the chain saw, are part of American
iconography and are routinely used for satire. *The Texas Chain Saw Massacre* is as ubiquitous in the American landscape as McDonald's.

2. Humor has also been long associated with Hitchcock. Since the
1950s and 1960s television programs, the text "Hitchcock-as-auteur"
has had a connotation of having a morbid sense of humor.[18] As Robert
Kapsis points out, Andrew Sarris' 1960 review of *Psycho* counsels
watching it a second time for "the macabre comedy inherent in the conception of the film."[19] Allusions to Hitchcock texts are now available to
be associated with the prospects of irony, parody, and the comic. Thus,
despite Wood's appeal in the opening sentence of his book *Hitchcock's
Films* that we take Hitchcock seriously, we can't take Hitchcock "seriously"—or at least only seriously.[20]

Of course, cognitive priming is only part of the matter. As Freud
notes about jokes, the economies of expenditure of energy are related to
inhibition—either preventing an inhibition from being constructed or
circumventing an inhibition already present. I do not have space in this
essay to draw out the psychoanalytical mechanisms at stake, but obviously my personal invoking of the intertext of *Psycho* has been a means
to defend myself from the sadomasochistic fantasies I am also constructing in viewing the text. By using the intertextual frame "Tobe
Hooper has used Hitchcock's *Psycho* as an intertext for *Texas Chain Saw
Massacre* and I am smart enough to see this," I am constructing for myself the role of a listener to a joke I am attributing to Hooper. Thus, I become complicit with Hooper in the mechanisms of a tendentious joke,
rather than the joke's victim—the "average" viewer of the movie. I can

laugh at the intertextual jokes rather than end up assaulted by the non-stop intensity of the plot.

I do not suppose that everyone laughing during *The Texas Chain Saw Massacre* is laughing for the reason that I have just suggested. The operations of the economies of the comic and the joke, particularly in the face of blood and gore, are quite complex. However, I would conclude by noting that scholars have produced substantial work on the types of intertextuality. Yet we have done very little work on the functions of intertextuality for the viewing subject. This is a worthy challenge as we try to sort out the political effects of texts on social subjects. The process of intertextuality clearly serves cognitive functions: we comprehend texts based on the series of other texts in which we insert the one we are viewing. Intertextuality also serves sociological functions such as the one implied by Koch's remarks: intertextuality permits scholars to align texts with other texts for the purposes of praising them as art or denigrating them as trash. Finally, intertextuality obviously serves affective functions, here to give me cultural capital and to let me laugh when I see the horror and humor of Hitchcock in Texas.

NOTES

1. Robin Wood, "Return of the Repressed," *Times Educational Supplement*, no. 3213 (31 December 1976), 12. A longer version is in *Film Comment* 14 (July–August 1978): 24–31, and becomes "An Introduction to the Horror Film." Also see "The American Film Comedy from *Meet Me in St. Louis* to *The Texas Chainsaw Massacre*," *Wide Angle* 3, no. 2 (1979): 5–11.

2. Michael Goodwin, "A Real Nightmare Makes a Great Horror Film," *Village Voice*, 9 February 1976, 115.

3. John H. Dorr, "*The Texas Chain Saw Massacre*," *Hollywood Reporter*, 29 October 1974, 3–4.

4. Linda Gross, "'Texas Massacre' Grovels in Gore," *Los Angeles Times*, 30 October 1974, sect. 4, 14.

5. "Mack," *Variety*, 6 November 1974. The only other early review in the *Motion Picture Product Digest* took *Texas Chain Saw Massacre* to be based on a 1973 event, exploiting its horror potentials; "The Texas Chain Saw Massacre," *Motion Picture Product Digest* 2, no. 12 (13 November 1974): 47.

6. Julian Smith, "Getting Stuck in America: Two Interrupted Journeys," *Journal of Popular Film* 5, no. 2 (1976): 95–108.

7. Michael Wolff, "What Do You Do at Midnight? You See a Trashy Movie," *New York Times*, 7 September 1975, sect. 2, 17.

8. Stephen Koch, "Fashions in Pornography: Murder as an Expression of Cinematic Chic," *Harper's Magazine* 253 (November 1976), 108. Apparently it was given by Hooper, not particularly solicited by MoMA as described by Koch. Roger Greenspun, "Carrie, and Sally and Leatherface among the Film Buffs," *Film Comment* 13 (January 1977): 14–17.

9. Guy Phelps, "Family Life," *Sight and Sound* 45, no. 2 (1976): 84–85.

10. Koch, "Fashions in Pornography," 110.

11. Greenspun, "Carrie, and Sally and Leatherface," 14–17. The mummified ancestor parallel is briefly mentioned in the BFI's November 1976 *Monthly Film Bulletin*. John [undecipherable in copy], "Texas Chain Saw Massacre, The," *Monthly Film Bulletin* 43, no. 515 (November 1976): 258.

12. Wood, "Return of the Repressed," 12.

13. Mary Mackey, "The Meat Hook Mama, the Nice Girl, and Butch Cassidy in Drag," *Jump Cut*, no. 14 (1977): 12–14.

14. Tony Williams, "American Cinema in the '70s: *The Texas Chainsaw Massacre*," *Movie*, no. 25 (Winter 1977/78): 12–16.

15. Tobe Hooper describes watching *Psycho* before making *The Texas Chain Saw Massacre* in Goodwin, "Real Nightmare Makes a Great Horror Film," 115.

16. For example, while I was working on this essay, Walter Metz pointed out to me that many of the parallels that I have seen in *The Texas Chain Saw Massacre* are about the maintenance of life, against the fact of death in *Psycho*. Why this should be would be interesting to consider, particularly in light of the transformation of this strand of the horror film with the release of *Halloween* in 1978.

17. Robert Stam, Robert Burgoyne, and Sandy Flitterman-Lewis, *New Vocabularies in Film Semiotics: Structuralism, Post-Structuralism and Beyond* (New York: Routledge, 1992), 204.

18. See Robert E. Kapsis, *Hitchcock: The Making of a Reputation* (Chicago: University of Chicago Press, 1992), 25–41.

19. Kapsis, *Hitchcock*, 64.

20. Robin Wood, *Hitchcock's Films* (New York: Paperback Library, 1965), 7.

PART IV

INTERPRETATION AND THE REPRESENTATION OF THE REAL

11

Securing the Fictional Narrative as a Tale of the Historical Real

The Return of Martin Guerre

IN THE FIRST sentence of his review of *The Return of Martin Guerre*,[1] Vincent Canby wrote: "This is, as they say, a true story."[2] Given contemporary philosophy and historiography's skepticism over using, much less combining, the words *true* and *story*, it seems pertinent to consider the ideological and psychoanalytical implications of our narrativization of the historical real and our repetitive compulsion to appropriate, mobilize, dramatize, and yet to fix in that movement the past for the present—"to fix" in a double sense as in "to halt" and "to cure." If narrative is understood as "taking place" and as operating on trajectories of desires, it is also a framing, an aggressive act of holding "in place," and a settling of those desires into their proper spaces. Additionally, if the narrativization of the past is symptomatic of the subject's search for a mastery and coherence of self and other and self-as-signifying, doubly pertinent, then, are cases of films which for all purposes might remain neatly entrenched in fictional narrative but are claimed for the historical real as "authentic," "realistic," a "true story." What is the meaning of saying: "This is, as they say, a true story"?

I am interested in exploring not only Canby's remark but also the American popular critical response to *The Return of Martin Guerre*. Specifically, the questions that mobilize my plot are: How was this fictional narrative secured as a tale of the historical real? What intertextual and textual processes and what ideological and psychoanalytical drives promoted the double fixing of a commercially released art film as some kind of "true story"? What has this to do with "who needs narrative"? The answers, I think, are embedded in—or perhaps, really, on the surface of—Canby's sentence.

I

The American critical response to *The Return of Martin Guerre* was generally positive. Of the nineteen reviews or review-background articles that I sampled, only one would fall into the "thumbs down" category. I shall have more to say about these reviews later, but for now I would like to localize what the American critics laid out as significant features of the film. In particular, a contradiction develops in their descriptions, and it is around and through that contradiction that I would like to explore the methodical neurosis of our compulsion to fix history.

Canby thought *The Return of Martin Guerre* was a "social history of an unusually rich sort." He wrote that Gérard Depardieu, who played one of the Martins, looked the way a sixteenth-century peasant should look and that the film was shot in southwest France, near the place where the events represented occurred between 1542 and 1561. Canby also remarked that the cinematographer lit the film in "the tones of amber, olive and umber associated with Brueghel's paintings of 16th-century village life." While pointing backward to all of this "historical accuracy," Canby at the same time referenced the present by claiming that the film had an "immediacy." Although set in the past, it speaks to us.

Annette Insdorf suggested that the film "gives new life to a legendary folk tale by insisting on its 'timelessness.'. . . With visual compositions that recall Flemish painting and music that blends medieval sounds with electronic instrumentation, the film conveys the flavor of the Middle Ages as well as the modernity of the tale's implications." Stanley Kauffmann said that for artful historical films—this one included—one is struck with the anachronistic problem of how a camera could be there to photograph the events: the film "enters a world of data communication to which it doesn't belong."

These responses suggest at least one contradiction. The critics speak of the believability and historical accuracy of certain details but also of a timelessness, a universality, something that transcends historical time. So one asks, can this film be both specific in time and place and also universal? How did the film seem to achieve a sense of historical accuracy and also seem to have some universality?

Intertextuality seems a useful notion for explaining this experience. Whether or not we believe that our knowledge of the world is totally mediated by language, few would argue that once we enter into representations of the real, we are embarked within semiotic activities and, hence, into all sorts of language systems. Our sense of the real becomes mediated by and through specific sociohistorical discourses. In fact, other texts suggest what the real is to us, and every kind of a text is in some sense a representation of the real. In English, the word *representation* means to "re-present" something else, but it also has a possibility of meaning "to refer to." That is, in a representation the original is never there but always absent, a representation is a referring to some authentic or original real. The semiotic process, then, is a compulsive attempt to point to and to fix the real, a kind of valiant but vain talking cure for the split subject. This proposition about semiotics is well known in our poststructuralist era. Despite this, however, semiotic gestures continue—not the least of which are conference papers and articles about semiotic gestures.

Whole sets of knowledges are accepted as providing us with our notions of the real. These include scientific discourses, popular knowledges, religious beliefs, and the kinds of pointings we produce from paintings, sculptures, novels, and, of course, from films. Let me suggest an instance of how crucial this intertextuality is in merely comprehending a narrative. When we read a story or view a film, no innate comprehension occurs. Even so simple an act as organizing the chronology of events requires the intertextual discourse available from scientific texts about time. Specifically, Western religions and Western science assume that geocentered time has particular characteristics. It is unidirectional, continuous, regular, and unique. Other ways of thinking about time have existed in other cultures, some believing that time is cyclical, returning to an eternal beginning.

This conjunction between Western religious and geocentered scientific discourses about temporality is a powerful one—these intertextual discourses not only inflect the production of our narrative texts but also their reception. Obviously, because of the potentials of plot manipulation, story events can be put in nonchronological order. In addition, temporal gaps are common for dramatic intensification. It is not uncommon, either, for texts to represent the same story event two or more times—motivated usually as partial or conflicting accounts of that event.

Martin Guerre can be segmented into forty-one plot scenes.[3] Scenes 1 through 4 occur on "one Sunday in August in 1542" in the small village of Artigat when the very youthful Martin Guerre weds, but apparently does not bed, the similarly young Bertrande de Rols, consolidating the properties and wealth of two peasant families. Scene 5 depicts the arrival some eighteen years later of Jean de Coras, a magistrate from the region, who has entered the village to conduct an investigation, to make an account of and to account for the past. He proceeds to take the oral testimony of Bertrande, now an older woman. Scenes 5 through 27 alternate between this moment of the magistrate's lawful and forceful acquisition of a tale of the past and a series of flashbacks motivated as Bertrande's story of the families' history. Represented in visual images, then, are the villagers' ridicule of Martin at Candlemas when no children are produced from the union, as well as Bertrande's humiliation because she remains with Martin; the successful use of exorcism to cure Martin of impotence; the birth of a son but the continuing emotional distance of Martin; Martin's quarrel with his father; Martin's disappearance for eight years, contributing to his parents' death and removing Bertrande from her social position as wife of the major village landowner. Then a man arrives—I shall label him Martin 2— whom, after some hesitation, the villagers and Bertrande accept as the "returned" Martin. This is the first return of Martin Guerre.

The changes in Martin 2 seem positive: he is now the center of the family social life through his storytelling, his ability to read and write, and his acts as a good husband and father. Any questions about his identity are quelled through his apparent knowledge of so many facts of the past public and private life of the villagers. A daughter is born. For some three years or so, all goes well, until two vagabonds enter the village and declare that the "real" Martin lost a leg in a war and that Martin 2 is Arnaud from Tiel. Martin 2 requests an accounting from his uncle Pierre of the profits from Martin's lands during his absence. The conversation deteriorates when Martin 2 threatens to turn to the law to obtain these assets, and Pierre responds through the authority of the vagabonds' insinuations that Martin 2 is an impostor. The mood of the village becomes acrimonious as sides are chosen, and Martin's cousins physically attack Martin 2, trying to murder him.

In scene 28 Coras concludes the trial, arguing that no document— oral or written—exists that would prove Martin 2 is not who he says is, that would split the body of this man from the name of Martin Guerre. Furthermore, Pierre is fined for slandering Martin 2. Scene 29 shows Martin 2 and Bertrande in bed that evening. The following morning, in scene 30, Pierre, Martin's cousin, and the village priest arrive with a document that they claim Bertrande has signed, saying this is not the real Martin. Scenes 31 through 39 constitute the taking and weighing of more testimony in the second trial, with the surprise appearance at just the last moment of a one-legged man—for our purposes Martin 3—who is finally declared the "true" Martin, stripping the appellation from Martin 2 and affixing, halting, and curing the unstable relation between proper name and body. This is the second return of Martin Guerre.

The trial's drama has centered on varieties of documents—physical, written, and oral—as well as hypothesized explanations of the individuals' actions, including witchcraft, greed, bribery, and sexual desire, to establish the "facts." In particular, the village priest is represented as supportive of doctrines of witchcraft, whereas Coras is impressed, and in some sense awed, by Martin 2's rationality and appeal to logic. Martin 2's defeat finally comes when Coras discovers a contradiction in Martin 2's storytelling. Upon Martin 3's arrival, Martin 2 denies ever seeing him before, but later Martin 2 explains Martin 3's knowledge of intimate domestic details as based on information from conversations with Martin 2. The incoherent discourse about the past sunders the bond of name and body, but the court reattaches the sign to a newly returned Martin Guerre. Scenes 40 and 41, in a classic denouement, cover Coras' final questioning of Bertrande, seeking what she really knew and her interiorized motivations, as well as Martin 2's public execution. A short voice-over postscript informs us that Coras "found this prodigious imposture so awesome that he recorded it for posterity." We learn as well that twelve years later during the St. Bartholomew's Day massacre, Coras was hung, "a victim of his Protestant convictions."

The digressory accounting of the "facts" is a good instance of the function of intertextual discourses in mediating comprehension of semiotic systems. In particular, *Martin Guerre* displays some very common characteristics of Western cinematic narratives: the technique of flashbacks not only provides critical expositional information but also clothes that information in all the glory of the visual rather than the dry oral testimony of Bertrande. Our film experience also is quite at odds with what it might have been had the events been ordered sequentially.

Actually, not only have intertextual discourses on "real time" mediated the filmic experience, so too have discourses on narratives, character psychology, and the cinematic apparatus. Because of knowledges of the way a camera works, the processes of printing, and the potentials of editing, no spectator is surprised when films present events out of order, in fast or slow motion, with gaps, or multiple times. The technological apparatus has permitted the representation of the events that way.

Additionally, Gerard Genette explains that "public opinion" provides a norm against which events in a text are judged for their plausibility: "To understand the behavior of a character (for example), is to be able to refer it back to an approved maxim, and this reference is perceived as a demonstration of cause and effect."[4] In the case of *The Return of Martin Guerre,* Coras acts for the reader as a textual interrogator, especially as he seeks to correlate Bertrande's behavior with some accepted rationale, in particular trying to locate it in a discourse about woman's sexual desire. As Genette suggests, this attempt by "public opinion" to locate is ideological, or as Roland Barthes might express it, it is the desire for a myth which "transforms history into nature" so that history "is immediately frozen."[5]

Such a fixing, securing, or pinning down of the past as coherent is attempted not for the past's sake but for the sake of the present—such a representation appears to ward off the threatening anxiety of having to recognize the inability of an individual to control and master the self-as-subject. In this way, Coras' standing-in-for-the-reader is not innocent; he functions to propose and affirm contemporary twentieth-century bourgeois and patriarchal ideologies of character motivation, cultural stereotypes, and sexual difference.

So the intertextuality I have in mind is not simply a moment in a text or some relation between two texts, but rather a fundamental and unceasing spectatorial activity, the semiotic action of processing a filmic narrative by repeated referencing and referring to other texts. Intertextuality as understood from a poststructuralist perspective is a constant and irretrievable circulation of textuality, a returning to, a pointing toward, an aggressive attempt to seize other documents. The results of this procedure of referencing other texts are also complicitly and irrevocably circular and ideological. For although the activity of intertextuality is neutral and without cessation, none of the discourses invoked nor the real is ever fixed, halted, and cured but only referred to, compulsively and repetitiously.[6]

II

One of my questions has been why *The Return of Martin Guerre* managed to secure in its U.S. critical reception the reputation of being historically specific yet universal. Understanding the processes of intertexuality is useful in beginning to answer that question. In a more substantial way, I would return to Canby's sentence, "This is, as they say, a true story," to focus on "as they say" as a gesture provoking intertextuality. The "they" is, no doubt, no specific group of people; "they" are a set of texts in circulation in the social formation that give authenticity to the notion that "this" is "a true story"; "they" are its adjacent texts, including publicity articles, talk show interviews, advertising, and, of course, reviews.

"They" are something else as well. For the "they" of Canby is ironically, and with some subterfuge, not only a set of texts but also "me"— Vincent Canby—the author of a text which will be read by hundreds of thousands of potential filmgoing spectators. "This is, as they/I say, a true story."

How does Canby know that "this" film is an instance of "as they say, a true story"? It might seem simple to pin down this "they" to a single text—the press book distributed with the film.[7] In fact, Canby's review was not unique. Of the nineteen reviews sampled, fifteen specifically mentioned that the film was based on past events, two reviews clearly did not, and two were somewhat ambiguous. The two reviewers who ignored the "truth" of the story were Roger Ebert, who stressed *Martin Guerre* as a "perceptive mystery, a charming love story," and Janet Maslin, who doted on the congruence between the body of Depardieu and the role of Martin 2. Now if the "they" is circulating and replacing "I," and "I" replaces "they," from where did the press book derive its knowledges? In part from social historian Natalie Zemon Davis, who served—we are told in four of the film reviews, in two book reviews, an interview, and the film's credits—as "historical consultant." But also from a number of other texts, ranging through the genres of two novels, a play, an operetta, and the original Jean de Coras' narrative. His story, the film tells us, came from the oral testimony of the participants who recounted the events during the two trials. All we have as "origin" is another text: the oral history and testimony of "eye" witnesses.

Turning back to the present, I would note a second feature of the reviews besides their general claim that *Martin Guerre* recounts a true

story. The reviews also emphasized that the film had specific characteristics making it historically authentic. These included facts about the
film's production as well as one other set of texts. Ten of the reviewers
considered this film authentic in part because it reminded them of other
representations created in the same period. Such a proposition derives
from the notion that somehow Brueghel, La Tour, and Flemish paintings should be considered reasonably authentic representations of the
people of the sixteenth century because of the adjacent date of their
manufacture. Since we do not assume that early Egyptian paintings
faithfully mimic real Egyptians, our assumption that Brueghel's or the
Flemish paintings might do so must result from our pointing to other
texts: discourses on art history. Brueghel is, "as they say," a "representational" painter. Yet our knowledge of this period's visible, physical
surface is dependent wholly on paintings and sculptures: we have—as
Kauffmann reminds us—no photographs.

I stress the point of intertextuality so much, particularly for this
film, because of the critical attention the reviewers paid to what might
be called surface or physical or visible features: that is, features such as
props, sets, costumes, lighting, bodies, and bodily gestures. They described its physical world as authentic and consequently true; they
pointed to and fixed its visible world as specifically historical. What has
been used by the film and its contextualizing discourses to authenticate
its claim to be a "true story" is, as one reviewer put it, "a surface sheen."

My subtext may already be apparent. Even if one could say that the
film in some sense really did represent completely the physical or visible world of the 1500s, it would be said within an ideology that what is
visible is what is real. The gesture of saying, "this is, as they say, a true
story," has been complemented by texts pointing to the authentic as
"visible," unmediated, with knowledges apparent to the perceiving
subject's eye and ear—from "eye and ear witnesses": the oral testi-
monies of the villagers and Bertrande de Rols as recorded by Coras.

Thus, on the one hand, this film and its adjacent texts promote spectatorial activities of reference to other "authentic" texts, hoping to secure for a fictional narrative a status of being a tale of the historical real,
of fixing it as a coherent representation and of bonding the body of the
past and its name. This referencing is primarily accomplished through
pointers related to texts about the visible or physical world. In fact, this
process duplicates the film's obsession with the returning Martin Guerres—where matching witnesses' accounts of visible bodily features is

considered critical empirical evidence in establishing Martin's identity. At the same time, however, and perhaps more significantly, aspects other than visible authenticity can very easily, by something of a parasitic attachment, be dragged along as seemingly part of the real. Not the least of these is the fictional narrative as a distortion through elision, conversion, emphasis, and incompleteness of the real. Although I previously mentioned ironically, I would now say that only Ebert's review resisted this fallacious procedure, refusing as it did to consider *The Return of Martin Guerre* as other than "a charming love story."

On the other hand, although this film and its readers may aggressively attempt to secure *The Return of Martin Guerre* for the historical real through surrounding texts ("this is, as they say"), its "realism" is also pursued through the film's narrative structure and narrational procedures. Although I do not have space to consider all of the textual features operating, two seem particularly significant: the voice-over narrator and the flashbacks.

As indicated above, plot scenes 1 through 4 represent the major events of Martin and Bertrande's marriage day. More particularly, over the third scene when a marriage broker arrives, the voice-over narrator says the following: "You won't regret having taken the time to follow this narrative, for it is neither a tale of adventure nor an extravagant fantasy that you will hear but a true story in all its purity. It all began on one Sunday in August in 1542." We must add to our list of "theys" this narration as one of those "saying" this is a true story. But the words of this narration are only of minor note in the more subtle operations. Beside the statement's content is its procedure. For one thing, the narration is highly specific. It is not "sometime in the sixteenth century" but Sunday, August 1542. It isn't just any place in France but Artigat. And the voice of this narrator is masculine. It is a voice of some authority, being neither weak nor high-pitched, and it is nondiegetic: this masculine narrator never appears in the story itself. Because the narrator is not a participant, a typical reader would tend to assume that the narrator has no motivation for lying to us. Not only that, but through "public opinion," patriarchal structures, narrational conventions, and intertextual knowledges, the narrator is positioned as all-knowing. Thus the function of this voice-over, nondiegetic narration is to get us to believe what it says.

Beginning a film with a voice-over, nondiegetic narrator is a common device, and sometimes this function is served by intertitles. Those intertitles take on a kind of distance from the events which are embedded and presented as diegetic. Because framing information is a "separate" text, at a distance and not part of the enclosed story, it can easily take on an authenticity in comparison with that which it embeds. When this voice-over of masculine authority assures (or perhaps reassures) us of an educational value of this true story, it doubles and redoubles its claims.

Thus the voice-over narrator acts here in a subtle way as a textual device compulsively repeating, "this is, as 'I' say, a true story." And, equally subtly, so do the flashbacks. In the fifth scene, Coras, the magistrate, begins an interrogation of Bertrande, who recalls—in chronological sequence—the events following her marriage. Alternating between the questioner and filmic visualizations of Bertrande's oral speech, scenes 6 through 26 represent the events leading up to and including the dispute between Martin 2 and Pierre over the truth of Martin 2's identity and of Pierre's greed. Each accuses the other of lying. In some sense, scene 26 is the cause of scene 5: village life has been so destabilized over the issue of property rights that the state, in the form of Coras, must enter the conflict between the two versions of "the true story." The rest of the film, scenes 27 through 41, operates as a consequence of scene 5.

I am interested in the fact that much of the film's exposition used later to authenticate Martin 2's claims relies upon a reader's matching Bertrande's visions and Martin 2's oral references to the events represented in those visions. Specifically, scenes 6, 8, 10, 11, 13, 15, 16, and 18 through 26 are motivated as visual versions of her oral testimony— from the woman's voice. I would ask, why flashbacks? Why not just have Bertrande testify? Yes, it is pleasurable (from conventional standards and psychoanalytical processes) to "watch" Bertrande's discourse for fifteen or thirty minutes. But more pertinent to my analysis is that the flashbacks, by which we seem to "see" the events, lend them some implicit authenticity. The visible is conventionally more believable than the aural. Furthermore, the way the flashbacks are put together tends to elide the fact that this is Bertrande's testimony, one version of the story, perhaps abetted by stereotypes of sixteenth-century peasant women. Very little overlap exists between Bertrande's or Coras' voice and the space of the images, as the sound track rapidly converts to a diegetically synchronized voice. That is, the image-sound coordination as well as Bertrande's testimony under oath seems, if not actually to authenticate the images, at least not to raise the possibility of their being anything but what they seem to be—representations, a fixing of visual space as narrative real. By diminishing the role of Bertrande's voice and by using the ideology of an apparent truth in the visible, the flashbacks operate much as the adjacent texts and the voice-over narrator to say, "this is/was, as they/I say, a true story." Nevertheless, in spite of the activity of intertextuality as well as the textual devices of a voice-over narrator and flashbacks that claim this film is pointing to, referring to, historical authenticity, there remains a contradiction in the critical response, one which, not surprisingly, overthrows this attempt to make coherent the name of "true story" and the body, *The Return of Martin Guerre*.

III

A period film points toward a particular moment and place, while a film that implies universality references a much wider body of time and space. How can both references exist simultaneously? The answer is, through a very typical strategy. The film implies that what's historical is a physical reality. It is the mise-en-scène, the props, the costumes, and the people that are historical. What is universal is "inside" or "beneath" this—essences of humanity and relations among people. What is really being claimed as universal and hence real is constant social relations and explanations of human beings. Physical particularities, though "true," provide only surface sheen; they are transitory; they are merely of the moment, and not the "real truth." Thus, a sign points to a sign that stands for another sign—the fixing, halting, curing of our desire to reference the real. That final sign is a "myth," a public opinion certified only by social contract and hegemonies of ideological discourses.

Martin Guerre can be said to propose two conflicting explanations of the significant "depth" relation, or "essence of humanity," upon which or from which social relations and institutions work and function: medieval Catholicism and bourgeois liberal humanism. Like our two returned Martins, the true identities of these ideologies (and their respective "universality") are at stake. In fact, however, just as the claim of historical authenticity in this film is questionable, so too is the narrative's purported explanation of the causal chain of events.

202 SECURING THE FICTIONAL NARRATIVE

The story's precipitating event is Martin 2's request for an accounting of assets, which provokes overt violence and the entrance of institutions to resolve the family's differences. Intriguingly, notions of the separation between the private sphere and the public are dissolved in the sequences of these events. The family cannot solve the dispute because it is not separated from the public; its very structure has been set up upon an economic contract—the marriage agreement. The family is an institution based in the economic sphere, incapable of settling its own dispute because it is within the problem. Yet the institution that is called in is not neutral either. In fact, in a major displacement of the final voice-over narration, this dispute—this war of the Guerres—is not merely about the truth of one potential patriarchy, but about dominance among institutions. At a transitional time when the Catholic church was losing sectors of its power to insurgent Protestants, and as the liberal state were assuming authority over the economic base, *Martin Guerre* traces wide disturbances in discourses of "the truth."

I have said that the final voice-over narration is significantly displaced, putting at the end of the film what is the narrative's teleological origin. In this conclusion which is also a beginning, our authoritative masculine nondiegetic narrator gives us only two small bits of information: he explains how the story managed to be recorded (Coras was so impressed with it) and informs us that in the religious persecutions twelve years later, Coras was killed: "a victim of his Protestant convictions. But as surely as death awaits all mortals, the spirit lives on forever."

Retrospectively, the opposition between the village priest and Coras reproduces the larger conflict. The narrative represents the priest as believing in witchcraft, demons, and spirits; he argues that Martin 2's actions have been controlled by the devil. Coras seeks other explanations, appealing, as the priest does, to public opinion: it is plausible that people have such good memories, that the past is a text that the subject can reference, and that Martin's logic and reasoning could come only from an innocent. In the denouement, Coras' final interrogation of Bertrande seeks a source or explanation for her testimony, which he finally provides for her through his suggestion that sexual desire is the cause. The Catholic church is thus associated with the irrational past, the judge with future rational humanism—which the narrator claims still exists.

Subtending the film, then, is the proposition that the conflict is over explaining the subject within the social. Now it is not by chance that it is Coras' record that remains for our history; it is not to the priest's account that we refer for our "true story." The film explicitly sides with Coras' version, his spirit, his rational, humanistic version of the subject as a unified speaking subject, cohering in mind, body, and speech. Yet Coras falls into the ideological difficulties of empiricism, taking the document to say what it appears to say, to match signs and referents. "This was and is, as they/I say, a true story." Strangely enough, "the true story" contradicts him (and itself and the reader) as the "true Martin" arrives in a deus ex machina climax.

IV

Yet I would agree that, in another sense, this is a true story. For *The Return of Martin Guerre* might well be said to represent history as an ideological struggle over power and hegemony whose actors are driven by instincts of desire and death. The film points to the real, or true, in the sense that it represents human beings within the social formation as split subjects. Anxiety about the subject's helplessness within this state of affairs, I would argue, compulsively propels the narrative's repetition, my own repetition as a reader analyzing it, and the drive to order the past.

Having said this, I need to step back once more, turning this film and my argument around one more time. Pierre Macherey has written:

> We understand then what we must seek in texts; not signs of their cohesion and of their autonomy, but the material contradictions which produce them and which are produced there in the form of conflicts. If literature is an objective reflection of reality, it is because literature is determined by the antagonisms which constitute it not as a totality, but as a historical and social material reality. Literature expresses these conflicts and adds to them an imaginary resolution; but these solutions, these compromises which are finally the texts, continue to bear the mark of the divisions which give them a real base, a reality, and also an interest.[8]

Although a number of Macherey's remarks are valuable, for my purposes two points stand out as I return to my questions about securing

204 SECURING THE FICTIONAL NARRATIVE

together narratives and the historical real and about who needs narratives and why. For one thing, Macherey assumes a relation between literature and the historical real, but with literature "add[ing] to [the material conflicts] an imaginary resolution." Although I have only implied how I might define a narrative, if I were to note one feature, it would be "resolution," if not outright closure. Macherey's comments also indicate that the major distinction between texts and the real is not any real coherence or autonomy in either case, but an imaginary coherence or autonomy for the textual—imaginary in the double sense of not real and pre-oedipal. If I have just said that this film does represent the real, it is because I have employed the process of intertextuality and have claimed the authority of my textual representation of the real (historical materialism and poststructuralism) in so doing. I have narrativized the historical real into a resolution of imaginary coherence in order to compare the propositions of the text before me with the text of the historical real which I believe to be "a true story." This compromise bears its mark in my circulating around and around "this was/is, as they/I say, a true story." I am securing my fictional narrative, this article, as a tale of the historical real as have *Martin Guerre* and its adjacent texts. Not content with allowing the fictional narrative to be the only narrative, the critics, the film, the voice-over diegetic narrator, and I have narrativized history. And, I would add, so has Macherey.

Macherey's remarks about imaginary resolutions, however, contain a gesture directed in a second way. Any text will bear the traces of its own compulsion to point to an imaginary coherence since its compromises "continue to bear the mark of the divisions" which produced them. Perhaps here Freud's observations about the compulsion to repeat will now make sense as more than one of the controlling motifs for this essay. It is in his later work in relation to the famous reformulation and postulation of the death instinct that he uses the concept of repetition compulsion as part of his proof.[9] The death instinct as aggressive, potentially directed outward or inward toward the self, operates in conflict with Eros, but also at times in conjunction. This instinct is functionally critical for cessation of tension but also, for Freud, for the survival of the species. Freud writes, for instance, that "order is a kind of compulsion to repeat" in which "one is spared hesitation and indecision."[10] In this thesis, sadism and masochism "contain an element distinct from sexuality in the form of a desire for mastery or subjugation."[11] The death instinct can also be seen in dreams, in the child's *fort-da* game,

and in any compulsive repetition where repetition is a form of dis-
charge which, when carried to extremes (that is, as a compulsion), functions "to restore a state that is historically primitive and also marked by
the total draining of energy, i.e., death." What is repeated and transformed rather than remembered is the repressed material. The neurotic
"repeats instead of remembering."[12] Freud considers masochism as
older than sadism, but when the instinct is directed aggressively against
the external world, sadism may be how we avoid our own self-destruc-
tion. In fact, it is the cohesion of an outward aggression and Eros that
permits our continued living. This sadism, Freud notes, is "accompanied by an extraordinarily high degree of narcissistic enjoyment, owing
to its presenting the ego with a fulfillment of the latter's old wishes for
omnipotence."[13]

In so many ways, while *Martin Guerre* displays the trajectories of
desire associated with Eros, it also aggressively turns outward and then
inward to try to master and order the Self's history, to order plot and
past, to contain separations of body and name, to restore, finally, a primitive and imaginary narcissistic state in which the subject is presumed
whole.

Peter Brooks applies the notion of compulsive repetition to the text
of *Great Expectations* and expands it to include both narrative structure
and the reader's relation to the narrative. For Brooks, "repetition is a
symbolic enactment referring back to unconscious determinants, progressive in that it belongs to the forward thrust of desire . . . but regressive in its points of reference."[14] The climax and resolution of a narrative becomes the "scene that decisively re-enacts both a return of the repressed and a return to the primal moment of childhood [that was
forgotten]" (p. 127). It is an attempt to master the past—which is ultimately the "return to the quiescence of the inorganic, of the non-tex-
tual," of death (p. 139). Hence Brooks argues that "*Great Expectations* is
exemplary in demonstrating both the need for plot and its status as deviance, both the need for narration and the necessity to be cured from
it": a desire to plot "the meaning of life," and when that proves unavailable, the condemnation to "repetition, rereading" (p. 140).

If Macherey and Brooks are correct, the resolution of a narrative
should still bear the marks of its primary divisions, pointing back to the
forgotten past, if not necessarily reproducing it. The opposition that an-
imates *Martin Guerre* is marked not only in the text, but also in the critical discourse in and surrounding the film. Is the real surface or

essence? How is it knowable? Here another aspect of Freud's work is of use: his revised understanding of anxiety in relation to the crises of the individual, whereby anxiety becomes a cause (not an effect). If the individual forecasts the possibilities of a dangerous situation, anxiety can be used as signal mechanism which the subject hopes will prevent the future difficulty. In terms of the psychic functions of narrative, telling stories may be pleasurable as they serve the aggressive instinct; they also may be acting as signals when the individual thinks the future holds the danger of the helplessness associated with loss of coherency as self. If narratives are about the past, they are also about the present and the future.

V

In Alfred Hitchcock's film *Stagefright*, the plot is structured around a flashback, but in the resolution of the film we discover that the flashback was a lie told by one of the protagonists who turns out to be the sought-after murderer. In *Martin Guerre*, I do not believe that the audience questions the testimony of Bertrande as it is presented. Yet the final encounter between Coras and Bertrande requires a reevaluation of this presumption. The conversation leaves a strong sense that Bertrande lied throughout the trials and either suspected or knew all along that Martin 2 was not her husband. Significant to this interpretation is the telling absence of any scenes in which Martin 2 and Bertrande discuss the events through which they are living.

If it is possible that Bertrande lied, then it is highly probable that all of her testimony and all of the flashbacks are colored, subjective, and incomplete. More broadly put, it is reasonable to conclude that the visible (as physical surface and as photograph) refers inadequately or not at all to the reality of the subject's discursive interiorized social utterances which motivate his or her actions and discourse in human relations; that the visible, through cinematic narrative, can point only subjectively and distortingly toward the real. Phrased in another way, all there is is surface, text, representation, rather than recollection, return, and reconstitution.

As deceptive as the subjective flashbacks and the omission of events is the implication of the climax, the imaginary resolution. Note that Martin 2 maintains his credibility by his knowledge and use of small details about the past—that is, surface features. In particular, for instance, he references Bertrande's accounts of events to authenticate his identity. The film tries to gain its credibility similarly. Using props, sets, costumes, and lighting to give the appearance of authenticity, of telling through these visible features that its representation of the past is the truth, it employs small details of the visible just as Martin 2 does in his attempt to secure his narrative fiction as a tale of the historical real. "This is/was, as they/I say, a true story."

But it turns out that Martin 2 lied as well, that according to all standards of judgment of the institutions, he was merely a simulacrum of Martin Guerre. If he lied, contradicting what he said he saw and said, then, as in the case of Bertrande, the truth of the story's fiction is suspect. And surface reality, the visible reality of cinema, may lie too: the potential for lying is something endemic to representations as semiotic systems. A cinema that relies on the visible or that requires intertextuality for its credibility is always involved in representations, and how can cinema not do this? Representations, while possibly referring to a historical real, will always be imaginary references and resolutions, "compromises," as Macherey says.

And once discourse can lie, can point elsewhere, and once the speaking subject can be elsewhere, then Western rational humanism meets its crisis. Is it by accident that a text so grounded in the visual real should also conclude itself by referring to the death of Coras-as-believer-in-narrative-as-historical-document? An imaginary resolution of coherence of name and body, torn asunder by the speaking subject as subjective and potential liar, symptomatically concludes in the return of the oral testimony of an omniscient nonbodied masculine narrator, compulsively and repetitiously "fixing" history. The narrative ends, doubly self-destructively, in the death not only of Martin 2 but also of Coras, the liberal humanist who hoped to account for the past and who stood in for us the viewers, who try unsuccessfully to know the truth through two trials, an ex post facto interrogation of Bertrande, and a final written history. It ends with the death of visible surface as document, in a cessation of desire to master the past as reproducible for the present, to retrieve narcissistically the self-as-signifying-and-unified. As a text built upon intertextual circulations, its origins continue to refer to, to point to, but not to recollect and remember as it asserts that Coras' essence lives on. Again, the repetitions symptomatic in the duplicating returns of Martin Guerre mark out this text's neurosis just as our own neuroses are marked out by vain attempts to fix by representing the text via intertextuality as historical real.

If I were to ask, then, "who needs narrative?" Freud would, I think, say, "everyone." The drive to narrativize the past and to secure the fictional tale as pointing to that historical real is understandable as a repetitious desire to fix, to halt and cure. It is the death instinct aligned with Eros, a signal anxiety of our time. In some sense, then, I can only end with a small final amending of Vincent Canby's sentence: "This is/was, as they/I say, maybe kind of a true story." That's the imaginary resolution that I desire for the end of this passage through the narrative.

NOTES

This essay is a revision of a lecture presented at the "Film: Who Needs Narrative?" Conference at the City University Graduate Center, New York, NY, 24 April 1987. I would like to thank participants for their comments. In particular, I thank Ann Kaplan and assure her that I do believe in history even if knowing it is somewhat complicated. Additionally, I thank Vincent Rocchio, whose thoughts about anxiety were very stimulating to me at just the right time.

1. *Le Retour de Martin Guerre,* produced by Société Française de Production Cinématographique, Société de Production de Films Marcel Dassault, and FR3; directed by Daniel Vigne; French release in May 1982; U.S. release through European International Distribution in June 1983.

2. Vincent Canby, "Film: 'Martin Guerre,'" *New York Times,* 10 June 1983, sect. 3, 5. Two review/background articles and seventeen reviews composed the sampling for this study. The review/background articles are Michael Blowen, "'Martin Guerre' Director Vigne Surprised at Film's U.S. Success," *Boston Globe/Independent Press,* rpt. in *Chicago Sun-Times,* 21 August 1983, 4; and Annette Insdorf, "A Medieval Tale Is Relived on Film," *New York Times,* 5 June 1983, sect. 2, 1, 19. Besides Canby's, the reviews are David Ansen, "Great Pretender?" *Newsweek,* 27 June 1983, 80; Lewis Archibald, "*The Return of Martin Guerre,*" *Aquarian,* 25 May 1983, 4; Edward Benson, "*Le Retour de Martin Guerre,*" *Film Quarterly* 38, (Fall 1984): 34–37; Michael Blowen, "'Martin Guerre' Is One of Year's Best," *Boston Globe,* 24 June 1983, 30; David Denby, "*The Return of Martin Guerre,*" *New York/Cue,* 23 May 1983, 91; Roger Ebert, "'Martin Guerre' Is Perceptive Mystery, Charming Love Story," *Chicago Sun-Times,* 18 August 1983, 74; Michael Feingold, "Peasant under Glass," *Village Voice,* 14 June 1983, 54; Stanley Kauffmann, "The Historical Present," *New Republic,* 2 May 1983, 24–25; "Len," "*Le Retour de Martin Guerre,*" *Variety,* 9 June 1982, 16; Ernest Leogrande, "A Moving, Sensitive 'Martin Guerre,'" *New York Daily News,* 10 June 1983, Friday

section, 5; Mark Levinson, *"The Return of Martin Guerre,"* *Cineaste* 13 (1984): 47–49; Janet Maslin, "When Role and Actor Are Perfectly Matched," *New York Times,* 21 August 1983, sect. 2, 17; Marcia Pally, *"The Return of Martin Guerre,"* *New York Native,* 9–22 May 1983, 49; David Sterritt, "Disappointing French Films," *Christian Science Monitor,* 26 May 1983, 16; Judy Stone, "'Martin Guerre'—Bed and Bored," *San Francisco Chronicle,* 1 July 1983, 64; Archer Winsten, "'Guerre' Crackles with French Suspense," *New York Post,* 10 June 1983, 43. It should be pointed out that this is not an unbiased sample, relying as it does on the indexing and clipping services of the New York Public Library–Lincoln Center Performing Arts Research Center. It does, however, have the advantage of covering many of the sources of U.S. taste making. It might have been useful as well to have explored television and radio reviews.

3. By "plot" I mean the events as represented in the text; by "story" I refer to the chronology that we mentally produce through textual and intertextual semiosis and which has existence only as an ex post facto generalization.

4. Gerard Genette, *Figures II* (1969), 174–75, cited in and trans. by Nancy K. Miller, "Emphasis Added: Plots and Plausibilities in Women's Fictions" (1981), rpt. in *The New Feminist Criticism: Essays on Women, Literature, and Theory,* ed. Elaine Showalter (New York: Pantheon Books, 1985), 340.

5. Roland Barthes, *Mythologies* (1957), trans. Annette Lavers (New York: Hill and Wang, 1972), 129.

6. It is "neutral'" in so far as it occurs in multiple modes of production and, thus, should not be characterized as a symptom of bourgeois capitalism or patriarchy.

7. See Benson, *"Retour,"* 34.

8. Pierre Macherey, "The Problem of Reflection," *Substance,* no. 15 (1976): 18.

9. Sigmund Freud, *New Introductory Lectures on Psychoanalysis* (1933), ed. and trans. James Strachey (New York: W. W. Norton, 1965), 102–8; Sigmund Freud, *Civilization and Its Discontents* (1930), ed. and trans. James Strachey (New York: W. W. Norton, 1961); *Abstracts of the Standard Edition of the Complete Psychological Works of Sigmund Freud,* ed. Carrie Lee Rothgeb (New York: International Universities Press, 1973), 329–30, 368–75, 454–55; and Richard Wollheim, *Sigmund Freud* (New York: Viking Press, 1971), 201–13.

10. Freud, *Civilization and Its Discontents,* 40.

11. Wollheim, *Sigmund Freud.*

12. Freud cited in Wollheim, *Sigmund Freud,* 150.

13. Freud, *Civilization and Its Discontents,* 68.

14. Peter Brooks, *Reading for the Plot: Design and Intention in Narrative* (1984) (New York: Vintage Books, 1985), 124.

12

Cinematic Shots

The Narration of Violence

IN THE ESSAY "The Modernist Event," historian Hayden White tackles the problem of the representation of history in contemporary moving images, dealing in part with Oliver Stone's 1991 film *JFK*.[1] Previously, White asked whether moving images could represent historical thinking, concluding that moving images can do just so.[2] Now, he is interested in considering whether a particular time period (the twentieth century—or at least what he marks as certain "modernist" moments in it) can be represented. He wonders, for instance, if the twentieth century has witnessed events unlike those that nineteenth-century historians had as their subjects, events such as massive famines, ecological disasters, nuclear explosions, or the Holocaust. These violent experiences are not only difficult to *describe* verbally but also impossible to *explain* in terms of traditional human agency. The nature, scope, and implications of these events give them a new dimension.

At the same time, White argues that modernism and what he considers as its extension, postmodernism, provide new ways to represent and investigate such twentieth-century events and catastrophes.[3] In a (post)modernist representation of real events, meaning and event run together, producing new genres such as the "docudrama," "faction," "infotainment," "the fiction of fact," and historical metafiction such as Doctorow's *Ragtime* (1975), Thomas' *The White Hotel* (1981), Syberberg's *Our Hitler* (1977), Visconti's *The Damned* (1969). These metafictions are about events that cannot be remembered *nor* can they be forgotten.

JFK, for White, is symptomatic of these new metafictions. Critics castigated the film because it "seemed to blur the distinction between fact and fiction by treating an historical event as if there were no limits on what could legitimately be said about it." In particular, White remarks on the critical reception of the film by David Armstrong, who chastised *JFK* for the "mix 'n' match of recreated scenes and archival footage" or by Richard Grenier, who wrote that Stone directed "his film in a pummelling style, a left to the jaw, a right to the solar plexus, flashing forward, flashing backward, crosscutting relentlessly, shooting 'in tight,' blurring, obfuscating, bludgeoning the viewer until Stone wins, he hopes by a TKO."[4]

An implicit psychoanalytical dimension to White's thesis parallels the homology being created here between the content of the violent acts and the brutal style of shooting and editing. If people do try to describe such unrepresentable events through a more traditional, linear narrative, the attempt itself may be seen to produce a fetishism of the event. Since such a description is impossible, the substitute narrative serves as the description's replacement, trying to fill in for the lack of an ability to describe or explain the events. This attempt to narrativize thus undoes the necessary process of mourning for the loss of explanation. In trying to master the impossible story, the historian unwittingly and ironically is unable to psychically master the event. Thus, only anti-narrative non-stories of the literary (post)modernist kind are able to represent such traumatic events; the antinarrative form of representation is not totalizing and permits mourning to occur.

White's grand allegory is typical of the kind of provocative work he has produced for historiographers for the last quarter century. As usual, the proposition he has produced is an intriguing one, capable of generating a rather interesting narrative about twentieth-century representations of modernity's historical realities. What I wish to consider, however, is not the truth of White's narrative, but whether, in fact, Oliver Stone did something particularly unusual in his docudrama practice in *JFK* and whether that supposed unusual practice is (post)modernist—for White leaves the answers to these questions tantalizingly unclear. In proceeding with this investigation, then, I shall have some more angles from which to (re)view shots—both historical and edited—in *JFK*.

First of all, did Oliver Stone do something unusual in his docudrama practice in *JFK*? To answer this question, I think it is necessary to pose a series of four subquestions which together seem to me to characterize discussions about docudramas, reenactments, films that mix types of source material, and adequate subjects for re-presentation in film.

IS IT UNUSUAL TO DRAMATIZE HISTORICAL EVENTS?

Is it reality? No. It's better.
—Tom Shales, 1989, on television documentaries

Narrativizing historical events is as old as the Bible or the *Iliad* and the *Odyssey*. In fact, Jerome Bruner argues in "The Narrative Construction of Reality" that narrative is one of several "cultural tool kits" that permit mastery and transfer of knowledges and skills from person to person, culture to culture. Bruner claims that

> we organize our experience and our memory of human happenings mainly in the form of narrative—stories, excuses, myths, reasons for doing and not doing, and so on. Narrative is a conventional form, transmitted culturally and constrained by each individual's level of mastery. . . . Unlike the constructions generated by logical and scientific procedures that can be weeded out by falsification, narrative constructions can only achieve verisimilitude.[5]

While White may be accurate in describing the psychological desire to narrativize events as connected to the Oedipal complex, the death principle, and issues of aggression and mastery, Bruner claims the narrativizing process is also ecologically necessary for social order.

This subquestion about dramatizing historical events, however, is not really precisely about narrative but instead about dramatization—or about interpretation. One might claim that narrating is "normal" but that anything other than a virtual copy of the real event must emphasize certain aspects of the event and neglect others, and thus produce both drama and a point of view.

Thousands of instances of dramatizing reality exist in print and moving images. In fact, as soon as movies started, they began dramatizing contemporary affairs. An early silent film such as *The Sampson-Schley Controversy* might be considered an interpretative docudrama. In 1901, Edwin S. Porter, who had produced many short films based on real events, filmed a three-shot movie in such a way as to take a position about a controversy over whether Captain Schley had inappropriately exceeded his command during the Battle of Santiago Bay and deserved to be court-martialed for cowardice. Porter aligned his point of view with that of the *New York Journal*, whose editorial cartoon served as the source of Porter's visual imagery. In the first two shots, Porter depicted Captain Schley commanding the battleship that led the fray against the enemy and fighting alongside his sailors. Porter then cut to a third shot showing Admiral Sampson drinking tea several hundred miles away.[6]

Why would Porter bother to organize the narrative by crosscutting to Sampson? Because dramatizing and interpreting the events not only are inherently necessary (all narratives are selective) but are much more engaging if the drama produced emphasizes conflict between individuals. In this case, the conflict was merely political and legal, but conflict that becomes physically violent is even more fascinating spectacle. Echoing centuries of Western dramatic theory, books on how to write movies would continue to emphasize conflict as the fuel for viewer interest because the causes for and effects of conflict and violence are debatable, reproducing aggression for mastery among spectators who struggle over the depictions and points of view. Like the accusations made against Stone for his cutting in *JFK*, Porter dramatically jabbed at the opponent Sampson, landing a quick right to his chin. Was it reality? No, it was better. Even at the start of cinema, narration through editing provided a specific dramatization of conflict, with the filmmaker taking his shot at explaining and interpreting a historical event.

IF DRAMATIZING HISTORICAL EVENTS WITH EDITING IS STANDARD CINEMATIC PRACTICE, IS IT UNUSUAL TO MIX DOCUMENTARY FOOTAGE WITH REENACTMENTS?

Hollywood has never been the land of footnotes.
—Bob Katz, 1991, review of *JFK*

The activity of combining moving images shot at the same time as the event (i.e., documentary footage) with staged scenes (i.e., what are called in the industry "reenactments") is a practice nearly as old as the movies, with early newsreels employing the two types of materials to create a narrative of the events for the viewer.[7] However, this practice has become a major issue during the past several years, in part because of the significant rise of so-called reality-based television.

Reality-based television has been remarkably successful in audience ratings and in syndication. As of April 1993, at least fourteen reality shows were on the four major networks, including, for example, *Rescue: 911, Unsolved Mysteries, Cops,* and *How'd They Do That?*[8] Industry personnel consider these programs to have emerged from documentary practice and to have taken off during the six-month writers' strike in 1988 when the networks turned to them in order to fill airtime.

Reality-based TV producers make a major distinction between their genre and the docudrama. On the one hand, the docudrama is seen as a "pure" reenactment of a historical event. Examples might include the movie bio-pic *The Glenn Miller Story* (Anthony Mann, 1954) or the three television versions of the Amy Fisher story. Docudramas are based on real events, but the entire text is reenacted.

On the other hand, reality TV uses the interview and voices of original historical people to tell the story of the event. Moreover, reality TV mixes documentary footage, still photos, news clips, and sound bites with reenactments. The reenactments are based upon "what actually happened," but they use actors instead of the original people, or, lately, the original people may even play themselves in a reconstruction of the event. Arnold Shapiro, a producer of some of these documentaries, suggests that such a mixture goes back in U.S. television news practices to at least the 1950s and the show *You Asked for It.* The reason proffered for doing these reenactments is, however, not merely to give narrative information but to create dramatic interest. Although producers of these programs claim to be very careful not to create dialogue that is unsubstantiated, some producers have also indicated that they will create a reenacted dramatization even when they have archival footage of the event. This happens when it is determined that the reenactment will produce a better visual impact or will be stronger dramatically than the documentary footage.[9] Such re-enactments must still adhere to the network standards for veracity which pertain when no documentary footage is available.

Obviously, given the popularity of reality-based TV, the question of blurring fact and fiction has taken on an urgency for TV networks. Shapiro points out that "in the past, documentary makers labeled all dramatizations as such," but lately that convention has ceased. Another way to differentiate the ontological status of the material has been to shoot in black and white for the dramatized past and in color for the current interviews. Even that practice has disappeared. Documentary filmmaker Harrison Engle, who is also president of the International Documentary Association, points out that *The Thin Blue Line* (Errol Morris, 1988) "blended what one critic called 'the B-movie re-enactment' of a bizarre Texas murder with the traditional talking heads of those involved in the crime." Engle's own latest documentary "mixes re-enactments with archival footage."[10]

The problem with mixing documentary and reenactment material is not that mixing creates a less accurate interpretation of the event. What results is still thought to be a point of view. Rather, the issue is that the mixing may confuse the audiences as to what is documentary evidence and what is speculation or hypothesis by the filmmaker. It is supposed that audiences will be less capable of judging the validity of the interpretation if they are confused into perceiving the reenactment as an authentic "trace" of the real. What is at stake is the credibility of the image as it relates to spectatorial understanding of the technology of the camera, for even if the meaning of a documentary image is ambiguous (as appears to have been the case in the Rodney King footage), it still has a higher credibility claim than a reenactment. Audience perception and memory are what matters.[11]

Evidence does exist that audiences are not particularly discriminating viewers. Statistics indicate, for example, that "almost half the watchers considered . . . 'America's Most Wanted' . . . to be news."[12] Thus, problems exist because of the presumption of audience gullibility and the belief that a reenactment is "more subjective" than documentary footage—as well as likely more dramatic and entertaining. Consequently, networks have faced a dilemma about how to deal with such popular and revenue-generating programs. What is causing their difficulty is that viewers often refuse to distinguish between entertainment and news in the way networks feel obliged to insure that they do.

One way for producers to avoid the problem of meeting network standards about the authenticity of material for news programs is to move any questionable programs out of that category and into "entertainment." Networks maintain little documentation for docudramas— only enough to prevent the threat of lawsuits for infringement on personal story rights. Thus, a solution for the news ethics problem has been recategorizing many reality-based programs and consequently implying different standards for referring to the real. A striking example of this was when a producer for NBC's *Dateline* (a "news" program) enhanced a story about a Chevy pickup truck by adding explosives to the vehicle and failing to make evident that the subsequent crash had been staged. Besides firing the executive producer, NBC shifted *Dateline* from its news division to the entertainment section to prevent any further innuendo that NBC's standards for news practices were degenerating.

A second protective strategy has been to label the reenactment (or the docudrama) as having been derived from a specific person's point of view. Here, (post)modernist practices of recognizing and representing the existence of various subjectivities enter and are coopted by commercial interests. While *Rashomon* and many other twentieth-century texts may have challenged the idea that any cohesive representation of reality can be said to exist, now television and movies can appropriate the multiperspective narrational device to their own purposes. Three made-for-TV movie versions of the Amy Fisher story make perfect sense. One is Amy Fisher's; one is Joey Buttafucco's; and the third represents the court transcription.

Such a *Rashomon*-like strategy has already been parodied. During April 1993 in the *Doonesbury* comic strip, Uncle Duke staged his own dramatic rescue from an avalanche in hopes of selling the story to television. However, his version was scooped by versions from the rescue crew and his assistant, Honey. This satire is even funnier if the reader recalls that the character Duke is based on Hunter Thompson, founder of "gonzo journalism," itself an earlier example of the journalistic dramatizing of fact. Additionally, a comic book series, He Said/She Said, provides a cartoon version of the Fisher/Buttafuoco story. One side tells "her story in her words"; the flip side is "his story." Apparently a Mia Farrow/Woody Allen comic was also in preparation shortly after the publicity around their conflict.[13]

Thus, the practice of mixing documentary and reenacted footage for entertainment purposes is widespread, even if somewhat debated as a legitimate practice for use in the news division on network TV. In the case of *JFK*, we cannot consider the controversy that erupted as primarily generated merely by the film's cross-editing of shots of mixed heritage. Moreover, aligning a dramatization with a particular perspective is so common as to be susceptible to satire. Stone positioned *JFK* as Garrison's version of the events, and, as I shall discuss below, reviewers routinely took the film to be from his perspective. Moreover (although after the fact), Stone and co-writer Zachary Sklar published the script with footnotes to substantiate every reenacted scene in the movie as reality-based, thus claiming to adhere to traditional standards of authenticating claims. We never asked such a proof for the Amy Fisher stories. Something else besides the hybridizing of material for dramatizing the narrative must be involved.[14]

IS IT UNUSUAL TO REPRESENT VIOLENCE AS THE PRODUCT OF A CONSPIRACY?

The President's brain is missing.

—J. Hoberman, 1991, review of *JFK*

Perhaps it really was the subject matter of *JFK* that was the unusual practice. Was this perhaps the first case of a major Hollywood studio making a reality-based movie that claimed a conspiracy was behind certain violent historical events? Well, again, the answer is no. However, comparison with an earlier film which does so may be particularly helpful in thinking about why such a controversy developed around *JFK*.

In 1939 Warner Bros. produced *Confessions of a Nazi Spy* (Anatole Litvak, 1939). As described by Clayton Koppes and Gregory Black in *Hollywood Goes to War*, "*Confessions* was based on a real incident: Nazi spies who came to the United States had been caught and convicted by a federal court in New York City."[15] According to Koppes and Black, when Warner Bros. sent the script to the Production Code office, "a hot debate" ensued.

> One faction objected strenuously, arguing that the screenplay depicted Hitler and his government unfairly. There was no proof that German agitators had come to the United States with the intention of seizing control of the country; after all, they said, every country has spies. Nor was it fair to show Hitler only as "a screaming madman." The film should acknowledge "his unchallenged political and social achievements." Such European events as the dismemberment of Czechoslovakia and the abolition of Christian schools in the Third Reich were "extraneous" to the spy story. Even if everything in the script were true, this group said, it would be "one of the most lamentable mistakes ever made by the industry."(p.28)

Warner Bros. proceeded with the film which "identif[ied] the German-American Bund as an arm of the German government whose purpose was to destroy the American Constitution and Bill of Rights"(p.29). Moreover, they populated the film with major studio stars—Edward G. Robinson, George Sanders, Paul Lukas—and gave it to Anatole Litvak to direct. As Koppes and Black point out, the critical response was mixed, and the film enjoyed only moderate box office success. Among the negative comments were those of the *Variety* reviewer, who scoffed at the melodrama presented:

> Brutality, calloused inhumanity, kidnapping, beating, kicking in the groin and every evidence of disagreeable behavior is included. Two dominant impressions of the film may perhaps be: (a) that every outgoing German liner has kidnapped victims of Nazi sadism hidden away in dungeons, and (b) that the bunds are expressions of open treason. A third over-all impression is that any café with the waiters in leather shorts and tables in checkered linen is a nest of conspirators. It should be bad for biz in such taverns.[16]

Confessions of a Nazi Spy is similar to *JFK* in that it too mixes documentary footage with reenactments. The *New York Times* reviewer described this: "the film's quasi-documentary character has been supported by its employment of newsreel shots of Hitler haranguing his Brownshirts, a commentator's voice, maps and other factual pictorial matter." The reviewer continued, "But its editorial bias, however justified, has carried it to childish extremes."[17]

Editing in *Confessions*, then, functioned much like Stone's editing strategy of intercutting documentary footage with reenactments to fill in gaps and connect the conspiratorial players into a coherent, masterful plot. Missing shots were supplied to create a causal chain rhetorically explaining the Germans' violence. Thus, just as with *JFK*, *Confessions* suggested that it could reveal how events seemingly unconnected and threatening to the integrity of the United States were actually related to one another. In such conspiracy discourse, covert activities in the real world are presumed capable of being plotted into a master narrative to which every sinister event relates.[18]

Shortly after the film's opening, Fritz J. Kuhn, president of the German Bund, initiated a request for an injunction against distribution of the film in advance of a five-million-dollar libel suit against Warner

Bros. claiming the Bund was a "loyal American organization." Warner Bros. responded by indicating that they would prove that "scenes of spying and perversive activity portrayed there are true."[19] The injunction was denied, although Kuhn was allowed to proceed with the libel suit. Unfortunately for Kuhn, he was arrested at about the same time on perjury charges connected to other events.[20]

JFK follows in a line of conspiracy stories, most of which are wholly fictional, that focus on a group's intent to subvert a government and its representatives. A number of these appeared in the 1970s, including *The Parallax View* (Alan Pakula, 1974), *Marathon Man* (John Schlesinger, 1976), and *Three Days of the Condor* (Sydney Pollack, 1976). Most of the conspiracy movies were made after the conspiracy in question had been proven to be true, and eventually Watergate generated its own docudrama, *All the President's Men* (Alan Pakula, 1976).

Confessions, however, is somewhat unusual in the history of movies in its claims to dramatize a true conspiracy. *Confessions* was under congressional investigation in 1941 when the bombing of Pearl Harbor cut short the need to prove the charges against the Nazis. At this point state policy changed, making the plot not only credible, but useful in mobilizing public sentiment for war. But as in the case of *JFK*, however, since the history was not the official history, it was contested.

IS IT UNUSUAL TO PRESENT UNOFFICIAL VERSIONS OF HISTORY?

Doublespeak Appendix

Conspiracy Theory: A critique or explanation I find offensive.

Historical Lies: Lies, partial lies, or truths that conflict with well-established official lies.

—Edward S. Herman, 1992, on *JFK*

Usually unofficial versions of history are not released by major studios. They tend to like authorized ones. Many of the statements of concern over *JFK* expressed the worry that the movie manipulated viewers into accepting Stone's thesis. In one version of this, it was held that if viewers think a reenactment has documentary status, they may become confused about what is known as a fact and what is as yet merely a speculative assertion. Additionally, viewers might miss the point that the story is told from one person's point of view (in the case of *JFK*, Garrison's perspective). Finally, rapid editing is particularly aggressive. Recall Grenier's vocabulary about *JFK*'s editing: Stone directs "his film in a pummelling style, a left to the jaw, a right to the solar plexus, flashing forward, flashing backward, crosscutting relentlessly, shooting 'in tight,' blurring, obfuscating, bludgeoning the viewer until Stone wins, he hopes by a TKO." These worries hinge on the assumption that viewers have to be tricked or even beaten up to accept the conspiracy thesis.

This might be the case if viewers actually did believe the official version of Kennedy's assassination. However, adequate evidence exists that massive portions of the U.S. population already assume that Oswald was not the sole author of Kennedy's death. A Gallup poll in July 1991 indicated that only sixteen percent of Americans thought that Oswald acted alone. Seventy-three percent "suspect others were involved."[21] A *Washington Post* survey in May 1991 revealed that fifty-six percent of the population believed in a conspiracy; only nineteen percent agreed with the official Warren Commission thesis.[22] Further, it is not only recently that significant numbers of Americans have believed in a conspiracy theory in regard to the assassination. Less than a year after Kennedy's death, "in the spring of 1964, one-third of Americans believed Lee Harvey Oswald acted in concert with others. Within two years the figure had doubled. Every poll taken over the last quarter century has shown between 60% and 80% of the public favoring a conspiratorial explanation."[23]

What Stone has provided, then, is not merely an unofficial version of the assassination but one that happens to be a very popular version. As Andrew O'Hehir suggested, "Those who are enraged at Oliver Stone's film *JFK* for its heavily fictionalized blending of various assassination theories are missing the point. As Stone has apparently grasped in his blockhead populist way, the J.F.K. killing has been fiction for a long time." O'Hehir proposed that "[Kennedy's assassination is] the creation myth we use to understand the discords of contemporary America: the tale of the fall from grace, for which we keep vainly seeking redemption. If it hadn't happened, we would have had to invent it."[24]

While I do not wish to argue that Kennedy's assassination has become fictional—it really happened—I do believe that most individuals in the United States already embrace some dramatic plot for the events of that day. Individuals may attribute parts of the conspiracy to various institutions or persons, or they may just generally think more of the story exists than has been recognized officially.

What is at stake in the *JFK* controversy, then, is not a bludgeoning of the spectator by the editing style or the hybrid documentary/reenactment material but fear that the official Warren Commission story will finally fall to a new and popularly produced "authorized" history. This fear is particularly obvious in the way an article in the *Washington Post* presented a series of interviews with persons coming out of the film.

> —"I came out of the movie feeling different about the government," said Russell Reed, 21. . . .
>
> —"I really see what the movie said could be possible," said Amanda Peel, 17. . . .
>
> —"The government should unlock the documents and let people find out what is in the documents," said David Buell, 30.[25]

Clearly, by stressing the ages of the interviewees, the *Washington Post* proposed that while the generation of baby boomers may believe the story of a conspiracy behind the Kennedy assassination, *JFK* threatens to promote that belief into the next generation.

Some writers have pointed out that the media attack on Stone may have been a defensive move by certain journalists out to protect their failure to criticize the government's version of the assassination. Two *Village Voice* writers argued,

> The bashing of Oliver Stone's movie *JFK* by the bastions of the American media—CBS, *The New York Times, Time, Newsweek,* and *The Washington Post*—is said to spring from the sincere desire on the part of the keepers of America's memory to see that our sacred history does not fall prey to revisionist charlatans. While Stone's film does take serious liberty with history, the virulence with which the film has been attacked seems to say more about a defensive press that missed and continues to miss a major story than it does about any flaws in *JFK*.[26]

If, then, we return to my first question, did Oliver Stone do something particularly unusual in his docudrama practice in *JFK*, I think we have to conclude that he did not. Dramatizing historical events, mixing documentary footage with reenactments, representing conspiracy theories, and telling unauthorized histories have all occurred in the past.

They have not occurred without incident or question, but they are normal media practices, as are other of Stone's dramatic strategies. These would include hiring Kevin Costner, who had dinner with George Bush and danced with wolves, to play the sympathetic lead actor.

All of these observations, however, do not necessarily suggest a negative answer to the second large question: are these practices (post)modernist? After all, all of my examples are derived from two quintessential twentieth-century media—film and television. Perhaps, as White suggests, these examples are merely other instances of (post)modernist responses to the traumas of the era. In which case, I think we need to move to that question.

UNSOLVED MYSTERIES

Thus, *should we understand any of these practices as (post)modernist*? I think that this question ultimately implies a textual effects hypothesis and not a formalist analysis of style and content. To consider certain practices of cinematic or televisual editing as symptomatic of (post)modernism as White does is to miss the point. What is really at stake is the *effect* of a potentially (post)modernist strategy of mixing documentary shots and reenactments. Is the *effect* on the audience one of confusing fact and fiction, commenting on the medium of inscription, and thus leaving the event untotalized—which would make it (post)modernist? Or is the effect something else?

Modern theory warns us against master narratives, narratives that attempt to essentialize specific historical events into an every-time-and-every-place. I would suggest that we should never confuse a formal device such as rapid editing or editing together materials of different ontological status with the device's social or cultural functions or ignore such a device's function within its historical context. Editing of hybrid material might leave an event ambiguous, but it might permit the confirmation of what many spectators already believe to be real: in the case of *JFK*, Oswald was either a patsy or part of a conspiracy of some small or larger scale.

In reading critical responses to the movie, I observe that consistently the negative reviewers simply disagreed with the story they perceived Stone was telling. That is, they were not confused and knew that what was on the screen was Stone's mixture of documentary and reen-

actment footage cast into a dramatic narrative.[27] Moreover, they believed the story of Kennedy's assassination was tellable and explainable. The debate was not about whether one could describe the event
verbally or visually because *everyone thought he or she could*. They just
did not think the Stone/Garrison story was correct. Nor were they
(more than slightly) confused about what they thought Stone/Garrison
was claiming. For example, the *Newsweek* writer described the film's
plot:

> The assassination . . . was a grand conspiracy involving the CIA, the
> FBI, the Army and Navy, anti-Castro Cubans, New Orleans lowlifes
> and the Dallas police force. The motive: to thwart the dovish tenden-
> cies of John F. Kennedy who, if he had lived, would have pulled all
> American troops out of Vietnam, settled the cold war with the Soviet
> Union and patched up relations with Castro's Cuba.[28]

Furthermore, whether critical or admiring of the film, reviewers did not
find Kennedy's assassination an event equivalent to the Holocaust or
nuclear war, although many considered it to have produced a national
trauma. A sense of causality is also apparent. For those holding the
madman-Oswald-did-it-alone point of view, a psychiatric discourse
operates to explain human agency. For those holding the Oswald-as-
patsy-or-conspirator point of view, a conspiracy discourse functions to
fill in the missing parts of the Zapruder footage.

In a discussion about social drama, Victor Turner argues that three
phases characterize social relations during a conflict among members of
a group. The first phase "begins with a breach of regular norm-gov-
erned social relations, signalized by a public transgression of a salient
rule normally binding on members of the group." This breach is followed by a crisis and finally by the deployment of "adjustive and re-
dressive mechanisms . . . to seal off or heal the breach—a phase call[ed]
'redress.'" Turner notes that each participant in the social conflict creates a social drama. "Soon I realized," he writes, "that it was their very
bias that was of central importance. For the aim of the social drama is
not to present a seemingly objective recital of a series of events; it is concerned, rather, with the different interpretations put upon those events,
and the ways in which these give subtle expression to divergent interests or switches in the balance of power."[29] Turner continues that psychological factors are also involved in the drama presented.

Representing a historical event as a subjective social drama between contesting sides is not a new idea. It is, however, very different
from the radical notion that history is itself fictional. In her work on
postmodernist literature as "historiographic metafiction," Linda
Hutcheon suggests that postmodern works are those that "deny the
possibility of a clearly sustainable distinction between history and fiction."[30] This does not mean that historical events did not happen but
that authors of postmodern literature are pointing out that history texts
are interpretative dramatizations, that history texts are sites of contestation and social drama. As Hutcheon writes,

> In challenging the seamless quality of the history/fiction (or
> world/art) join implied by realist narrative, postmodern fiction does
> not, however, disconnect itself from history or the world. It fore-
> grounds and thus contests the conventionality and unacknowledged
> ideology of that assumption of seamlessness and asks its readers to
> question the processes by which we represent our selves and our
> world to ourselves and to become aware of the means by which we
> make sense of and construct order out of experience in our particular
> culture. We cannot avoid representation. We can try to avoid fixing our
> notion of it and assuming it to be transhistorical and transcultural.[31]

The reviewers of *JFK* certainly seem to have operated at a metafictional level in responding to the film. However, they did so not specifically because of its "(post)modernist" editing style but rather because
the reviewers were already accustomed to the notion that history is
dramatized from various points of view and thus debatable.[32]
The overt and metafictional recognition of the interpretative activities of those engaged in creating and reading social dramas like *JFK*
does not, however, explain a disturbing finding: twenty-two percent of
adults polled in the United States in April 1993 thought it possible that
the Holocaust had never happened. In the postmodernism theory, the
distance between the representation and the real has become such a
widely available and misunderstood notion that it is possible for people to doubt accounts of events of the magnitude of those described by
White as a "(post)modernist event."[33]
However, questioning the actual existence of a past event is not
what is happening in the case of *JFK*, whose reviewers and audiences
clearly read the movie as a drama about a real past. White may be right

about his allegory for events such as the Holocaust—trying to represent them as coherent narratives attributed to human agency may delay the mourning process or allow them to be ignored altogether. But the assassination of Kennedy does not belong to that category of events and responses. *JFK*'s represented violence is still considered real and explainable, even if debatable. We are still attempting to dramatize, master, and heal the breach of that traumatic event. We are still in conflict over that violence with various members of the audience who take a metafictional reading stance that looks at the film as presenting only one perspective on the past, a social drama with which they do or do not associate themselves.

Thus, White may be right in seeing that *JFK* poses a problem for postmodern historiography, but for the wrong reason. Like the postmodern historiographer, critics and spectators of twentieth-century histories have learned the rules of representation. They can read the movie as a dramatic narration. Thus it is not the formal properties of the editing strategies that make the movie (post)modern; rather, it is the reading strategies of the viewers who recognize that the movie is a subjective version of the past, created through shots put together by some agent. What is undecidable, finally, is who is appropriately authorized to fill in the missing narrative material. Spectators of the assassination have not stopped struggling over the story of Kennedy's violent death, permitting every version to stand as equally official. Thus, White may be right in his psychoanalytical reading of our relation to the historical event: we are not yet able to let that past event go, to move on to mourning the loss of J.F.K. This is because we still think we might be able to represent that event with some verisimilitude. Like the program that stimulated "reality-based TV," the assassination remains a violent plot whose cinematic shots do not yet produce a satisfying narrative resolution—it is still an "unsolved mystery."

NOTES

I would like to thank the audience at the Institute for Humanities, State University of New York–Stony Brook, for their comments on a draft of this chapter.

1. Hayden White, "The Modernist Event," Patricia Wise Lecture (1992), rev. in *The Persistence of History: Cinema, Television, and the Modern Event*, ed. Vivian Sobchack (New York: Routledge, 1996), 17–38.

2. Hayden White, "Historiography and Historiophoty," *American Historical Review* 93, no. 5 (December 1988): 1193–99.

3. I do not personally agree with theorizing "postmodernism" as an extension of "modernism," but arguing the point here is unnecessary; I will accept White's position.

4. David Armstrong and Todd Gitlin, "Killing the Messenger," *Image,* 16 February 1992; Richard Grenier, *TLS,* 24 January 1992 quoted by White, "Modernism Event."

5. Jerome Bruner, "The Narrative Construction of Reality," *Critical Inquiry* 18, no. 1 (Autumn 1991): 4.

6. Charles Musser, *Before the Nickelodeon: Edwin S. Porter and the Edison Manufacturing Company* (Berkeley: University of California Press, 1991), 182.

7. "Faking the Early News Films," in Raymond Fielding, *The American Newsreel, 1911–1967* (Norman: University of Oklahoma Press), 37–45. Fielding uses the term "faking" as though he assumes the producers hoped the viewers would be unable to differentiate between the documentary and reenacted footage. More work on assumptions about viewers and goals of the producers is necessary before concluding that "faking," as we might take the term to mean, is an adequate description of the situation. Additionally, in this essay, I am assuming two points: (1) that historical events have happened, and we are concerned not to prove their existence but to understand the problems of retrieval of descriptions and interpretations of meaning; and (2) that while documentary footage is selective and thus interpretative, it does have an ontological status different from that of reenactments of historical events.

8. Steve Coe, "Networks Serve Up Heavy Dose of Reality," *Broadcasting and Cable,* 12 April 1993, 26.

9. Mike Mathis, producer-director for "Unsolved Mysteries," Directors' Guild of America Workshop, August 1992; "Nightline," ABC, 6 February 1990; Diane Haithman, "Drawing the Line between Tabloid TV and Re-Enactments," *Los Angeles Times,* 20 February 1989, part 6, 1.

10. Haithman, "Drawing the Line." Because of the reenactments, *The Thin Blue Line* was ruled ineligible for inclusion in the documentary category for awards from the Academy of Motion Picture Arts and Sciences.

11. Andre Bazin's arguments about the ontology of the photographic image can be turned to here.

12. Thomas B. Rosenstiel, "TV Blurs Facts and Filminess; Infotainment: Seeing Really Is Believing," *Los Angles Times,* 3 December 1989, part M, 4. The source is unclear about how TV genres were defined in the survey; hence, we do not know if audiences had choices beyond "news" and "entertainment." Obviously, that would help to interpret these results.

13. The *Doonesbury* strip was published during April 1993. The comic book described was also published in April 1993. It asserted "the events depicted

herein have been presented in the exact order and manner in which they occurred. Character dialogue is based solely on statements made by the persons involved in the affair. First Amendment Publishing attests to the veracity and accuracy of the activities and events portrayed in this comic book."

14. *Malcolm X*, released after *JFK*, had something of the same trouble, although the adherence by Spike Lee to the authorized autobiography perhaps muted the potential for controversy.

15. Clayton R. Koppes and Gregory D. Black, *Hollywood Goes to War: How Politics, Profits, and Propaganda Shaped World War II Movies* (New York: Free Press, 1987), 27.

16. "Land," "*Confessions of a Nazi Spy,*" *Variety*, 3 May 1939.

17. Frank S. Nugent, "*Confessions of a Nazi Spy,*" *New York Times*, 29 April 1939, 13.

18. See Richard Hofstadter, *"The Paranoid Style in American Politics" and Other Essays* (New York: Knopf, 1965); Paul Michael Rogin, *Ronald Reagan, The Movie* (Berkeley: University of California Press, 1987).

19. "German Bund Sues," *Motion Picture Herald*, 20 May 1939, 9; "Answers Kuhn," *Motion Picture Herald*, 9 September 1939, 9.

20. The federal court ruled that no injunction could be issued to prevent or stop the publication of something deemed libelous; if libel exists, the party can file a damage suit and merits of fact would be heard at the trial. *Kuhn v. Warner Bros.*, 19 June 1939, District Court, S. D. New York Federal Supplement 29 (1940): 800.

21. Tamar Vital, "Who Killed J.F.K.?" *Jerusalem Post*, 31 January 1992.

22. "Twisted History," *Newsweek*, 23 December 1991, 46.

23. Jefferson Morley, "The Political Rorschach Test," *Los Angeles Times*, 8 December 1991, rpt. in *JFK: The Book of the Film/The Documented Screenplay*, ed. Oliver Stone and Zachary Sklar (New York: Applause Books, 1992), 231.

24. Andrew O'Hehir, "*JFK*: Tragedy into Farce," *San Francisco Weekly*, 18 December 1991, rpt. in *JFK*, ed. Stone and Sklar, 270.

25. Robert O'Harrow, Jr., "Conspiracy Theory Wins Converts," *Washington Post*, 2 January 1992, rpt. in *JFK*, ed. Stone and Sklar, 370–71.

26. Robert Hennelly and Jerry Policoff, "*JFK*: How the Media Assassinated the Real Story," *Village Voice*, 31 March 1992, rpt. in *JFK*, ed. Stone and Sklar, 497.

27. Whether they perceive this to be "news" or "entertainment" is another issue.

28. "Twisted History," *Newsweek*, 23 December 1991, 46.

29. Victor Turner, *On the Edge of the Bush: Anthropology as Experience* (Tucson: University of Arizona Press, 1985), 121.

30. Steven Connor summarizing Hutcheon's position in *Postmodernist Culture: An Introduction to Theories of the Contemporary* (Cambridge, MA: Basil Blackwell, 1989), 127.

31. Linda Hutcheon, *The Politics of Postmodernism* (London: Routledge, 1989), 53–54.

32. If we really wanted to find a film that in a postmodern way blurred fiction and fact, we might turn instead to Haskell Wexler's *Medium Cool* (1969), a movie in which an integral shot "contains" both documentary narrative and fictional narrative. Since the fiction story existed alongside the real events in the Chicago park, the fiction may have even affected the reality.

33. Michiko Kakutani, "When History Is a Casualty," *New York Times,* 30 April 1993, C1 and 31. To lay the lack of belief in the Holocaust directly at the feet of deconstructionism, as Kakutani does in the essay, is, however, irresponsible.

Permissions

1. "Modes of Reception," in *Le cinéma en histoire: Institution cinématographique, réception filmique, et réconstitution historique,* ed. André Gaudreault, Germain Lacasse, and Isabelle Raynauld (Quebec, Canada: Éditions Nota Bene, 1999), 305–23.

2. "The Perversity of Spectators: Expanding the History of the Classical Hollywood Cinema," in *Moving Images, Culture, and the Mind,* ed. Ib Bondebjerg (Luton, England: University of Luton Press, forthcoming).

3. "Writing the History of American Film Reception," in *Hollywood and Its Spectators, Vol. 3: History and Theory,* ed. Melvyn Stokes and Richard Maltby (London: British Film Institute, forthcoming).

4. "Hybrid or Inbred: The Purity Hypothesis and Hollywood Genre History," *Film Criticism* 22, no. 1 (Fall 1997): 5–20.

5. "The Romances of the Blonde Venus: Movie Censors versus Movie Fans," *Canadian Journal of Film Studies* 6, no. 2 (Fall 1997): 5–20.

6. "The Cultural Productions of 'A Clockwork Orange,'" in *Stanley Kubrick's "A Clockwork Orange,"* ed. Stuart Y. McDougal (New York: Cambridge University Press, forthcoming). Reprinted with the permission of Cambridge University Press.

7. "The Places of Empirical Subjects in the Event of Mass Culture: Jeanie Bueller and Ideology" (previously unpublished).

8. "Finding Community in the Early 1960s: Underground Cinema and Sexual Politics," in *Swinging Single: Representing Sexuality in the 1960s,* ed. Hilary Radner and Moya Luckett (Minneapolis, MN: University of Minnesota Press, 1999), 38–74.

9. "Taboos and Totems: Cultural Meanings of *The Silence of the Lambs,*" in *Film Theory Goes to the Movies,* ed. Jim Collins, Hilary Radner, and Ava Collins (New York: Routledge, 1993), 142–54.

10. "Hitchcock in Texas: Intertextuality in the Face of Blood and Gore," in *"As Time Goes By": Festskrift i anledning Bjorn Sorenssens 50-arsday,* ed. Gunnar Iversen, Stig Kulset, and Kathrine Skretting (Trondheim, Norway: Tapir, 1996), 189–97.

11. "Securing the Fictional Narrative as a Tale of the Historical Real: *The Return of Martin Guerre*," *South Atlantic Quarterly* 88, no. 2 (Spring 1989): 393–413.

12. "Cinematic Shots: The Narration of Violence," in *The Persistence of History*, ed. Vivian Sobchack (New York: Routledge, 1996), 39–54.

Index

Performance, 15–17, 53, 138
Personal Best, 37
Perverse. *See* Spectators
Phelps, Guy, 94, 183
Physique magazines, 98
Pickford, Mary, 50
Playboy, 101
Plot, 3, 5, 17–18, 23, 33–34, 36–38, 43, 67, 104, 108, 167, 193, 205, 209n, 225. *See also* Narrative; Story
Polan, Dana, 69
Polanski, Roman, 96, 156n
Politics. *See* Evaluation; Ideology
Pollack, Sydney, 219
Polysemy, 39, 77, 83
Pop art, 141–48
Popcorn Venus, 105
Popular culture, 12–13, 17–18, 24, 44, 115, 122, 125–26, 131, 137–39, 146–47
Pornography, 37, 95–102, 105, 107, 139–41, 144, 147–49, 159n
Porter, Edwin S., 212–13
Possessed, 80
Postcolonial theory, 72
Post-Fordian Hollywood, 62, 74n. *See also* Classical Hollywood cinema
Postmodern cinema, 15–18, 20, 21, 43
Postmodernism, 210–12, 216, 222, 224
Poststructural theory, 63, 65–66, 78, 82–83, 162, 193, 196, 204, 222, 228n. *See also* Structuralism
Power, 54, 73, 203
Pre-Oedipal. *See* Psychoanalytical theory
Production: by minority groups, 74; modes of, 16, 28, 30, 40, 132, 152n. *See also* Fan, production by
Production Code, 96, 130; office, 217
Progressivism, 80, 82, 88, 90n
Promotion. *See* Advertising
Psycho, 5–6, 20, 69, 128, 179–87
Psychoanalytical theory, 2, 5, 167, 170–71, 177n, 185, 191, 204–8, 211–12
Public Enemy, 70
Publicity. *See* Advertising
Public sphere, 15, 18–19, 21, 23, 45, 47, 49, 51
Pull My Daisy, 132, 152–53n
Pulp Fiction, 11–12, 17–18, 21
Puns, 165–66, 177n
Purity thesis, 62–63, 65, 68–69, 71–72

Quayle, Dan, 115, 118, 120
Queen of Sheba Meets the Atom Man, The, 136, 139

Rabinovitz, Lauren, 132, 135
Race, 24, 30, 39, 46, 48, 77. *See also* Ethnicity
Racism, 102, 123, 126
Rape, 100, 106, 138
Rapf, Harry, 68
Rashomon, 216
Ratings system, 96
Ray, Nicholas, 69
Readers, types of, 39, 41n
Reading. *See also* Reception
Reagan, Ronald, 119
Realism, 34–35, 101, 107, 143, 145, 191, 198. *See also* Verisimilitude
Reality-based television, 213–17
Rebel Without a Cause, 124n
Reception: contextual factors, 1, 5, 23, 29–30, 44, 77–78, 162, 167–68, 171–72; deviant, 32, 78, 89, 107, 184; historical materialist approach, 1, 23–24, 30–31, 118, 162–63, 173–74; modes of, 2, 11, 13–14, 16, 20–24, 44, 77–78, 89; normative, 3, 32–41; schemata for analysis, 1, 3, 55, 162–63, 173–74, 184; symptomatic interpretation, 35
Red-Headed Woman, 81
Reed, Rex, 183
Re-enactment, 211, 213–16, 218, 221–22
Reflexivity. *See* Self-referentiality
Regina v. Hicklin, 97–98, 100
Regulation, of content, 77, 88, 89n, 94
Repetition compulsion, 191, 193, 196, 200, 203–5, 207
Representation, 193, 207, 224
Republicans, 130
Rescue: 911 (TV), 214
Resnais, Alain, 141–42
Resolution. *See* Endings
Return of Martin Guerre, The, 4, 191–209
Reviewers, 67–68, 88–89, 102, 164, 176n, 181
Reviews, 82, 91n, 166, 197
Reynolds, Debbie, 141
Rhodes, Chip, 115–16, 118, 120–23
Rice, Ron, 136
Rice, Susan, 93

About the Author

Janet Staiger is William P. Hobby Centennial Professor of Communication in the Department of Radio-Television-Film at the University of Texas at Austin. Her books include the landmark study *Interpreting Films: Studies in the Historical Reception of American Cinema* as well as *Bad Women: Regulating Sexuality in Early American Cinema* and *The Classical Hollywood Cinema* (with David Bordwell and Kristin Thompson).